RURAL BANKING AND OVERDUES MANAGEMENT

RURAL BANKING AND OVERDUES MANAGEMENT

Anshu Rohtagi

CYBER TECH PUBLICATIONS
4264/3, Ansari Road, Daryaganj, New Delhi-110002 (India)
Ph.: 011-23244078, 011-43559448 Fax: 011-23280028
E-Mail: cyberpublicationsdelhi@yahoo.com
Website: www.cybertechpublications.com

RURAL BANKING AND OVERDUES MANAGEMENT

Anshu Rohtagi

First Edition 2010

Published by : Asian Offset Printers

G.S. Rawat for **Cyber Tech Publications**
4264/3, Ansari Road, Daryaganj, New Delhi-110002 (India)
Ph.: 011-23244078, 011-43559448 Fax: 011-23280028
E-Mail: cyberpublicationsdelhi@yahoo.com
Website: www.cybertechpublications.com

Preface

Within the framework of marketing concept the present study has examined in detail various efforts by the agencies concerned like sponsor banks, state government, RBI and Government of India with regards to need-based service package in rural India, branch location issues, rural banking, communication, customer-friendly bank personnel, procedural simplification, etc. The issues have been studied empirically on the basis of information gathered, on self-developed five-point Lickert-scaled schedule, from randomly selected respondents. The reliability and validity of findings have been tested transparently and objectively. Besides the aforesaid nature and scope of original addition to the knowledge on rural bank marketing, thc conceptual background of the concept of marketing orientation in rural banking made in the beginning of the study justifies the necessity of the work as RRBs are said to have combined concepts of both comparative and commercial banking in real rural settings.

This book throws adequate light on various aspects of lending by RRBs in both agricultural as well as non-agricultural sectors. It also highlights the overdues of the RRBs which is a burning problem of the country. This book will be of much use to the planners, government, research scholars, financing institutions and others.

—*Author*

CONTENTS

1

INTRODUCTION

In any economy Banks play a pivotal role. Without a sound and effective banking system in India it cannot have a healthy economy. The banking system of India should not only be hassle free but it should be able to meet new challenges posed by the technology and any other external and internal factors. For the past three decades India's banking system has several outstanding achievements to its credit. The most striking is its extensive reach. It is no longer confined to only metropolitans or cosmopolitans in India. In fact, Indian banking system has reached even to the remote corners of the country. This is one of the main reason of India's growth process.

The government's regular policy for Indian bank since 1969 has paid rich dividends with the nationalisation of 14 major private banks of India. Not long ago, an account holder had to wait for hours at the bank counters for getting a draft or for withdrawing his own money. Today, he has a choice. Gone are days when the most efficient bank transferred money from one branch to other in two days. Now it is simple as instant messaging or dial a pizza. Money have become the order of the day.

The first bank in India, though conservative, was established in 1786. From 1786 till today, the journey of Indian Banking System can be segregated into three distinct phases. They are as mentioned below:

- Early phase from 1786 to 1969 of Indian Banks
- Nationalisation of Indian Banks and up to 1991 prior to Indian banking sector Reforms.

- New phase of Indian Banking System with the advent of Indian Financial & Banking Sector Reforms after 1991.

To make this write-up more explanatory, I prefix the scenario as Phase I, Phase II and Phase III.

Phase I

The General Bank of India was set up in the year 1786. Next came Bank of Hindustan and Bengal Bank. The East India Company established Bank of Bengal (1809), Bank of Bombay (1840) and Bank of Madras (1843) as independent units and called it Presidency Banks. These three banks were amalgamated in 1920 and Imperial Bank of India was established which started as private shareholders banks, mostly Europeans shareholders. In 1865 Allahabad Bank was established and first time exclusively by Indians, Punjab National Bank Ltd. was set up in 1894 with headquarters at Lahore. Between 1906 and 1913, Bank of India, Central Bank of India, Bank of Baroda, Canara Bank, Indian Bank, and Bank of Mysore were set up. Reserve Bank of India came in 1935.

During the first phase the growth was very slow and banks also experienced periodic failures between 1913 and 1948. There were approximately 1100 banks, mostly small. To streamline the functioning and activities of commercial banks, the Government of India came up with The Banking Companies Act, 1949 which was later changed to Banking Regulation Act 1949 as per amending Act of 1965 (Act No. 23 of 1965). Reserve Bank of India was vested with extensive powers for the supervision of banking in india as the Central Banking Authority. During those days public has lesser confidence in the banks. As an aftermath deposit mobilisation was slow. Abreast of it the savings bank facility provided by the Postal department was comparatively safer. Moreover, funds were largely given to traders.

Phase II

Government took major steps in this Indian Banking Sector Reform after independence. In 1955, it nationalised Imperial

Bank of India with extensive banking facilities on a large scale specially in rural and semi-urban areas. It formed State Bank of india to act as the principal agent of RBI and to handle banking transactions of the Union and State Governments all over the country.

Seven banks forming subsidiary of State Bank of India was nationalised in 1960 on 19th July, 1969, major process of nationalisation was carried out. It was the effort of the then Prime Minister of India, Mrs. Indira Gandhi. 14 major commercial banks in the country was nationalised.

Second phase of nationalisation Indian Banking Sector Reform was carried out in 1980 with seven more banks. This step brought 80% of the banking segment in India under Government ownership.

The following are the steps taken by the Government of India to Regulate Banking Institutions in the Country:

- 1949 : Enactment of Banking Regulation Act.
- 1955 : Nationalisation of State Bank of India.
- 1959 : Nationalisation of SBI subsidiaries.
- 1961 : Insurance cover extended to deposits.
- 1969 : Nationalisation of 14 major banks.
- 1971 : Creation of credit guarantee corporation.
- 1975 : Creation of regional rural banks.
- 1980 : Nationalisation of seven banks with deposits over 200 crore.

After the nationalisation of banks, the branches of the public sector bank India rose to approximately 800% in deposits and advances took a huge jump by 11,000%.

Banking in the sunshine of Government ownership gave the public implicit faith and immense confidence about the sustainability of these institutions.

Phase III

This phase has introduced many more products and facilities in the banking sector in its reforms measure. In 1991, under the chairmanship of M Narasimham, a committee was set up by his name which worked for the liberalisation of banking practices. The country is flooded with foreign banks and their ATM stations. Efforts are being put to give a satisfactory service to customers. Phone banking and net banking is introduced. The entire system became more convenient and swift. Time is given more importance than money.

The financial system of India has shown a great deal of resilience. It is sheltered from any crisis triggered by any external macroeconomics shock as other East Asian Countries suffered. This is all due to a flexible exchange rate regime, the foreign reserves are high, the capital account is not yet fully convertible, and banks and their customers have limited foreign exchange exposure.

NATIONALISATION OF BANKS IN INDIA

The nationalisation of banks in India took place in 1969 by Mrs. Indira Gandhi the then prime minister. It nationalised 14 banks then. These banks were mostly owned by businessmen and even managed by them.

- Central Bank of India
- Bank of Maharashtra
- Dena Bank
- Punjab National Bank
- Syndicate Bank
- Canara Bank
- Indian Bank
- Indian Overseas Bank
- Bank of Baroda
- Union Bank
- Allahabad Bank
- United Bank of India
- UCO Bank
- Bank of India

Befor the steps of nationalisation of Indian banks, only State Bank of India (SBI) was nationalised. It took place in July 1955 under the SBI Act of 1955. Nationalisation of Seven State Banks of India (formed subsidiary) took place on 19th July, 1960. The State Bank of India is India's largest commercial bank and is ranked one of the top five banks worldwide. It serves 90 million customers through a network of 9,000 branches and it offers -- either directly or through subsidiaries -- a wide range of banking services.

The second phase of nationalisation of Indian banks took place in the year 1980. Seven more banks were nationalised with deposits over 200 crores. Till this year, approximately 80% of the banking segment in India were under Government ownership.

After the nationalisation of banks in India, the branches of the public sector banks rose to approximately 800% in deposits and advances took a huge jump by 11,000%.

- 1955 : Nationalisation of State Bank of India.
- 1959 : Nationalisation of SBI subsidiaries.
- 1969 : Nationalisation of 14 major banks.
- 1980 : Nationalisation of seven banks with deposits over 200 crores.

Scheduled Commercial Banks In India

The commercial banking structure in India consists of:

- Scheduled Commercial Banks in India
- Unscheduled Banks in India

Scheduled Banks in India constitute those banks which have been included in the Second Schedule of Reserve Bank of India(RBI) Act, 1934. RBI in turn includes only those banks in this schedule which satisfy the criteria laid down vide section 42 (6) (a) of the Act.

As on 30th June, 1999, there were 300 scheduled banks in India having a total network of 64,918 branches.The scheduled commercial banks in India comprise of State bank of India and its associates (8), nationalised banks (19), foreign banks (45), private sector banks (32), co-operative banks and regional rural banks.

"Scheduled banks in India" means the State Bank of India constituted under the State Bank of India Act, 1955 (23 of 1955), a subsidiary bank as defined in the State Bank of India (Subsidiary Banks) Act, 1959 (38 of 1959), a corresponding new bank constituted under section 3 of the Banking Companies (Acquisition and Transfer of Undertakings) Act, 1970 (5 of 1970), or under section 3 of the Banking Companies (Acquisition and Transfer of Undertakings) Act, 1980 (40 of 1980), or any other bank being a bank included in the Second Schedule to the Reserve Bank of India Act, 1934 (2 of 1934), but does not include a co-operative bank".

"Non-scheduled bank in India" means a banking company as defined in clause (c) of section 5 of the Banking Regulation Act, 1949 (10 of 1949), which is not a scheduled bank".

The following are the Scheduled Banks in India (Public Sector):

- State Bank of India
- State Bank of Bikaner and Jaipur
- State Bank of Hyderabad
- State Bank of Indore
- State Bank of Mysore
- State Bank of Patiala
- State Bank of Saurashtra
- State Bank of Travancore
- Andhra Bank
- Allahabad Bank
- Bank of Baroda
- Bank of India
- Bank of Maharashtra
- Canara Bank
- Central Bank of India

- Corporation Bank
- Dena Bank
- Indian Overseas Bank
- Indian Bank
- Oriental Bank of Commerce
- Punjab National Bank
- Punjab and Sind Bank
- Syndicate Bank
- Union Bank of India
- United Bank of India
- UCO Bank
- Vijaya Bank

The following are the Scheduled Banks in India (Private Sector):

- Vysya Bank Ltd
- Axis Bank Ltd
- Indusind Bank Ltd
- ICICI Banking Corporation Bank Ltd
- Global Trust Bank Ltd
- HDFC Bank Ltd
- Centurion Bank Ltd
- Bank of Punjab Ltd
- IDBI Bank Ltd

The following are the Scheduled Foreign Banks in India:

- American Express Bank Ltd.
- ANZ Gridlays Bank Plc.
- Bank of America NT & SA
- Bank of Tokyo Ltd.
- Banquc Nationale de Paris

- Barclays Bank Plc
- Citi Bank N.C.
- Deutsche Bank A.G.
- Hongkong and Shanghai Banking Corporation
- Standard Chartered Bank.
- The Chase Manhattan Bank Ltd.
- Dresdner Bank AG.

Banks in India

In India the banks are being segregated in different groups. Each group has their own benefits and limitations in operating in India. Each has their own dedicated target market. Few of them only work in rural sector while others in both rural as well as urban. Many even are only catering in cities. Some are of Indian origin and some are foreign players.

All these details and many more is discussed over here. The banks and its relation with the customers, their mode of operation, the names of banks under different groups and other such useful informations are talked about.

One more section has been taken note of is the upcoming foreign banks in India. The RBI has shown certain interest to involve more of foreign banks than the existing one recently. This step has paved a way for few more foreign banks to start business in India.

Major Banks in India

- ABN-AMRO Bank
- Abu Dhabi Commercial Bank
- American Express Bank
- Andhra Bank
- Allahabad Bank
- Axis Bank (Earlier UTI Bank)
- Bank of Baroda
- Bank of India

- Bank of Maharastra
- Bank of Punjab
- Bank of Rajasthan
- Bank of Ceylon
- BNP Paribas Bank
- Canara Bank
- Catholic Syrian Bank
- Central Bank of India
- Centurion Bank
- China Trust Commercial Bank
- Citi Bank
- City Union Bank
- Corporation Bank
- Dena Bank
- Deutsche Bank
- Development Credit Bank
- Dhanalakshmi Bank
- Federal Bank
- HDFC Bank
- HSBC
- ICICI Bank
- IDBI Bank
- Indian Bank
- Indian Overseas Bank
- IndusInd Bank
- ING Vysya Bank
- Jammu & Kashmir Bank
- JPMorgan Chase Bank
- Karnataka Bank

- Karur Vysya Bank
- Laxmi Vilas Bank
- Oriental Bank of Commerce
- Punjab National Bank
- Punjab & Sind Bank
- Scotia Bank
- South Indian Bank
- Standard Chartered Bank
- State Bank of India (SBI)
- State Bank of Bikaner & Jaipur
- State Bank of Hyderabad
- State Bank of Indore
- State Bank of Mysore
- State Bank of Saurastra
- State Bank of Travancore
- Syndicate Bank
- Taib Bank
- UCO Bank
- Union Bank of India
- United Bank of India
- United Bank Of India
- United Western Bank
- Vijaya Bank

Public Sector Banks in India

Among the Public Sector Banks in India, United Bank of India is one of the 14 major banks which were nationalised on July 19, 1969.

Its predecessor, in the Public Sector Banks, the United Bank of India Ltd., was formed in 1950 with the amalgamation of four banks viz. Comilla Banking Corporation Ltd. (1914),

Bengal Central Bank Ltd. (1918), Comilla Union Bank Ltd. (1922) and Hooghly Bank Ltd. (1932).

Oriental Bank of Commerce (OBC), a Governmet of India Undertaking offers Domestic, NRI and Commercial banking services. OBC is implementing a GRAMEEN PROJECT in Dehradun District (UP) and Hanumangarh District (Raiasthan) disbursing small loans.

This Public Secotor Bank India has implemented 14 point action plan for strengthening of credit delivery to women and has designated 5 branches as specialized branches for women entrepreneurs.

The following are the list of Public Sector Banks in India

- Allahabad Bank
- Andhra Bank
- Bank of Baroda
- Bank of India
- Bank of Maharastra
- Canara Bank
- Central Bank of India
- Corporation Bank
- Dena Bank
- Indian Bank
- Indian Overseas Bank
- Oriental Bank of Commerce
- Punjab & Sind Bank
- Punjab National Bank
- Syndicate Bank
- UCO Bank
- Union Bank of India
- United Bank of India
- Vijaya Bank

List of State Bank of India and its subsidiary, a Public Sector Banks

- State Bank of India
  - o State Bank of Bikaner & Jaipur
  - o State Bank of Hyderabad
  - o State Bank of Indore
  - o State Bank of Mysore
  - o State Bank of Saurastra
  - o State Bank of Travancore

Private Sector Banks in India

Private banking in India was practiced since the begining of banking system in India. The first private bank in India to be set up in Private Sector Banks in India was IndusInd Bank. It is one of the fastest growing Bank Private Sector Banks in India. IDBI ranks the tength largest development bank in the world as Private Banks in India and has promoted a world class institutions in India.

The first Private Bank in India to receive an in principle approval from the Reserve Bank of India was Housing Development Finance Corporation Limited, to set up a bank in the private sector banks in India as part of the RBI's liberalisation of the Indian Banking Industry. It was incorporated in August 1994 as HDFC Bank Limited with registered office in Mumbai and commenced operations as Scheduled Commercial Bank in January 1995.

ING Vysya, yet another Private Bank of India was incorporated in the year 1930. Bangalore has a pride of place for having the first branch inception in the year 1934. With successive years of patronage and constantly setting new standards in banking, ING Vysya Bank has many credits to its account.

List of Private Banks in India

- Bank of Punjab
- Bank of Rajasthan

- Catholic Syrian Bank
- Centurion Bank
- City Union Bank
- Dhanalakshmi Bank
- Development Credit Bank
- Federal Bank
- HDFC Bank
- ICICI Bank
- IDBI Bank
- IndusInd Bank
- ING Vysya Bank
- Jammu & Kashmir Bank
- Karnataka Bank
- Karur Vysya Bank
- Laxmi Vilas Bank
- South Indian Bank
- United Western Bank
- UTI Bank

Co-Operative Banks in India

The Co operative banks in India started functioning almost 100 years ago. The Cooperative bank is an important constituent of the Indian Financial System, judging by the role assigned to co operative, the expectations the co operative is supposed to fulfil, their number, and the number of offices the cooperative bank operate. Though the co operative movement originated in the West, but the importance of such banks have assumed in India is rarely paralleled anywhere else in the world. The cooperative banks in India plays an important role even today in rural financing. The businessess of cooperative bank in the urban areas also has increased phenomenally in recent years due to the sharp increase in the number of primary co-operative banks. Co operative Banks in India are registered under the

Co-operative Societies Act. The cooperative bank is also regulated by the RBI. They are governed by the Banking Regulations Act 1949 and Banking Laws (Co-operative Societies) Act, 1965.

Cooperative banks in India finance rural areas under:

- Farming
- Cattle
- Milk
- Hatchery
- Personal finance

Cooperative banks in India finance urban areas under:

- Self-employment
- Industries
- Small scale units
- Home finance
- Consumer finance
- Personal finance

Some facts about Cooperative banks in India

- Some cooperative banks in India are more forward than many of the state and private sector banks.
- According to NAFCUB the total deposits & lendings of Cooperative Banks in India is much more than Old Private Sector Banks & also the New Private Sector Banks.
- This exponential growth of Co operative Banks in India is attributed mainly to their much better local reach, personal interaction with customers, their ability to catch the nerve of the local clientele.

Regional Rural Banks in India

Rural banking in India started since the establishment of banking sector in India. Rural Banks in those days mainly focussed upon the agro sector. Regional rural banks in India penetrated every corner of the country and extended a helping hand in the growth process of the country.

SBI has 30 Regional Rural Banks in India known as RRBs. The rural banks of SBI is spread in 13 states extending from Kashmir to Karnataka and Himachal Pradesh to North East. The total number of SBIs Regional Rural Banks in India branches is 2349 (16%). Till date in rural banking in India, there are 14,475 rural banks in the country of which 2126 (91%) are located in remote rural areas. Apart from SBI, there are other few banks which functions for the development of the rural areas in India. Few of them are as follows.

Haryana State Cooperative Apex Bank Limited

The Haryana State Cooperative Apex Bank Ltd. commonly called as HARCOBANK plays a vital role in rural banking in the economy of Haryana State and has been providing aids and financing farmers, rural artisans, agricultural labourers, entrepreneurs, etc. in the state and giving service to its depositors.

NABARD

National Bank for Agriculture and Rural Development (NABARD) is a development bank in the sector of Regional Rural Banks in India. It provides and regulates credit and gives service for the promotion and development of rural sectors mainly agriculture, small scale industries, cottage and village industries, handicrafts. It also finance rural crafts and other allied rural economic activities to promote integrated rural development. It helps in securing rural prosperity and its connected matters.

Sindhanur Urban Souharda Co-operative Bank

Sindhanur Urban Souharda Co-operative Bank, popularly known as SUCO BANK is the first of its kind in rural banks of India. The impressive story of its inception is interesting and inspiring for all the youth of this country.

United Bank of India

United Bank of India (UBI) also plays an important role in regional rural banks. It has expanded its branch network in a big way to actively participate in the developmental of the rural and semi-urban areas in conformity with the objectives of nationalisation.

Syndicate Bank

Syndicate Bank was firmly rooted in rural India as rural banking and have a clear vision of future India by understanding the grassroot realities. Its progress has been abreast of the phase of progressive banking in India especially in rural banks.

Foreign Banks In India

Foreign Banks in India always brought an explanation about the prompt services to customers. After the set up foreign banks in India, the banking sector in India also become competitive and accurative.

New rules announced by the Reserve Bank of India for the foreign banks in India in this budget has put up great hopes among foreign banks which allows them to grow unfettered. Now foreign banks in India are permitted to set up local subsidiaries. The policy conveys that forign banks in India may not acquire Indian ones (except for weak banks identified by the RBI, on its terms) and their Indian subsidiaries will not be able to open branches freely. Please see the list of Foreign banks in India till date.

List of Foreign Banks in India

- ABN-AMRO Bank
- Abu Dhabi Commercial Bank
- Bank of Ceylon
- BNP Paribas Bank
- Citi Bank
- China Trust Commercial Bank
- Deutsche Bank
- HSBC
- JPMorgan Chase Bank
- Standard Chartered Bank

- Scotia Bank
- Taib Bank

By the year 2009, the list of foreign banks in India is going to become more quantitative as number of foreign banks are still waiting with baggage to start business in India.

Upcoming Foreign Banks in India

By 2009 few more names is going to be added in the list of foreign banks in India. This is as an aftermath of the sudden interest shown by Reserve Bank of India paving roadmap for foreign banks in India greater freedom in India. Among them is the world's best private bank by EuroMoney magazine, Switzerland's UBS.

The following are the list of foreign banks going to set up business in India

- Royal Bank of Scotland
- Switzerland's UBS
- US-based GE Capital
- Credit Suisse Group
- Industrial and Commercial Bank of China

Merrill Lynch is having a joint venture in Indian investment banking space -- DSP Merrill Lynch. Goldman Sachs holds stakes in Kotak Mahindra arms. GE Capital is also having a wide presence in consumer finance through GE Capital India.

India's GDP is seen growing at a robust pace of around 7% over the next few years, throwing up opportunities for the banking sector to profit from. The credit of banks has risen by over 25% in 2004-05 and the growth momentum is expected to continue over the next four to five years. Participation in the growth curve of the Indian economy in the next four years will provide foreign banks a launch pad for greater business expansion when they get more freedom after April 2009.

Banking Services in India

With years, banks are also adding services to their customers. The Indian banking industry is passing through a phase of customers market. The customers have more choices in choosing their banks. A competition has been established within the banks operating in India.

With stiff competition and advancement of technology, the services provided by banks has become more easy and convenient. The past days are witness to an hour wait before withdrawing cash from accounts or a cheque from north of the country being cleared in one month in the south. This section of banking deals with the latest discovery in the banking instruments along with the polished version of their old systems.

Bank Account

Open bank account - the most common and first service of the banking sector. There are different types of bank account in Indian banking sector. The bank accounts are as follows:

- Bank Savings Account - Bank Savings Account can be opened for eligible person / persons and certain organisations / agencies (as advised by Reserve Bank of India (RBI) from time to time)
- Bank Current Account - Bank Current Account can be opened by individuals / partnership firms / Private and Public Limited Companies / HUFs / Specified Associates / Societies / Trusts, etc.
- Bank Term Deposits Account - Bank Term Deposits Account can be opened by individuals / partnership firms / Private and Public Limited Companies / HUFs/ Specified Associates / Societies / Trusts, etc.
- Bank Account Online - With the advancement of technology, the major banks in the public and private sector has faciliated their customer to open bank account online. Bank account online is registered through a PC with an internet connection. The advent of bank account online has saved both the cost of operation for banks as well as the time taken in opening an account.

Note :- A minor account can be opened but jointly with a guardian and only the guardian would is allowed to operate the account.

General Procedure to Open an Account

- The Bank will provide you with details of various types of accounts that you may open with the Bank.
- You can have your choice on what type of account would best suit you, based on your needs and requirements
- The Bank will, prior to opening an account, require documentation and information as prescribed by the "Know Your Customer" (KYC) guidelines issued by RBI and or such other norms or procedures adopted by the Bank prior to opening the account.
- The due diligence process that the Bank would follow, will involve providing documentation verifying your identity, verifying your address, and information onyour occupation or business and source of funds. As part of the due diligence process the Bank may also require an introduction from a person acceptable to the Bank if they so deem necessary and will need your recent photographs.
- The Bank is required by law to obtain Permanent Account Number (PAN) or General Index Register (GIR) Number or, where you do not possess such registration, declaration in Form No. 60 or 61 as specified under the Income Tax Rules.
- In the event that the account opening process is likely to take longer than normal, the Bank will inform you of the revised timeline.
- You can also call your branch or the executive for any queries that you may have and the branch / executive will revert on the query at the earliest.
- The Bank will provide you with the account opening forms and other relevant material to enable you open the account. Bank personnel will advise you on the complete details of information that would be required by the Bank for the verification process.
- The Bank reserves the right, at its sole discretion, to open any account and at such terms as the Bank may prescribe from time to time

Plastic Money

Credit cards in India is gaining ground. A number of banks in India are encouraging people to use credit card. The concept of credit card was used in 1950 with the launch of charge cards in USA by Diners Club and American Express. Credit card however became more popular with use of magnetic strip in 1970. Credit card in India became popular with the introduction of foreign banks in the country.

Credit cards are financial instruments, which can be used more than once to borrow money or buy products and services on credit. Basically banks, retail stores and other businesses issue these.

Major Banks issuing Credit Card in India

- State Bank of India credit card (SBI credit card)
- Bank of Baroda credit card or BoB credit card
- ICICI credit card
- HDFC credit card
- IDBI credit card
- ABN AMRO credit card
- Standard Chartered credit card
- HSBC credit card
- Citibank Credit Card

Precautions Taken after Receiving Credit Card

To Avoid:

- Bending the Card.
- Exposure to electronic devices and gadgets.
- Direct exposure to sunlight.
- Be cautious about disclosing your account number over the phone unless you know you're dealing with a reputable company.
- Never put your account number on the outside of an envelope or on a postcard.

- Draw a line through blank spaces on charge or debit slips above the total so the amount cannot be changed.
- Don't sign a blank charge or debit slip.
- Tear up carbons and save your receipts to check against your monthly statements.
- Cut up old cards - cutting through the account number - before disposing of them.
- Open monthly statements promptly and compare them with your receipts. Report mistakes or discrepancies as soon as possible to the special address listed on your statement for inquiries. Under the FCBA (credit cards) and the EFTA (ATM or debit cards), the card issuer must investigate errors reported to them within 60 days of the date your statement was mailed to you.
- Keep a record - in a safe place separate from your cards- of your account numbers, expiration dates, and the telephone numbers of each card issuer so you can report a loss quickly.
- Carry only those cards that you anticipate you'll need.

To Do:

- Please sign on the signature panel on the reverse of the Card immediately with a non-erasable ball-point pen (preferably in black ink). This will ensure that the benefits of membership are yours and yours alone.
- Keep the Card in a prominent place in your wallet. You will notice if it is missing.

Resons credit card being rejected at retail outlet:

- One may have exceeded the borrowing limit or defaulted (constantly) on minimum payment due.
- The Card is hotlisted.
- The card has crossed its expiration date.
- Non-receipt of dues of one-card blocks future transactions on any other card(s) held of the same card-issuing bank.

- The magnetic stripe on the reverse of the card is damaged i.e. has been scratched or exposed to continuous heat/ direct sunlight or magnetic field-like card kept near a TV set / other electronic appliances.
- Systems or technology failures have in rare instances also led to non acceptance of cards when swiped through an Electronic Terminal.

Global Player in Credit Card Market

MasterCard

MasterCard is a product of MasterCard International and along with VISA are distributed by financial institutions around the world. Cardholders borrow money against a line of credit and pay it back with interest if the balance is carried over from month to month.

Its products are issued by 23,000 financial institutions in 220 countries and territories. In 1998, it had almost 700 million cards in circulation, whose users spent $650 billion in more than 16.2 million locations.

VISA Card

VISA cards is a product of VISA USA and along with MasterCard is distributed by financial institutions around the world. A VISA cardholder borrows money against a credit line and repays the money with interest if the balance is carried over from month to month in a revolving line of credit. Nearly 600 million cards carry one of the VISA brands and more than 14 million locations accept VISA cards.

American Express

The world's favorite card is American Express Credit Card. More than 57 million cards are in circulation and growing and it is still growing further. Around US $ 123 billion was spent last year through American Express Cards and it is poised to be the world's No. 1 card in the near future. In a regressive US economy last year, the total amount spent on American Express cards rose by 4 percent. American Express cards are very popular in the U.S., Canada, Europe and Asia and are used widely in the retail and everyday expenses segment.

Diners Club International

Diners Club is the world's No. 1 Charge Card. Diners Club cardholders reside all over the world and the Diners Card is a alltime favourite for corporates. There are more than 8 million Diners Club cardholders. They are affluent and are frequent travelers in premier businesses and institutions, including Fortune 500 companies and leading global corporations.

JCB Cards

The JCB Card has a merchant network of 10.93 million in approximately 189 countries. It is supported by over 320 financial institutions worldwide and serves more than 48 million cardholders in eighteen countries world wide. The JCB philosophy of "identify the customer's needs and please the customer with Service from the Heart" is paying rich dividends as their customers spend US$43 billion annually on their JCB cards.

Grace / Interest Free Period

The number of days you have on a card before a card issuer starts charging you interest is called grace period. Usually this period is the number of days between the statement date and the due date of payment. Grace periods on credit cards are usually 2-3 weeks. However, there is likely to be no grace for balances carried forward from previous month and fresh purchases thereafter if any.

The following are some of the varieties of credit cards in India

- ANZ - Gold
- ANZ - Silver
- Bank Of India - Indiacard
- Bol - Taj Premium
- Bol - Gold
- BoB - Exclusive
- BoB - Premium
- Canara Bank - Cancard

- Citibank - Gold
- Citibank - Silver
- Citibank WWF Card
- Citibank Visa Card for Women
- Citibank Cry Card
- Citibank Silver International Credit Card
- Citibank Women's International Credit Card
- Citibank Gold International Credit Card
- Citibank Electronic Credit Card
- Citibank Maruti International Credit Card
- Citibank Times Card
- Citibank Indian Oil International Credit Card
- Citibank Citi Diners Club Card
- HSBC - Gold
- HSBC - Classic
- ICICI Sterling Silver Credit Card
- ICICI Solid Gold Credit Card
- ICICI True Blue Credit Card
- SBI Card
- Stanchart - Gold
- Stanchart - Executive
- Stanchart - Classic

Thomas Cook Standard Chartered Global Credit Card

Standard Segregation of Credit Cards

- Standard Card - It is the most basic card (sans all frills) offered by issuers.
- Classic Card - Brand name for the standard card issued by VISA.
- Gold Card/Executive Card - A credit card that offers a higher line of credit than a standard card. Income

eligibility is also higher. In addition, issuers provide extra perks or incentives to cardholders.

- Platinum Card - A credit card with a higher limit and additional perks than a gold card.
- Titanium Card - A card with an even higher limit than a platinum card.

The following are some of the plus features of credit card in India

- Hotel discounts
- Travel fare discounts
- Free global calling card
- Lost baggage insurance
- Accident insurance
- Insurance on goods purchased
- Waiver of payment in case of accidental death
- Household insurance

Some facts of credit cards

- The first card was issued in India by Visa in 1981.
- The country's first Gold Card was also issued from Visa in 1986.
- The first international credit card was issued to a restricted number of customers by Andhra Bank in 1987 through the Visa program, after getting special permission from the Reserve Bank of India.
- The credit cards are shape and size, as specified by the ISO 7810 standard. It is generally of plastic quality. It is also sometimes known as Plastic Money.

Debit Card

Debit cards, also known as check cards look like credit cards or ATM cards (automated teller machine card). It operate like cash or a personal check. Debit cards are different from credit cards. Credit card is a way to "pay later," whereas debit card is a way to "pay now." When we use a debit card, our money is quickly deducted from the bank account. Debit cards are accepted at many locations, including grocery stores, retail stores, gasoline stations, and restaurants. Its an alternative to carrying a checkbook or cash.

With debit card, we use our own money and not the issuer's money. In India almost all the banks issue debit card to its account holders.

Features of Debit Card

- Obtaining a debit card is often easier than obtaining a credit card.
- Using a debit card instead of writing checks saves you from showing identification or giving out personal information at the time of the transaction.
- Using a debit card frees you from carrying cash or a checkbook.
- Using a debit card means you no longer have to stock up on traveler's checks or cash when you travel.
- Debit cards may be more readily accepted by merchants than checks, especially in other states or countries wherever your card brand is accepted.
- The debit card is a quick, "pay now" product, giving you no grace period.
- Using a debit card may mean you have less protection than with a credit card purchase for items which are never delivered, are defective, or were misrepresented. But, as with credit cards, you may dispute unauthorized charges or other mistakes within 60 days. You should contact the card issuer if a problem cannot be resolved with the merchant.
- Returning goods or canceling services purchased with a debit card is treated as if the purchase were made with cash or a check.

Tips for responsible use of Debit Card

- If your card is lost or stolen, report the loss immediately to your financial institution.

- If you suspect your card is being fraudulently used, report it immediately to your financial institution.
- Hold on to your receipts from your debit card transactions. A thief may get your name and debit card number from a receipt and order goods by mail or over the telephone. Your card does not have to be missing in order for it to be misused.
- If you have a PIN number, memorize it. Do not keep your PIN number with your card. Also, don't choose a PIN number that a smart thief could figure out, such as your phone number or birthday.
- Never give your PIN number to anyone. Keep your PIN private.
- Always know how much money you have available in your account. Don't forget that your debit card may allow you to access money that you have set aside to cover a check which has not cleared your bank yet.
- Keep your receipts in one place -- for easy retrieval and better oversight of your bank account.

Loans

Banks in India with the way of development have become easy to apply in loan market. The following loans are given by almost all the banks in the country:

- Personal Loan
- Car Loan or Auto Loan
- Loan against Shares
- Home Loan
- Education Loan or Student Loan

In Personal Loan, one can get a sanctioned loan amount between Rs 25,000 to 10,00,000 depending upon the profile of person applying for the loan. SBI, ICICI, HDFC, HSBC are some of the leading banks which deals in Personal Loan.

Almost all the banks have jumped into the market of car loan which is also sometimes termed as auto loan. It is one of the fast moving financial product of banks. Car loan / auto loan are sanctioned to the extent of 85% upon the ex-showroom price of the car with some simple paper works and a small amount of processing fee. Loan against shares is very easy to get because liquid guarantee is involved in it.

Home loan is the latest craze in the banking sector with the development of the infrastructure. Now people are moving to township outside the city. More number of townships are coming up to meet the demand of 'house for all'. The RBI has also liberalised the interest rates of home loan inorder to match the repayment capability of even middle class people. Almost all banks are dealing in home loan. Again SBI, ICICI, HDFC, HSBC are leading.

The educational loan, rather to be termed as student loan, is a good banking product for the mass. Students with certain academic brilliance, studying at recognised colleges/universities in India and abroad are generally given education loan / student loan so as to meet the expenses on tuition fee/ maintenance cost/books and other equipment.

Money Transfer

Beside lending and depositing money, banks also carry money from one corner of the globe to another. This act of banks is known as transfer of money. This activity is termed as remittance business. Banks generally issue Demand Drafts, Banker's Cheques, Money Orders or other such instruments for transferring the money. This is a type of Telegraphic Transfer or Tele Cash Orders.

It has been only a couple of years that banks have jumped into the money transfer businessess in India. The international money transfer market grew 9.3% from 2003 to 2004 i.e. from US$213 bn. to US$233 bn. in 2004. Economists say that the market of money transfer will further grow at a cumulative 10.1% average growth rate through 2008.

With the use of high technology and varieties of product it seems that "Free" money transfers will become commonplace. We will see more bundling of tailored money services by banks and non-traditional entrants that will include "free" money transfers. Many banks will even use money transfer services as loss-leaders inorder to generate account openings and cross-sell opportunities. The price evolution of money transfer products for banks will be similar to that of consumer bill pay-the product is worth giving away as an account acquisition tool to win overall market share and establish banking relationships.

ATM money transfer card products have had terrible bank adoption rates since being introduced in the last three to four years. Remittees who are highly educated and have been already been exposed to ATM technology in receiving countries tend to have an interest in this product. Money transfer to India is one of the most important part played by the banks. This service provide peace of mind to either the NRIs or to the visitors to India. Many Indian banks have ATM'S (automatic teller machine), enable to draw foreign currency in India.

By 2007, we will see a good percent of all foreign-born households doing some level of online banking. First-mover banks will start having a window of opportunity to include online transfer functionality within the next couple of years, which currently frequents traditional money transmitters such as Western Union. There is a terrific opportunity for banks and non-banks to offer more robust global inter-institutional funds transfer services online. More than half of Western Union's customers today are already banked, and most do not have an alternative product marketed by their bank that is painless, quick, and cost-effective. That will change as banks offer transfer services through their online channel.

Money Transfer to India

Apart from banks few financial institutions and online portals gives services of money transfer to India. Some of them are as under:

- Western Union Money Transfer
- Union Money Transfer
- IKobo Money Transfer
- Cash2india.com
- Remit2india

- Samachar Money Transfer
- Timesofmoney.com
- Wells Fergo International Money Transfer
- Travellers Express
- Money Gram International

Visa Money Transfer

Visa has recently introduced the 'Visa Money Transfer' option for its savings and current account holder of any bank with a visa debit card. This facility helps its customer to transfer funds from his bank account to any visa card, either debit or credit within India.

A Visa Money Transfer is of similar kind, in many respects, to the third-party fund transfer option given by some banks to its account holders through e-cheque, but this is restricted to only visa cardholders.

How to transfer money?

- Log on to your bank account through your respective bank websites.
- Fill the beneficiary details like visa card numbers, name, address and then specify the amount that needs to be transferred. For bank account specify the visa card number and credit card number for paying credit card bill.
- Click on to VISA Transfer Payments button.
- Transfer immediately or on schedule date. Your account will be debited according to the date mentioned.

Notable points of Visa Money Transfer

- The time taken for money transfers could be the same or even more than that of a demand draft i.e. two or three days or even more.
- Currently there are no charges but limits has been set by certain banks on the current transfers.
- It is available in 150 cities across the country now.

- The transferred amount can neither be changed nor stopped once it is initiated.

Financial and Banking Sector Reforms

The last decade witnessed the maturity of India's financial markets. Since 1991, every governments of India took major steps in reforming the financial sector of the country. The important achievements in the following fields is discussed under serparate heads:

- Financial markets
- Regulators
- The banking system
- Non-banking finance companies
- The capital market
- Mutual funds
- Overall approach to reforms
- Deregulation of banking system
- Capital market developments
- Consolidation imperative

Now let us discuss each segment seperately.

Financial Markets

In the last decade, Private Sector Institutions played an important role. They grew rapidly in commercial banking and asset management business. With the openings in the insurance sector for these institutions, they started making debt in the market. Competition among financial intermediaries gradually helped the interest rates to decline. Deregulation added to it. The real interest rate was maintained. The borrowers did not pay high price while depositors had incentives to save. It was something between the nominal rate of interest and the expected rate of inflation.

Regulators

The Finance Ministry continuously formulated major policies in the field of financial sector of the country. The

Government accepted the important role of regulators. The Reserve Bank of India (RBI) has become more independant.

Securities and Exchange Board of India (SEBI) and the Insurance Regulatory and Development Authority (IRDA) became important institutions. Opinions are also there that there should be a super-regulator for the financial services sector instead of multiplicity of regulators.

The Banking System

Almost 80% of the business are still controlled by Public Sector Banks (PSBs). PSBs are still dominating the commercial banking system. Shares of the leading PSBs are already listed on the stock exchanges. The RBI has given licences to new private sector banks as part of the liberalisation process. The RBI has also been granting licences to industrial houses. Many banks are successfully running in the retail and consumer segments but are yet to deliver services to industrial finance, retail trade, small business and agricultural finance.

The PSBs will play an important role in the industry due to its number of branches and foreign banks facing the constrait of limited number of branches. Hence, in order to achieve an efficient banking system, the onus is on the Government to encourage the PSBs to be run on professional lines.

Development Finance Institutions

FIs's access to SLR funds reduced. Now they have to approach the capital market for debt and equity funds.

Convertibility clause no longer obligatory for assistance to corporates sanctioned by term-lending institutions.

Capital adequacy norms extended to financial institutions.

DFIs such as IDBI and ICICI have entered other segments of financial services such as commercial banking, asset management and insurance through separate ventures. The move to universal banking has started.

Non-banking Finance Companies

In the case of new NBFCs seeking registration with the RBI, the requirement of minimum net owned funds, has been raised to Rs.2 crores. Until recently, the money market in India was narrow and circumscribed by tight regulations over interest rates and participants. The secondary market was underdeveloped and lacked liquidity. Several measures have been initiated and include new money market instruments, strengthening of existing instruments and setting up of the Discount and Finance House of India (DFHI). The RBI conducts its sales of dated securities and treasury bills through its open market operations (OMO) window. Primary dealers bid for these securities and also trade in them. The DFHI is the principal agency for developing a secondary market for money market instruments and Government of India treasury bills. The RBI has introduced a liquidity adjustment facility (LAF) in which liquidity is injected through reverse repo auctions and liquidity is sucked out through repo auctions.

On account of the substantial issue of government debt, the gilt- edged market occupies an important position in the financial set- up. The Securities Trading Corporation of India (STCI), which started operations in June 1994 has a mandate to develop the secondary market in government securities.

Long-term debt market: The development of a long-term debt market is crucial to the financing of infrastructure. After bringing some order to the equity market, the SEBI has now decided to concentrate on the development of the debt market. Stamp duty is being withdrawn at the time of dematerialisation of debt instruments in order to encourage paperless trading.

The Capital Market

The number of shareholders in India is estimated at 25 million. However, only an estimated two lakh persons actively trade in stocks. There has been a dramatic improvement in the country's stock market trading infrastructure during the last few years.

Expectations are that India will be an attractive emerging market with tremendous potential. Unfortunately, during recent times the stock markets have been constrained by some unsavoury developments, which has led to retail investors deserting the stock markets.

Mutual Funds

The mutual funds industry is now regulated under the SEBI (Mutual Funds) Regulations, 1996 and amendments thereto. With the issuance of SEBI guidelines, the industry had a framework for the establishment of many more players, both Indian and foreign players.

The Unit Trust of India remains easily the biggest mutual fund controlling a corpus of nearly Rs.70,000 crores, but its share is going down. The biggest shock to the mutual fund industry during recent times was the insecurity generated in the minds of investors regarding the US 64 scheme. With the growth in the securities markets and tax advantages granted for investment in mutual fund units, mutual funds started becoming popular.

The foreign owned AMCs are the ones which are now setting the pace for the industry. They are introducing new products, setting new standards of customer service, improving disclosure standards and experimenting with new types of distribution.

The insurance industry is the latest to be thrown open to competition from the private sector including foreign players. Foreign companies can only enter joint ventures with Indian companies, with participation restricted to 26 per cent of equity. It is too early to conclude whether the erstwhile public sector monopolies will successfully be able to face up to the competition posed by the new players, but it can be expected that the customer will gain from improved service.

The new players will need to bring in innovative products as well as fresh ideas on marketing and distribution, in order to improve the low per capita insurance coverage. Good regulation will, of course, be essential.

Overall Approach to Reforms

The last ten years have seen major improvements in the working of various financial market participants. The government and the regulatory authorities have followed a step-by-step approach, not a big bang one. The entry of foreign players has assisted in the introduction of international practices and systems. Technology developments have improved customer service. Some gaps however remain (for example: lack of an inter-bank interest rate benchmark, an active corporate debt market and a developed derivatives market). On the whole, the cumulative effect of the developments since 1991 has been quite encouraging. An indication of the strength of the reformed Indian financial system can be seen from the way India was not affected by the Southeast Asian crisis.

However, financial liberalisation alone will not ensure stable economic growth. Some tough decisions still need to be taken. Without fiscal control, financial stability cannot be ensured. The fate of the Fiscal Responsibility Bill remains unknown and high fiscal deficits continue. In the case of financial institutions, the political and legal structures hve to ensure that borrowers repay on time the loans they have taken. The phenomenon of rich industrialists and bankrupt companies continues. Further, frauds cannot be totally prevented, even with the best of regulation. However, punishment has to follow crime, which is often not the case in India.

Deregulation of Banking System

Prudential norms were introduced for income recognition, asset classification, provisioning for delinquent loans and for capital adequacy. In order to reach the stipulated capital adequacy norms, substantial capital were provided by the Government to PSBs.

Government pre-emption of banks' resources through statutory liquidity ratio (SLR) and cash reserve ratio (CRR) brought down in steps. Interest rates on the deposits and lending sides almost entirely were deregulated.

New private sector banks allowed to promote and encourage competition. PSBs were encouraged to approach the public for raising resources. Recovery of debts due to banks and the Financial Institutions Act, 1993 was passed, and special recovery tribunals set up to facilitate quicker recovery of loan arrears.

Bank lending norms liberalised and a loan system to ensure better control over credit introduced. Banks asked to set up asset liability management (ALM) systems. RBI guidelines issued for risk management systems in banks encompassing credit, market and operational risks.

A credit information bureau being established to identify bad risks. Derivative products such as forward rate agreements (FRAs) and interest rate swaps (IRSs) introduced.

Capital Market Developments

The Capital Issues (Control) Act, 1947, repealed, office of the Controller of Capital Issues were abolished and the initial share pricing were decontrolled. SEBI, the capital market regulator was established in 1992. Foreign institutional investors (FIIs) were allowed to invest in Indian capital markets after registration with the SEBI. Indian companies were permitted to access international capital markets through euro issues.

The National Stock Exchange (NSE), with nationwide stock trading and electronic display, clearing and settlement facilities was established. Several local stock exchanges changed over from floor based trading to screen based trading.

Private Mutual Funds Permitted

The Depositories Act had given a legal framework for the establishment of depositories to record ownership deals in book entry form. Dematerialisation of stocks encouraged paperless trading. Companies were required to disclose all material facts and specific risk factors associated with their projects while making public issues.

To reduce the cost of issue, underwriting by the issuer were made optional, subject to conditions. The practice of making preferential allotment of shares at prices unrelated to the prevailing market prices stopped and fresh guidelines were issued by SEBI. SEBI reconstituted governing boards of the stock exchanges, introduced capital adequacy norms for brokers, and made rules for making client or broker relationship more transparent which included separation of client and broker accounts.

Buy Back of Shares Allowed

The SEBI started insisting on greater corporate disclosures. Steps were taken to improve corporate governance based on the report of a committee. SEBI issued detailed employee stock option scheme and employee stock purchase scheme for listed companies.

Standard denomination for equity shares of Rs. 10 and Rs. 100 were abolished. Companies given the freedom to issue dematerialised shares in any denomination.

Derivatives trading starts with index options and futures. A system of rolling settlements introduced. SEBI empowered to register and regulate venture capital funds.

The SEBI (Credit Rating Agencies) Regulations, 1999 issued for regulating new credit rating agencies as well as introducing a code of conduct for all credit rating agencies operating in India.

Consolidation Imperative

Another aspect of the financial sector reforms in India is the consolidation of existing institutions which is especially applicable to the commercial banks. In India the banks are in huge quantity. First, there is no need for 27 PSBs with branches all over India. A number of them can be merged. The merger of Punjab National Bank and New Bank of India was a difficult one, but the situation is different now. No one expected so many employees to take voluntary retirement from PSBs, which at one time were much sought after jobs. Private sector banks will be self consolidated while co-operative and rural banks will be encouraged for consolidation, and anyway play only a niche role.

In the case of insurance, the Life Insurance Corporation of India is a behemoth, while the four public sector general insurance companies will probably move towards consolidation with a bit of nudging. The UTI is yet again a big institution, even though facing difficult times, and most other public sector players are already exiting the mutual fund business. There are a number of small mutual fund players in the private sector, but the business being comparatively new for the private players, it will take some time.

We finally come to convergence in the financial sector, the new buzzword internationally. Hi-tech and the need to meet increasing consumer needs is encouraging convergence, even though it has not always been a success till date. In India organisations such as IDBI, ICICI, HDFC and SBI are already trying to offer various services to the customer under one umbrella. This phenomenon is expected to grow rapidly in the coming years. Where mergers may not be possible, alliances between organisations may be effective. Various forms of bancassurance are being introduced, with the RBI having already come out with detailed guidelines for entry of banks into insurance. The LIC has bought into Corporation Bank in order to spread its insurance distribution network. Both banks and insurance companies have started entering the asset management business, as there is a great deal of synergy among these businesses. The pensions market is expected to open up fresh opportunities for insurance companies and mutual funds.

It is not possible to play the role of the Oracle of Delphi when a vast nation like India is involved. However, a few trends are evident, and the coming decade should be as interesting as the last one.

Reserve Bank of India (RBI)

Kindly Take Note : Reserve Bank of India (RBI) is the central bank of the country and is different from Central Bank of India.

The central bank of the country is the Reserve Bank of India (RBI). It was established in April 1935 with a share capital of Rs. 5 crores on the basis of the recommendations of the Hilton Young Commission. The share capital was divided into shares of Rs. 100 each fully paid which was entirely owned by private shareholders in the begining. The Government held shares of nominal value of Rs. 2,20,000.

Reserve Bank of India was nationalised in the year 1949. The general superintendence and direction of the Bank is entrusted to Central Board of Directors of 20 members, the Governor and four Deputy Governors, one Government official from the Ministry of Finance, ten nominated Directors by the Government to give representation to important elements in the economic life of the country, and four nominated Directors by the Central Government to represent the four local Boards with the headquarters at Mumbai, Kolkata, Chennai and New Delhi.

Local Boards consist of five members each Central Government appointed for a term of four years to represent territorial and economic interests and the interests of co-operative and indigenous banks.

The Reserve Bank of India Act, 1934 was commenced on April 1, 1935. The Act, 1934 (II of 1934) provides the statutory basis of the functioning of the Bank.

The Bank was constituted for the need of following:

- To regulate the issue of banknotes
- To maintain reserves with a view to securing monetary stability and
- To operate the credit and currency system of the country to its advantage.

Functions of Reserve Bank of India

The Reserve Bank of India Act of 1934 entrust all the important functions of a central bank the Reserve Bank of India.

Bank of Issue

Under Section 22 of the Reserve Bank of India Act, the Bank has the sole right to issue bank notes of all denominations. The distribution of one rupee notes and coins and small coins all over the country is undertaken by the Reserve Bank as agent of the Government. The Reserve Bank has a separate Issue Department which is entrusted with the issue of currency notes. The assets and liabilities of the Issue Department are kept separate from those of the Banking Department. Originally, the assets of the Issue Department were to consist of not less than two-fifths of gold coin, gold bullion or sterling securities provided the amount of gold was not less than Rs. 40 crores in value. The remaining three-fifths of the assets might be held in rupee coins, Government of India rupee securities, eligible bills of exchange and promissory notes payable in India. Due to the exigencies of the Second World War and the post-was period, these provisions were considerably modified. Since 1957, the Reserve Bank of India is required to maintain gold and foreign exchange reserves of Ra. 200 crores, of which at least Rs. 115 crores should be in gold. The system as it exists today is known as the minimum reserve system.

Banker to Government

The second important function of the Reserve Bank of India is to act as Government banker, agent and adviser. The Reserve Bank is agent of Central Government and of all State Governments in India excepting that of Jammu and Kashmir. The Reserve Bank has the obligation to transact Government business, via. to keep the cash balances as deposits free of interest, to receive and to make payments on behalf of the Government and to carry out their exchange remittances and other banking operations. The Reserve Bank of India helps the Government - both the Union and the States to float new loans and to manage public debt. The Bank makes ways and means advances to the Governments for 90 days. It makes loans and advances to the States and local authorities. It acts as adviser to the Government on all monetary and banking matters.

Bankers' Bank and Lender of the Last Resort

The Reserve Bank of India acts as the bankers' bank. According to the provisions of the Banking Companies Act of 1949, every scheduled bank was required to maintain with the Reserve Bank a cash balance equivalent to 5% of its demand liabilites and 2 per cent of its time liabilities in India.

By an amendment of 1962, the distinction between demand and time liabilities was abolished and banks have been asked to keep cash reserves equal to 3 per cent of their aggregate deposit liabilities. The minimum cash requirements can be changed by the Reserve Bank of India.

The scheduled banks can borrow from the Reserve Bank of India on the basis of eligible securities or get financial accommodation in times of need or stringency by rediscounting bills of exchange. Since commercial banks can always expect the Reserve Bank of India to come to their help in times of banking crisis the Reserve Bank becomes not only the banker's bank but also the lender of the last resort.

Controller of Credit

The Reserve Bank of India is the controller of credit i.e. it has the power to influence the volume of credit created by banks in India.

It can do so through changing the Bank rate or through open market operations. According to the Banking Regulation Act of 1949, the Reserve Bank of India can ask any particular bank or the whole banking system not to lend to particular groups or persons on the basis of certain types of securities. Since 1956, selective controls of credit are increasingly being used by the Reserve Bank.

The Reserve Bank of India is armed with many more powers to control the Indian money market. Every bank has to get a licence from the Reserve Bank of India to do banking business within India, the licence can be cancelled by the Reserve Bank of certain stipulated conditions are not fulfilled. Every bank will have to get the permission of the Reserve Bank before it can open a new branch. Each scheduled bank must send a weekly return to the Reserve Bank showing, in detail, its assets and liabilities. This power of the Bank to call for information is also intended to give it effective control of the credit system. The Reserve Bank has also the power to inspect the accounts of any commercial bank.

As supereme banking authority in the country, the Reserve Bank of India, therefore, has the following powers:

(a) It holds the cash reserves of all the scheduled banks.

(b) It controls the credit operations of banks through quantitative and qualitative controls.

(c) It controls the banking system through the system of licensing, inspection and calling for information.

(d) It acts as the lender of the last resort by providing rediscount facilities to scheduled banks.

Custodian of Foreign Reserves

The Reserve Bank of India has the responsibility to maintain the official rate of exchange. According to the Reserve Bank of India Act of 1934, the Bank was required to buy and sell at fixed rates any amount of sterling in lots of not less than Rs. 10,000.

The rate of exchange fixed was Re. 1 = sh. 6d. Since 1935 the Bank was able to maintain the exchange rate fixed at lsh.6d. though there were periods of extreme pressure in favour of or against the rupee. After India became a member of the International Monetary Fund in 1946, the Reserve Bank has the responsibility of maintaining fixed exchange rates with all other member countries of the I.M.F.

Besides maintaining the rate of exchange of the rupee, the Reserve Bank has to act as the custodian of India's reserve of international currencies. The vast sterling balances were acquired and managed by the Bank. Further, the RBI has the responsibility of administering the exchange controls of the country.

Supervisory Functions

In addition to its traditional central banking functions, the Reserve bank has certain non-monetary functions of the nature of supervision of banks and promotion of sound banking in India. The Reserve Bank Act, 1934, and the Banking Regulation Act, 1949 have given the RBI wide powers of supervision and control over commercial and co-operative banks, relating to licensing and establishments, branch expansion, liquidity of their assets, management and methods of working, amalgamation, reconstruction, and liquidation. The RBI is authorised to carry out periodical inspections of the banks and to call for returns and necessary information from them. The nationalisation of 14 major Indian scheduled banks in July 1969 has imposed new responsibilities on the RBI for directing the growth of banking and credit policies towards more rapid development of the economy and realisation of certain desired social objectives. The supervisory functions of the RBI have helped a great deal in improving the standard of banking in

India to develop on sound lines and to improve the methods of their operation.

Promotional Functions

With economic growth assuming a new urgency since Independence, the range of the Reserve Bank's functions has steadily widened. The Bank now performs a varietyof developmental and promotional functions, which, at one time, were regarded as outside the normal scope of central banking. The Reserve Bank was asked to promote banking habit, extend banking facilities to rural and semi-urban areas, and establish and promote new specialised financing agencies.

Accordingly, the Reserve Bank has helped in the setting up of the IFCI and the SFC; it set up the Deposit Insurance Corporation in 1962, the Unit Trust of India in 1964, the Industrial Development Bank of India also in 1964, the Agricultural Refinance Corporation of India in 1963 and the Industrial Reconstruction Corporation of India in 1972. These institutions were set up directly or indirectly by the Reserve Bank to promote saving habit and to mobilise savings, and to provide industrial finance as well as agricultural finance. As far back as 1935, the Reserve Bank of India set up the Agricultural Credit Department to provide agricultural credit.

But only since 1951 the Bank's role in this field has become extremely important. The Bank has developed the co-operative credit movement to encourage saving, to eliminate moneylenders from the villages and to route its short term credit to agriculture. The RBI has set up the Agricultural Refinance and Development Corporation to provide long-term finance to farmers.

Classification of RBIs Functions

The monetary functions also known as the central banking functions of the RBI are related to control and regulation of money and credit, i.e., issue of currency, control of bank credit, control of foreign exchange operations, banker to the Government and to the money market. Monetary functions of the RBI are significant as they control and regulate the volume of money and credit in the country.

Equally important, however, are the non-monetary functions of the RBI in the context of India's economic backwardness. The supervisory function of the RBI may be regarded as a non-monetary function (though many consider this a monetary function).

The promotion of sound banking in India is an important goal of the RBI, the RBI has been given wide and drastic powers, under the Banking Regulation Act of 1949 - these powers relate to licencing of banks, branch expansion, liquidity of their assets, management and methods of working, inspection, amalgamation, reconstruction and liquidation. Under the RBI's supervision and inspection, the working of banks has greatly improved. Commercial banks have developed into financially and operationally sound and viable units. The RBI's powers of supervision have now been extended to non-banking financial intermediaries. Since independence, particularly after its nationalisation 1949, the RBI has followed the promotional functions vigorously and has been responsible for strong financial support to industrial and agricultural development in the country.

Industrial Development Bank of India Ltd. (IDBI)

Industrial Development Bank of India (IDBI) is the tength largest bank in the world in terms of development.

The National Stock Exchange (NSE), The National Securities Depository Services Ltd. (NSDL), Stock Holding Corporation of India (SHCIL) are some of the institutions which has been built by IDBI. IDBI is a strategic investor in a plethora of institutions which have revolutionized the Indian Financial Markets.

IDBI Bank, promoted by IDBI Group started in November 1995 with a branch at Indore with an equity capital base of Rs. 1000 million.

Main Functions of IDBI

IDBI is vested with the responsibility of co-ordinating the working of institutions engaged in financing, promoting and developing industries. It has evolved an appropriate mechanism for this purpose. IDBI also undertakes/supports wide-ranging promotional activities including entrepreneurship development programmes for new entrepreneurs, provision of consultancy services for small and medium enterprises, upgradation of technology and programmes for economic upliftment of the underprivileged.

IDBI's Role as a Catalyst

IDBI's role as a catalyst to industrial development encompasses a wide spectrum of activities. IDBI can finance all types of industrial concerns covered under the provisions of the IDBI Act. With over three decades of service to the Indian industry, IDBI has grown substantially in terms of size of operations and portfolio.

Developmental Activities of IDBI

Promotional Activities

In fulfilment of its developmental role, the Bank continues to perform a wide range of promotional activities relating to developmental programmes for new entrepreneurs, consultancy services for small and medium enterprises and programmes designed for accredited voluntary agencies for the economic upliftment of the underprivileged. These include entrepreneurship development, self-employment and wage employment in the industrial sector for the weaker sections of society through voluntary agencies, support to Science and Technology Entrepreneurs' Parks, Energy Conservation, Common Quality Testing Centres for small industries.

Technical Consultancy Organisations

With a view to making available at a reasonable cost, consultancy and advisory services to entrepreneurs, particularly to new and small entrepreneurs, IDBI, in collaboration with other All-India Financial Institutions, has set up a network of Technical Consultancy Organisations (TCOs) covering the entire country. TCOs offer diversified services to small and medium enterprises in the selection, formulation and appraisal of projects, their implementation and review.

Entrepreneurship Development Institute

Realising that entrepreneurship development is the key to industrial development, IDBI played a prime role in setting up of the Entrepreneurship Development Institute of India for fostering entrepreneurship in the country. It has also established similar institutes in Bihar, Orissa, Madhya Pradesh and Uttar Pradesh. IDBI also extends financial support to various organisations in conducting studies or surveys of relevance to industrial development.

Easy Banking

This section is fully dedicated to the Tech Banking. A decade before, it was tough to belief that banking secctor will be at a finger tip. Now its possible. A mobile hand set with a connection is the only instrument needed to make a gateway to your banking transaction, the latest innovation of technology.

Apart from the Mobile Banking, including of SMS Banking, Net Banking and ATMs are the major steps taken by the banks in India towards modernisation. With all these devises and systems, there is a complete freedom to experience.

Check your account, transfer your fund, make payments and what more, do anything of everything what has been followed in physical banking since ages. But this time no standing for hours in front of cash counter and no time boundation in withdrawing your own money.

Indian Banks Association

The Indian Banks Association (IBA) was formed on the 26th September, 1946 with 22 members. Today IBA has more than 156 members comprising of Public Sector banks, Private Sector banks, Foreign banks having offices in India, Urban Co-operative banks, Developmental financial institutions, Federations, merchant banks, mutual funds, housing finance corporations, etc.

The functioning of IBA

- To promote sound and progressive banking principles and practices.

- To render assistance and to provide common services to members.
- To organise co-ordination and co-operation on procedural, legal, technical, administrative and professional matters.
- To collect, classify and circulate statistical and other information.
- To pool together expertise towards common purposes such as reduction in costs, increase in efficiency, productivity and improve systems, procedures and banking practices.
- To project good public image of banking through publicity and public relations.
- To encourage sports and cultural activities among bank employees.

The Organisational Structure of IBA

The Managing Committee manages the affairs, business and funds of IBA. The managing Committee is elected by the Ordinary members of the Association, and is the highest management and policy making body of the Association.

The Chairman of the Association heads upon the`working of the Association. He provides guidelines to the Association. The administrative head of IBA is the Chief Executive of IBA. He is also the Secretary to the Managing Committee. He leads a team of executives, officers and other staff members.

IBA constitutes standing committees/task forces/ small groups/ committees of experts from member banks for the examining of various aspects relating to industry level issues to get solutions.

Recommendations of these groups/committees, are communicated to members with the approval of the managing committee or taken up with the concerned authorities for action.

Proxy Banking In India

Indian villages were miles away from mutual funds, insurance and even equity trading. Thanks to Internet Kiosk and the ATM duo which has made it possible for rural India. This kiosk has been set up by ICICI Bank in partnership with network n-Logue Communications in remote villages of Southern part of the country. This is known as Proxi Banking. With the help of fibre optic cables, this kiosk works on wireless in local loop technology.

Reasons for setting-up of Proxi Banking

- 58% of rural households still do not have bank accounts.
- Only 21% of rural households have access to credit from a formal source.
- 70% of marginal farmers do not have deposit account.
- 87% households have no formal credit.
- Only 1% rural househlods rely on a loan from a financial intermediary. · The loans take between 24 to 33 weeks to get sanctioned.
- Consumers bribe officials to get loans approved which varies between 10 and 20 per cent of the loan amount.
- Branch banking in rurals is a loss-making.

Benefits to Rurals

- Small loans given for buying buffaloes.
- Loans for setting up a tea shop.
- Life and non-life insurance provided.
- Weather insurance given to farmers.
- Insurance policies sold to farmers like groundnut, castor, soya, paddy crop, etc.

The Proxy Banking is an innovative approach to rural lending and will add to the government's expanding base of kisan credit cards and the good old guidelines for agricultural lending.

Fact Files of Banks In India

- The first, the oldest, the largest, the biggest, get all such types of informations about Banking in India in this section.

- The first bank in India to be given an ISO Certification Canara Bank
- The first bank in Northern India to get ISO 9002 certification for their selected branches Punjab and Sind Bank
- The first Indian bank to have been started solely with Indian capital Punjab National Bank
- The first among the private sector banks in Kerala to become a scheduled bank in 1946 under the RBI Act South Indian Bank
- India's oldest, largest and most successful commercial bank, offering the widest possible range of domestic, international and NRI products and services, through its vast network in India and overseas State Bank of India
- India's second largest private sector bank and is now the largest scheduled commercial bank in India The Federal Bank Limited
- Bank which started as private shareholders banks, mostly Europeans shareholders Imperial Bank of India
- The first Indian bank to open a branch outside India in London in 1946 and the first to open a branch in continental Europe at Paris in 1974 Bank of India, founded in 1906 in Mumbai
- The oldest Public Sector Bank in India having branches all over India and serving the customers for the last 132 years Allahabad Bank
- The first Indian commercial bank which was wholly owned and managed by Indians Central Bank of India
- Bank of India was founded in 1906 in Mumbai. It became the first Indian bank to open a branch outside India in London in 1946 and the first to open a branch in continental Europe at Paris in 1974.

2

RURAL ECONOMY AND BANK CREDIT

Financial liberalization after 1991 decimated the formal system of institutional credit in rural India. It represented a clear and explicit reversal of the policy of social and development banking, such as it was, and contributed in no small way to the extreme deprivation and distress of which the rural poor in India have been victims over the last decade. This paper examines the impact of changes in banking policy and structure on the rural economy, and on the rural poor in particular.

Financial liberalization is a crucial component of the programmes of economic reforms that are being imposed on the people of less-developed countries. The demand that financial markets be liberalized quickly is high on the agenda of imperialism; in India as well, advocates of economic "reform" see financial liberalization as being at the core of structural adjustment. There are many components of the package of reforms associated with financial liberalization in India. Chandrasekhar and Ghosh (2002) classify the policies of financial liberalization in India into three types: first, policies to curtail government intervention in the allocation of credit, secondly, policies to dismantle the public sector and foster private banking, and thirdly, polices to lower capital controls on the Indian banking system.

It is well known that the burden of indebtedness in rural India is very great, and that despite major structural changes in credit institutions and forms of rural credit in the post-Independence period, the exploitation of the rural masses in the credit market is one of the most pervasive and persistent features of rural life in India. Rural households need credit for a variety of reasons. They need credit to meet short-term requirements of working capital and for long-term investment in agriculture and other income-bearing activities. Agricultural and non-agricultural activities in rural areas typically are seasonal, and households need credit to smoothen out seasonal fluctuations in earnings and expenditure. Rural households, particularly those vulnerable to what appear to others to be minor shocks with respect to income and expenditure, need credit as an insurance against risk. In a society that has no law of free, compulsory and universal school education, no arrangements for free and universal preventive and curative health care, a weak system for the public distribution of food and very few general social security programmes, rural households need credit for different types of consumption. These include expenditure on food, housing, health and education. In the Indian context, another important purpose of borrowing is to meet expenses on a variety of social obligations and rituals.

If these credit needs of the poor are to be met, rural households need access to credit institutions that provide them a range of financial services, provide credit at reasonable rates of interest and provide loans that are unencumbered by extra-economic provisions and obligations.

Historically, there have been four major problems with respect to the supply of credit to the Indian countryside. First, the supply of formal sector credit to the countryside as a whole has been inadequate.

Secondly, rural credit markets in India themselves have been very imperfect and fragmented. Thirdly, as the foregoing suggests, the distribution of formal sector credit has been unequal, particularly with respect to region and class, caste and gender in the countryside. Formal sector credit needs specially to reach backward areas, income-poor households, people of the oppressed castes and tribes, and women. Fourthly, the major source of credit to rural households, particularly income-poor working households, has been the informal sector. Informal sector loans typically are advanced at very high rates of interest. Further, the terms and conditions attached to these loans have given rise to an elaborate structure of coercion - economic and extra-economic - in the countryside.

That these constitute what may be called the "problem of rural credit" has been well recognized; recognized, in fact, in official evaluations and scholarship since the end of the nineteenth century. Given the issues involved, the declared objectives of public policy with regard to rural credit in the post-Independence period were, in the words of a former Governor of the Reserve Bank of India, "to ensure that sufficient and timely credit, at reasonable rates of interest, is made available to as large a segment of the rural population as possible". The policy instruments to achieve these objectives were to be, first, the expansion of the institutional structure of formal-sector lending institutions; secondly, directed lending, and thirdly, concessional or subsidized credit (ibid.). Public policy was thus aimed not only at meeting rural credit needs but also at pushing out the informal sector and the exploitation to which it subjected borrowers. Rural credit policy in India envisaged the provision of a range of credit services, including long-term and short-term credit and large-scale and small-scale loans to rural households.

BANKING POLICY IN RURAL INDIA: 1969 TO THE PRESENT

The period from 1969 to the present can be characterised as representing, broadly speaking, three phases in banking policy vis-à-vis the Indian countryside. The first was the period following the nationalization of India's 14 major commercial banks in 1969. This was also the early phase of the 'green revolution' in rural India, and one of the objectives of the nationalization of banks was for the state to gain access to new liquidity, particularly among rich farmers, in the countryside. The declared objectives of the new policy with respect to rural banking - what came to be known as "social and development banking" - were

(i) to provide banking services in previously unbanked or under-banked rural areas;

(ii) to provide substantial credit to specific activities, including agriculture and cottage industries; and

(iii) to provide credit to certain disadvantaged groups such as, for example, Dalit and Scheduled Tribe households.

The introduction of social and development banking policy entailed a radical shift from prevalent practice in respect of the objective and functioning of commercial banks. An important feature of the policy of social and development banking was that it recast completely the role of commercial banks in rural banking. Prior to 1969, the ountryside was not considered to be the problem of commercial banks.

It was only after 1969 that a multi-institutional approach to credit provision in the countryside became policy, with commercial banks, Regional Rural Banks and cooperative institutions establishing wide geographical and functional reach in the Indian countryside. The Reserve Bank of India (RBI) issued specific directives with respect to social and development banking. These included setting targets for the expansion of rural branches, imposing ceilings on interest rates, and setting guidelines for the sectoral allocation of credit.

Rural credit was an important component of the 'green revolution' package; the first post-nationalization phase of expansion in rural banking saw a substantial growth in credit advances for agriculture. Specifically, a target of 40 per cent of advances for the "priority sectors," namely agriculture and allied activities, and small-scale and cottage industries, was set for commercial banks. Advances to the countryside increased substantially, although they were, as was the green revolution itself, biased in respect of regions, crops and classes. The two main crops that gained from the green revolution, as is well recognized, were wheat and rice, and the application of the new technologies was primarily in the irrigated areas of the north-west and south of India, with the benefits concentrated among the richer classes of cultivators.

In 1975, the Government established by ordinance and then legislation a new network of rural financial institutions called the Regional Rural Banks (RRBs), which were promoted by the Government of India, State governments and commercial banks.

These were created on the basis of recommendations by a working group on commercial credit, also called the Narasimham Committee, and were intended to "combine the cooperatives' local feel and familiarity with the business acumen of commercial banks" (Jagan Mohan, 2004, p 22).

The number of such banks expanded rapidly, and covered 476 districts by 1987 (ibid.).

The second phase, which began in the late 1970s and early 1980s, was a period when the rhetoric of land reform was finally discarded by the ruling classes themselves, and a period when the major instruments of official anti-poverty policy were programmes for the creation of employment. Two strategies for employment generation were envisaged, namely wage-employment through state-sponsored rural employment schemes and self-employment generation by means of loans-cum-subsidy schemes targeted at the rural poor.

Thus began a period of directed credit, during which credit was directed towards "the weaker sections." The most important new scheme of this phase was, of course, the Integrated Rural Development Programme or IRDP, a scheme for the creation of productive income-bearing assets among the poor through the allocation of subsidized credit. The IRDP was initiated in 1978-79 as a pilot project and extended to all rural blocks of the country in 1980. There is much writing on the failure of IRDP to create long-term income-bearing assets in the hands of asset-poor rural households.

Among the many reasons for this failure were the absence of agrarian reform and decentralized institutions of democratic government, the inadequacy of public infrastructure and public provisioning of support services and the persistence of employment-insecurity and poverty in rural society. Nevertheless, the IRDP strategy did lead to a significant transfer of funds to the rural poor.

The second phase also involved an expansion and consolidation of the institutional infrastructure of rural banking.

"Even ardent critics of India's growth strategy," wrote a noted scholar of India's banking system, "would admit that what the country achieved in the area of financial sector development before the present reform process began, particularly after bank nationalization, was unparalleled in financial history". After bank nationalization, as Shetty points out, there was "an unprecedented growth of commercial banking in terms of both geographical spread and functional reach" (ibid.).

The third and current phase, which began in 1991, is that of liberalization. The policy objectives of this phase are encapsulated in the Report of the Committee on the Financial System, which was chaired, ironically, by the same person who recommended the establishment of Regional Rural Banks, M. Narasimham (RBI, 1991). In its very first paragraph, the report called for "a vibrant and competitive financial system...to sustain the ongoing reform in the structural aspects of the real economy." The Committee said that redistributive objectives "should use the instrumentality of the fiscal rather than the credit system" and, accordingly, that "directed credit programmes should be phased out." It also recommended that interest rates be deregulated, that capital adequacy norms be changed (to "compete with banks globally"), that branch licensing policy be revoked, that a new institutional structure that is "market-driven and based on profitability" be created, and that the part played by private Indian and foreign banks be enlarged.

Let us make it clear that, before the 1990s, the banking system was open to much criticism, particularly of its bureaucratic failures, its insensitivity to the social and economic contexts in which it functioned, and class and regional inequalities in lending patterns. The reforms proposed in 1991, however, were not attempts to bring rural banking closer to the poor, but to cut it back altogether and throw the entire structure of social and development banking overboard.

Record of Progress of Rural Banking

Policies of the current phase of financial liberalization have had an immediate, direct, and dramatic effect on rural credit. There has been a contraction in rural banking in general and in priority sector lending and preferential lending to the poor in particular.

Let us consider a few indicators. The impact of bank nationalization on the growth of scheduled commercial banks in rural areas is clear: the share of rural bank offices in total bank offices jumped from 17.6 per cent in 1969 to 36 per cent in 1972. The share then rose steadily, and attained a peak of 58.2 per cent in March 1990. From then onwards, there was a gradual decline in the share of rural bank offices, and the share fell below 50 per cent in 1998 and thereafter. In fact, there was an absolute contraction in the number of bank offices in the 1990s: 2,723 rural bank offices were closed between March 1994 and March 2000.

Official banking statistics do not, unfortunately, give us information on the volume of advances in a specific year. The basic source of data on banking is the Reserve Bank of India's annual Banking Statistics. Data in this document are provided on "credit outstanding," which is the total amount advanced, including all outstanding loans and non-performing assets, on March 31 of the reference year. Data under the head "credit sanctioned" do not represent the volume of advanced in a single year either; in fact, at the all-India level, the figures for "credit outstanding," "credit sanctioned," and "credit utilised" are equal. The consequence of this method of collection and presentation of data is that there are no data at all on loan advances by banks each year, that is, on the flow of credit The data on the stock of credit show a marked deceleration in credit provision to the countryside since 1991; had we data on the actual amount disbursed each year, we would have had a clearer picture of the collapse in rural banking in the period of liberalization.

The period after nationalization was characterized by an expansion of bank credit to rural areas: the credit outstanding from rural branches tripled in the 1970s, and continued to rise in the 1980s. After 1988, however, the credit outstanding from rural branches as a proportion of total credit outstanding declined, from around 15 per cent in 1987 and 1988 to 11 per cent in March 1999, and 10.2 per cent in March 2002. Turning to deposit mobilisation, rural deposits grew rapidly after nationalization; their share of aggregate deposits doubled in the 1970s, from 6.5 per cent in 1972 to 12.6 per cent in 1980 and continued to grow, although at a slower pace, in the 1980s. Once again, the peak was reached in 1990-91, when rural deposits accounted for 15.5 per cent of aggregate deposits.

The pace of deposit mobilization in rural areas fell in the 1990s. Given the pattern of growth of aggregate deposits and gross bank credit, it is no surprise that the credit-deposit ratio in rural areas rose after 1969. The ratio peaked at 68.6 per cent in 1984 and remained above 60 per cent until 1991. In the 1990s, the credit-deposit ratio fell sharply.

One of the objectives of banking policy after nationalization was to expand the flow of credit to agriculture and small industries, or what were termed "priority sectors." The share of priority sectors in the total credit outstanding of scheduled commercial banks rose from 14 per cent in 1969 to 21 per cent in 1972 and then went up to 33 per cent in 1980. The RBI set a target of 40 per cent for priority sector lending and by the mid-1980s this target was met. From 1985 to 1990, in fact, the target was over-achieved, that is, more than 40 per cent of total credit outstanding went to priority sectors. From 1991 to 1996, the share of priority sector credit fell, in line with the recommendations of the Narasimham Committee. At first glance, the direction in priority sector lending appears to have been reversed over the last five years. This is, however, a reversal by redefinition: "priority sector" lending now includes advances to newly-created infrastructure funds, to non-banking finance companies for on-lending to very small units, and to the food processing industry. Loans to multinationals like Pepsi, Kelloggs, Hindustan Lever and ConAgra now count as priority sector advances.

More recently, loans to cold storage units, irrespective of location, have been included in the priority sector. Chandrasekhar and Ray (2004) point to the growing presence of foreign banks in India, their direct presence and their indirect presence through the purchase of shares in existing private banks. This expansion is not good news for the priority sector. When data for scheduled commercial banks are disaggregated by type of bank (public sector banks, regional rural banks, private banks and foreign banks), we find that foreign banks did not lend to rural areas or agriculture.

Pallavi Chavan (2004) has examined the growth and regional distribution of rural banking over the period 1975-2002. Chavan's paper documents the gains made by the historically underprivileged regions of east, north-east, and central India during the period of social and development banking.

These gains were reversed in the 1990s: cutbacks in rural bank branches and in rural credit-deposit ratios were steepest in the eastern and north-eastern states of India. Policies of financial liberalization have unmistakably worsened regional inequalities in rural banking in India.

As already mentioned, one of our central concerns is the "credit starvation" (the term is S. L.Shetty's) of the rural economy, which resulted in shortages of credit for all purposes, including for productive investment in agricultural and non-agricultural activity. If we examine the term loans issued by scheduled commercial banks to agriculture between 1980-81 and 1997-98, then we observe that, inreal terms, credit outstanding rose from 1983-84 to 1990-91, but fell in the first four years after 1991 (although there was some recovery from 1995-96 onwards). It is instructive here to look at the distribution of total agricultural advances to cultivators by size classes of land holdings. The smallest cultivators i.e., those with land holdings of less than 2.5 acres or marginal cultivators, were the worst affected by the post-1991 decline in credit to agriculture.

Agricultural credit outstanding to marginal cultivators accounted for 30 per cent of total agricultural credit outstanding from commercial banks in 1990-91; its share fell to 23.8 per cent in 1999-2000 (Chavan, 2004, Table 10). At the same time, the share of credit outstanding to "small cultivators" (with between 2.5 and 5 acres) stagnated while that to large cultivators rose. Another indicator of the decline in credit to relatively poor rural households is the fact that the number of 'small borrowal accounts' (or accounts with a credit limit of Rs 25,000) fell in the 1990s.

The IRDP was a major component of the credit-led poverty alleviation strategy of the 1980s. The number of families assisted annually with IRDP loans rose from 2.7 million in 1980-81 to 4 million in 1984 and 4.2 million in 1987. Although the programme slackened after that, the number of beneficiaries in 1990-91 remained above the level of the early 1980s. After 1991, there was a steep decline in the number of IRDP beneficiaries: only 1.3 million families were assisted in 1998. If we index the number of families assisted in 1982 at 100, the number assisted in 1998 was a mere 37. The term credit disbursed by banks under IRDP followed a similar trajectory. With 1982 indexed at 100, total term credit mobilized for IRDP peaked at 113 in 1987 and went down to 52 in 1998 (ibid.).

Regional Rural Banks

Regional Rural Banks, as we have noted, were created in the 1970s exclusively to serve the credit needs of rural India, and specifically those individuals, social groups and regions most excluded by the formal system of credit. For all their weaknesses, these banks passed an important international test. A cross-country study of rural credit institutions threw up the important finding that, in the period 1988-1992, of all the institutions studied, Regional Rural Banks in India incurred the lowest costs of administration, 8.1 per cent of the total portfolio.

An important feature of banking reforms has been to alter the equation between different sectors of banking, in this case, to make the norms governing Regional Rural Banks indistinguishable from those governing commercial banks, thus undermining their capacity to serve the special needs of the rural economy and the rural poor. There has been a ban on recruitment to the staff of Regional Rural Banks since 1992 (Jagan Mohan, 2004).

At every discussion or seminar on problems of rural credit that we have attended in the recent past, bank officials speak of the impact on rural credit of the greying of bank personnel and the thinning of their ranks. Field officers of Regional Rural Banks in the 1970s and 1980s were relatively young and capable of spending substantial periods of time in the villages served by their branches.

Regional Rural Banks have also suffered because they are no longer permitted to recruit agricultural science and engineering graduates for specialised lending (see Shetty, 2004 and Jagan Mohan, 2004). Liberalization has had the effect of crippling Regional Rural Banks, rendering them incapable of fulfilling their original mandate.

MIRACLE CURE: MICRO-CREDIT AND SELF-HELP GROUPS

It is clear from the preceding sections that neo-liberal banking reform amounts, in theory and practice, to a reversal of the public policy objectives of extending the reach of rural credit, providing cheap and timely credit to rural households (particularly economically vulnerable households), overcoming historical problems of imperfect and fragmented rural credit markets, and displacing the informal sector from its powerful position in rural credit markets. As we have seen, there was a large-scale retreat by the formal sector from the Indian countryside in the post-1991 period. From official policy statements, it appears that the Government envisages only one major policy instrument to fill the gap left by the formal credit sector in the countryside: the establishment of micro-credit projects in rural India.

The micro credit approach is viewed as being able to rectify the major weaknesses of the banking system itself, most notably the "twin problems of non-viability and poor recovery performance" of existing rural credit institutions (Rangarajan 1996, p. 68). Micro-credit is the favoured alternative to the present system because, first, it is assumed that the transactions costs of banks and other financial institutions can be lowered significantly if these costs are passed on to NGOs or self-help groups, and secondly, because NGOs are expected to perform better than formal-sector credit institutions in respect of the recovery of loans.

The terms micro-credit and micro-finance have risen spectacularly to fame in the development profession and in development literature in the last decade and a half. The Declaration of the World-Bank-sponsored Micro-Credit Summit held in Washington, D. C. in 1997 defined micro-credit programmes as those "extending small loans to poor people for self-employment projects that generate income, allowing them to care for themselves and their families."

In India, the Task Force on Supportive and Regulatory Framework for Micro-Finance in India defined micro-finance as the "provision of thrift, credit and other financial services and products of very small amounts to the poor in rural, semi-urban or urban areas enabling them to raise their income levels and improve living standards" (NABARD 2000). The Reserve Bank of India uses the same definition (RBI 1999a).

While micro-credit loans are generally advanced for self-employment projects, they are sometimes advanced for consumption as well. Nevertheless, the advocates of micro-credit do consider it necessary for micro-credit institutions to get borrowers to make the transition from consumption loans to production loans (or loans for income-bearing projects) (Rangarajan 1997, p. 71).

The characteristic features of micro-credit operations are small loans to poor households in rural and urban areas for income generation through self-employment. Micro-credit institutions may also provide facilities for savings and otherfinancial services. Micro-credit, as discussed in the international literature, is associated with the following recurring empirical features:

- very small loans,
- no collateral,
- borrowers from among the rural and urban poor,
- loans for income-generation through market-based self-employment,
- the formation of borrower groups, and
- privatization, generally through the mechanism of NGO control over disbursement and the determination of the terms and conditions attached to each loan.

In an earlier paper, we reviewed the two claims in support of NGO-controlled micro credit, that is, lower transactions costs and a better repayment record than that of formal-sector financial institutions (Ramachandran and Swaminathan, 2002). The international evidence on administrative costs of NGOs shows that these costs were high (and administrative costs are, of course, the major component of total transactions costs) and relatively higher than those of commercial banks.

NGOs cannot match the economies of scale of a comprehensive system of banking (in the case of India, perhaps the best network of rural banks in the less developed world). Secondly, the costs of administration of NGO-controlled micro-credit have actually risen when NGO activity is scaled up.

Thirdly, repayment rates in NGO-controlled micro-credit projects are related directly to the level of administrative costs and mobilization efforts. High-cost NGO operations are financed either by donor funds or by raising interest rates to levels higher than those offered by the banking system or by doing both.

It is acknowledged widely that interest rates charged by micro-credit organizations are higher than the corresponding rates charged by commercial banks or other financial institutions.

Thus we argued that the transfer of the task of serving the credit needs of rural borrowers from the banking system to NGO-controlled micro-credit projects does not reducetransactions costs but, in effect, transfers transactions costs - higher transactions costs - to donors as well as borrowers.

Reviewing interest rates on micro-credit loans, R. Ramakumar and Pallavi Chavan (2004) observe that annual rates ranged from 24 to 36 per cent on bank-linked schemes refinanced by NABARD. Some studies, however, found rates of interest that were even higher, and as much as 60 per cent per annum. To sum up, interest rates for micro-credit loans are undoubtedly higher than those charged by the banking sector for agricultural loans, and the interest rate spread is also larger.

The other salient feature of micro-credit, high repayment, is not a costless achievement. First, a system based on the quick repayment of very small loans does not allow for funds to go into income-bearing activities that have a gestation period of any significance. Only projects with very quick rates of return and high rates of return relative to the tiny investment can meet existing repayment schedules. This pattern of repayment can put the poorest out of the pale of micro-credit, since the ability to pay the first few instalments depends on the initial resource base of the borrower. Secondly, high repayment is dependent on high transactions costs. As already mentioned, NGOs invest heavily in supervising, monitoring and enforcing loan repayments. When the activities of NGO-controlled micro-credit projects are scaled up, the relative burden of administrative costs tends to increase. An evaluation of SEWA bank, a bank set up by the Self Employed Women's Association (SEWA) showed that the proportion of overdues to total advances was actually marginally higher than the corresponding ratio for public-sector banks. Scaling up NGO-controlled micro-credit, it appears, can generate problems similar to those faced by traditional banking institutions. The corrective measures being taken by SEWA Bank to address the problem of overdue loans involve greater supervision and monitoring (Ghosh 2001). In short, higher and better repayment requires more staff and closer monitoring, or higher transactions costs.

In India, NGO-controlled micro-credit is not yet as widespread and does not represent as general a policy towards rural credit as it is and does, for instance, in Bangladesh. Nevertheless, the scale of bank finance through self-help groups has expanded rapidly in the last few years, and is even considered "the largest and fastest growing example of micro finance in the world" (RBI, 2004 a). Witness the proliferation of self help groups: from lessthan 10,000 in 1996-97, the number of self-help groups (SHGs) with bank finance has grown to 10 lakhs in 2004. And the total bank lending to self help groups has crossed Rs 3500 crores (RBI, 2004a). NABARD has set a goal of creating 1 million self help groups by 2007-8 in order to reach around 40 million persons.

Andhra Pradesh has been something of a leader in establishing self help groups: by 2002, over 50 per cent of the self help groups in the country (and 20 per cent of all self help groups in the world) were in Andhra Pradesh. Despite the growth in numbers - with over 3 lakh self help groups by 2002 - only 0.6 per cent of total bank credit in Andhra Pradesh was channelled to self help groups in 2002.

The results of a recent case study by Smriti Rao of the costs and benefits of participation in women's self-help groups in Andhra Pradesh are noteworthy (Smriti Rao 2004). Drawing on detailed interviews with women from different self help groups in two villages of the Telangana region, Rao describes various features of self help groups in practice, among them the exclusion of the poorest and the perpetuation of existing class and caste hierarchies by groups. She also shows that the State Government allocated very little by way of funds and manpower to monitoring self help groups. Transactions costs were inevitably borne by NGOs or members of groups themselves, including income-poor women. From these village studies, it emerges that micro-credit advances were small, short-term and high-cost. Interest rates on these loans were typically 30 per cent per annum, as compared to 36 per cent on loans from informal lenders. Rao writes that, in her study village, the benefits of participation were "limited to small, expensive and short term consumption loans." Rao's study also shows that self help groups in her study villages tend to reinforce the separateness of social groups along traditional lines.

There is as yet no large-scale evaluation of micro-credit institutions and finance as an alternative mechanism for meeting credit and banking needs in rural India. This is an important area for further research. The conclusions of the case study by Smriti Rao, however, are salutary, for they indicate the shortcomings of relying solely on micro-credit to alleviate poverty and empower women.

We have shown that, despite assertions to the contrary, NGO-controlled micro-credit organizations do not incur lower transactions costs than banks (they are able to transfer these costs to others). Banks have many advantages over private micro-credit organizations as providers of small-scale loans. They have advantages of scale; the banking system in India has a reach and spread that NGO-controlled micro-credit cannot begin to match; banks can cross-subsidize loans; banks are better placed to provide specialized training to their employees in development banking; banks are better placed to coordinate banking activity with development administrations, local governments and self-help groups; and banks are better able than private micro-credit organizations to offer a wide range of financial services to borrowers. For the state to withdraw from the field and hand over small-scale credit to NGO-controlled micro-credit organizations is, in effect, to undermine and weaken a major national asset, the widespread rural banking system.

Case studies based on primary data help identify the impact of changes in financial policy and banking structure on patterns of indebtedness among rural households. We shall attempt to review the major results from five papers, each reporting the findings of detailed village surveys on rural credit in the contemporary period.

The studies cover Baghra and Udaipur villages of Giridih district in Jharkhand, Panahar and Muidara villages of Bankura district in West Bengal, Morazha village of Kannur district in Kerala, Gokilapuram of Theni district in Tamil Nadu and Dhamar of Rohtak district and Birdhana of Fatehabad district in Haryana. Gokilapuram village in south-west Tamil Nadu is a highly-irrigated, agriculturally-advanced and commercialised village. The high development of productive forces is combined with a very unequal distribution of resources: a large proportion of households are landless while a small minority control the major share of land and other assets. The availability of data from two census-type surveys of Gokilapuram, the first in 1977 and the second in 1999, with smaller surveys in the interim, particularly in 1985, allows for a discussion of changes over a relatively long period of time (Ramachandran and Swaminathan, 2004b). Resurvey data are also available for the two villages in West Bengal. Vikas Rawal first studied the villages of Panahar and Muidara in 1995-96 and restudied them in 2002 (Rawal, 2004).

After land reform in the 1970s and 1980s, there were major changes in these two villages. Irrigated area, agricultural output and yields surged. As in other parts of West Bengal, agrarian structure in Panahar and Muidara is dominated by smallholders. In neighbouring Jharkhand, Surjit and Ramachandran conducted surveys of rural credit in the villages of Baghra and Udaipur in 2003. These villages are not only less developed in terms of agricultural production than Panahar and Muidara but also poorer in terms of general infrastructure and resources. Udaipur village, a village whose popoulation was almost entirely Adivasi (or Scheduled Tribe), had fewer landless households and less inequality in the distribution of land than Baghra, a multi-caste village. Rawal and Mukherjee (2004) present some features of credit among landless labour households in two villages of Haryana. In Dhamar village, their survey, which was conducted in 2002, covered 163 landless manual labour households. In Birdhana, a larger multi-caste village, their survey covered 282 households (this included households living in the village settlements and those that lived on the fields) and was conducted in June 2003.

The last case study is from northern Kerala. R. Ramakumar conducted a survey in 2001 of all landless households whose members participated in agricultural work in Morazha village (Ramakumar 2004). Morazha belongs to a region that was characterised by widespread and acute indebtedness among the peasantry during the British period. It is also a region where there were major struggles against British rule and against landlordism, and where the cooperative movement took strong roots. These village studies present some striking observations with respect to rural credit in the liberalization phase. First, all the village studies report high levels of indebtedness: 64 per cent of households in Morazha were indebted, the corresponding proportions were 66 per cent in Gokilapuram, 72 per cent in Baghra, 75 per cent in Dhamar and 83 per cent in Panahar and Muidara.

Secondly, with one exception, the village data combined with information on the banking sector indicate that the share of formal sources of credit, that is, commercial banks, regional rural banks and cooperatives, is extremely low. In Baghra village, for example, only 28 per cent of total credit was from the formal sector. In Panahar and Muidara, the formal sector accounted for 24 per cent of credit among all village households in 1995-96 but its share was nil among landless households. In Gokilapuram, formal sources of credit accounted for 14 per cent of loans taken and 40 per cent of the principal borrowed by all village households.

Class further differentiates access to credit. Among landless hired labour households in Gokilapuram, the formal sector accounted for only 22 per cent of total principal borrowed. Surprisingly, in the relatively advanced agricultural state of Haryana, landless labour households continued to depend on informal sources of credit.

Of total credit outstanding among landless households, formal sources accounted for 12 per cent in Dhamar and 8 per cent among manual labour households living in fields in Birdhana. In Udaipur village, somewhat paradoxically, it was observed that the formal sector accounted for 80 per cent of total principal borrowed. Given the limited scale of borrowing, this observation may be explained by the poverty of the village and the absence of informal lenders

The exception is the village of Morazha, where the cooperative movement is well established and where cooperative banks and societies are almost the sole source of credit for rural households. In 2001, 98 per cent of the principal borrowed by landless households was from cooperatives. Even here, though, cooperatives mainly met the needs of consumption credit and the issue of credit to landless households for productive purposes remained neglected. A most striking feature of the village data from Jharkhand was that the people at large had no access to the formal sector of credit.

In Baghra, only seven households received any formal sector credit at all in the five years prior to the survey. In each of the two study villages, only one household received any formal-sector credit in the year preceding the survey (Ramachandran and Surjit, 2004). The formal sector had virtually washed its hands of any responsibility to the villages.

Thirdly, the two studies that capture changes over time show a clear decline in access to formal sources of credit, particularly credit from scheduled commercial banks, in recent years. In Panahar and Muidara, the share of the formal sector in total debt fell from 24 per cent in 1995-96 to 7 per cent in 2001-02. In Gokilapuram, the share of the formal sector in the total principal borrowed by landless households fell from 80 per cent to 17 per cent between 1985 and 1999. It is worth noting that among landless labour households in Gokilapuram the share of principal borrowed for productive purposes fell from 44 per cent in 1985 to 14 per cent in 1999. Borrowing for consumption purposes dominated the loan portfolio of almost all classes of households.

In the study villages in West Bengal and Tamil Nadu, informal lenders are thriving and in fact gained ground after 1991 as a result of the withdrawal of the banking sector from rural areas. The village studies also indicate the gross inadequacy of credit, especially for crop cultivation and other productive activities. The growing and unmet demand for credit, both for direct production as well as for demands of health, education, and other needs, is resulting in what S. L. Shetty terms "credit starvation" among rural households.

This picture is confirmed by the latest report of the Rural Labour Enquiry, which shows both the weakening of banks in rural areas as well as the consolidation of moneylenders. In 1983, the formal sector, comprising government, cooperatives and banks accounted for 44 per cent of the debt of agricultural labour households. The share of the formal sector fell to 36 per cent in 1993 and further to 31 per cent in 1999-2000 (GOI, 2004). Over the same period, the share of moneylenders in the total debt incurred by agricultural labour households went up from 18.6 per cent in 1983 to 34 per cent in 1999-2000. During the period when the share of formal credit in total debt of rural households fell, the share of debt taken for productive purposes also fell sharply, from 41 per cent in 1983 to 21.5 per cent in 1999-2000 (ibid.).

Despite over three decades of systematic expansion of the banking infrastructure in the country, the village studies indicate that informal sources of credit - including usurious moneylenders -- remain important, and often dominant and growing, sources of credit for rural households.

In Panahar and Muidara, trader-moneylenders have come to dominate the informal credit market. In 1995-96, 32 per cent of the total principal borrowed by the surveyed households was borrowed from traders. Moneylenders accounted for 17 per cent of the total principal borrowed by households. In 2001-02, of the total principal borrowed by surveyed households, 50 per cent was advanced by agricultural traders and another 31 per cent was advanced by urban businessmen.

In Gokilapuram in 1977, of the total principal borrowed by landless labour households, 27 per cent was advanced by moneylenders and 23 per cent by landowners. By 1999, the share of landowners had fallen to 2.4, per cent while moneylenders accounted for 42 per cent. A major finding of this study is the phenomenal rise in the number of moneylenders, full time and part-time, village-based and town-based, operating in the area. In Baghra village too, among informal lenders, moneylenders dominated, accounting for 64 per cent of the total principal borrowed by households. The corresponding proportion in Udaipur was 46 per cent.

Landowner-employers were the dominant sources of credit for landless workers in Haryana. In Dhamar village, nearly 49 per cent of the total principal borrowed by landless households came from their agricultural employers. The rates of interest on loans from the informal sector, particularly from moneylenders, remain very high. In Panahar and Muidara, where traders were the major source of credit, explicit interest rates were not easy to unearth or compute though rates between 36 and 120 per cent per annum were reported. In Baghra, the modal interest rate range was 48-60 per cent per annum. In Gokilapuram, the modal interest rate range was 60-120 per cent for landless households and 36-48 per cent for all households. Among landless labour households in Gokilapuram, the share of principal borrowed at rates higher than 36 per cent per annum doubled between 1977 and 1999. In Dhamar, the modal rate of interest charged by employer-lenders was 36 per cent per annum. A distinctive feature of the Haryana villages was that the dependence of landless manual worker households on their employers for credit, together with conditions of severe unemployment, forced workers to enter into unfree labour relationships with their creditor-employers. It is particularly noteworthy that unfree labour relationships in these villages coexisted with significant technological advance and commercialisation in agriculture. The study found that, while unfreedom was widespread, there were considerable variations in its specific forms. The nature of unfreedom was closely linked to the high degree of concentration of ownership of land holdings in these villages. Casual workers were subject to various kinds of coercion by employer-creditors, and had also to perform various kinds of labour services. Siri workers in Dhamar village worked under conditions that were akin to bondage. They were not allowed to work for employers other than their creditors and restrictions were often imposed even on their physical mobility. In short, the study found that the dependence of manual workers households on employers for credit was an important factor in sustaining unfree conditions of employment.

In April-May 2004, the Indian electorate delivered a dramatic judgement on economic policy. Thirteen years of neoliberal economic policy (further intensified in the last five to six years) had taken their toll, and there is general agreement among serious political observers that the election results represented widespread protest, rural and urban, against the collapse of livelihoods among the mass of the people. If policy is to repair the damage done to the rural economy, India needs large-scale public investment in the countryside. The links between rural distress and the near-collapse of the formal sector of bank is well recognised, and it is no surprise that one of the promises of the new Government was that it would double the flow of rural credit in three years.

The purpose of this essay is not to evaluate the rural credit policy of the United Progressive Alliance government.

Nevertheless, it is clear that if any government is seriously to address the crisis in rural banking, it must reaffirm the commitment of the state to the policy of social and development banking, and reaffirm the part played by the credit system in redistribution and poverty alleviation. Commercial banks, Regional Rural Banks and cooperatives must lead rural credit revival, which is too serious and large-scale a task to be left merely to self help groups or NGO-controlled private-sector micro-credit organisations. The geographical and functional reach of public sector banking must be restored and extended, differential interest policies reinstated, and special loans-cum-subsidy schemes reintroduced on a large scale for all landless and poor and middle peasant households, scheduled caste and tribe households and other vulnerable sections of the rural population. Priority sector norms must be enforced, and, instead of an alternative such as investment in RIDF bonds, penalties must be imposed on any failure of banks to meet these public-interest targets.

If financial liberalization had the effect of damaging the system of formal credit severely, our case studies show that changes in national banking policy have had a rapid, drastic and potentially disastrous effect on the debt portfolios of the income-poor. In general, as formal sector credit withdrew, the informal sector rushed in to occupy the space that it had vacated.

Although it is clear that chronic indebtedness among the rural poor is a problem that cannot be solved by banking policy alone, and that the abolition of usury requires agrarian reform, a decisive change in banking policy is essential for the very survival of the working people in rural India.

STATE Bank of India, the country's largest bank, recently announced that it would shift its focus to Rural India to boost the retail portfolio. According to its Chairman, there is business opportunity in rural India. Similarly, ICICI Lombard plans to market weather insurance in the rural areas.

Urban-oriented banks and financial institutions see business prospects in shifting focus to the rural sector. They had not given this market much attention hitherto. A large pool of high net worth individuals, traders, entrepreneurs, processing industries, marketing and warehousing agencies, market intermediaries, professionals, educational institutions, plantations and so on provides a wide range of business avenues and market for these institutions to diversify the risks and also seek growth.

The development of the telecom infrastructure in the rural areas has made doing business easy. Marketing intermediaries and loan recovery agents have brought down the cost of operations. Recent studies indicate that the actual level of non-performing assets (NPAs) in the rural sector is less than elsewhere, and this coupled with the low cost of operations, less expensive labour, infrastructure, cost of living, and so on make Rural India an attractive market.

Success, however, depends on using the right strategies and the ability to foresee the growth of this sector. Many economists and policy-makers increasingly believe that future growth of the domestic economy to a large extent will depend on the robust performance of the agriculture and rural sector. The manufacturing and service sectors cannot sustain the economy's growth if the rural sector underperforms.

Despite decades of effort and experimentation in banking, the organised financial sector is still not able to meet the credit gap in the rural sector. It took time for banks to realise the potential of the rural markets. Lack of infrastructure in the rural areas and the focus in the urban sector were the reasons. Directed and subsidised lending, cumbersome procedures, delay in sanctioning loans and lack of statutory backing for recoveries were major impediments to the growth of banking in the rural sector.

The focus in the past has always been to make available cheaper credit. When banks are forced to lend cheap, there has been a tendency for a scramble for credit by the non-target group of beneficiaries. Empirical data indicate that various measures to make available cheaper source of credit have failed to achieve the desired results and led to wilful defaulting because such loans gets written off for reasons mainly political. This has really damaged the credit culture and structure in the rural sector. The rural sector needs timely credit. Due to the failure of the organised sector to make an impact in bridging the credit gap, the informal credit sector has been thriving and is able to lend as high as 24-36 per cent per annum depending on the borrowers' risk profile.

The concepts of lending based on credit history and risk perception being implemented in the organised sector now have been in vogue in Rural India's informal credit sector for long. It is time to find out why the informal credit sector thrives despite efforts to reduce the credit gap.

Banks need to make loan procedures simple and accessible if they want to make inroads into the rural sector. If banks can offer housing and car loans through simple procedures in urban markets, it is ridiculous to have cumbersome and complicated procedures in the rural sector. Simplification of loan procedures and credit accessibility will attract quality and high net worth borrowers.

Recent Budget announcements on the availability of agriculture credit at soft rates are welcome, but better credit delivery systems are required for Rural India. The success of the informal credit sector proves this point. To boost credit growth, banks should be permitted to lend at different rates depending on the borrower's risk profile. This will help develop a superior credit culture.

Recent measures to strengthen the loan recovery mechanism through the SARFESI Act will help develop the credit culture. Healthy competition and market forces will achieve free flow of credit at lower cost.

The Government should play a supportive and regulatory role in developing the investment climate. It should facilitate private and public sector investments for developing infrastructure in Rural India. Greater acceleration in development can be achieved through such direct incentives as exemption of tax on all private sector employment generation activities in the rural sector. As banking is the engine of growth, it would be worthwhile to exempt rural earnings from tax.

Maybe the Government, apart from its own involvement, ought also to work on schemes to attract corporate investment in infrastructure, education and health. Infrastructure is a key factor in the development of the rural sector and even the

President, Dr A. P. J. Abdul Kalam, has been advocating this aspect through PURA (providing urban infrastructure in the rural areas).

The Government and trade bodies should forge partnerships to attract domestic and foreign investment, because investments here will generate huge direct and indirect employment opportunities. Banks with their presence and exposure in the rural sector can play a creative role in such road shows.

Such projects as the Golden Quadrilateral and the proposed interlinking of rivers can boost Rural India's economy. Major economic activity should be set up along the project corridors to gainfully utilise the investments.

Domestic economic growth depends on the rural sector. Therefore, the corporate sector should focus on this sector. The external sector is attractive and offers exceptional opportunities, but in case of global economic slump, it is the rural sector than can sustain domestic growth. Advantages offered by the rural sector, such as cheap labour, need to be fully exploited by the domestic companies.

Banks should harness the rural savings, though smaller because of the lower income, and direct them towards productive sectors. Investment avenues for the urban population, such as government debt, mutual funds and capital market instruments, as also insurance products should be made available to the rural sector too. Information and communication technology can help banks convert rural networks into financial marts. Banks today have surplus liquidity and those that succeed in directing the surplus funds to productive sectors will gain. Banking is becoming increasingly complex and those that fail to tap the potential of the rural sector will stand to lose.

The overhead cost of operations for banks in Rural India will be more because of low business per employee and the large number of small clients. However, mechanisation and centralisation of accounting as also decentralisation, cheaper office premises, engagement of external agents for recovery of loans and marketing of products will make up for the other drawbacks. Taking the cue from a few banks and financial intermediaries that have big plans to make a foray into the rural sector, other banks also need to re-draw their strategies at the earliest.

BIOMETRIC ATMS FOR RURAL INDIA

To reach the rural masses, banks are going all out in providing a user-friendly banking experience. To boost micro financing initiatives, banks are deploying biometric solutions with ATMs. Establishing the identity of a rural depositor through biometrics makes it possible for illiterate or barely literate folks to become part of the banking user community. In recent years the importance of biometrics has grown tremendously with an increasing demand of security in accordance of unique identification of individuals.

Its use for identification in applications other than policing is on the rise. In view of the rapidly increasing applications, the scope of biometrics is also increasing, be it identification via face, voice, retina or iris. Fingerprinting, however, has the advantage of being a familiar concept worldwide.

In the retail payments arena, developments in biometric technology have made their presence felt in the pervasiveness of self service devices including Automated Teller Machines (ATMs) and Point of Service (POS) machines. Some of the new generation POS terminals are biometric enabled with smart card readers, allowing thumb-print based authentication. Some Indian banks have started implementing biometric applications in retail branch applications for officer authentication. Elsewhere in the world, efforts are on enabling payments through kiosks based on fingerprints (non-card based).

ATM enhancements with biometric support envisaged by vendors eliminate the need for PIN entry, and authenticate customer transactions by thumb-impressions. A simplified menu on ATMs coupled with possible audio guidance in local language enable easy use for rural masses. So far bank ATMs are dependent on PIN verification. The fingerprint authentication method is non-PIN based, and this requires enhancements to the standard Switch environment.

Securing Transactions with Fingerprints

With the development of biometric solutions for the ATMs there is no need to remember PIN numbers. Software vendors are coming up with finger print solutions for the rural masses. Chennai based Financial Software and Systems (FSS) has recently launched its Biometric ATM Interface Solution (BAIS) that enables connectivity of ATMs with biometric support to Electronic Financial Transaction (EFT) switches. Elaborating on the working of the biometric solutions, G. P. Shekar, Head - Consulting Practice, Financial Software and Systems (P) Ltd. says, "Customers opting for biometric authentication can visit a nearby kiosk or ATMs or bank, where his finger-print data would be scanned into a special PC with a finger-print scanner and the scanned fingerprint is then stored in an encrypted form in a central server. When a customer inserts (or swipes) his card in a biometric enabled ATM, he is prompted to set his finger in the fingerprint scanner. The transaction along with customer's biometric information is passed on to the switch. The switch verifies the fingerprint with the server, and if successful, requests the banking application to authorise the transaction." Based on the result, the Switch instructs the ATM to complete the transaction. FSS' BAIS solution meets this requirement, by performing requisite message translations as well as confirming authorisation.

CMC Limited which has its presence in the biometric space for nearly two decades has also developed solutions for banks. CMC's Fingerprint solution provides high level authentication for accessing ATMs. Fingerprint solutions provides an interface to integrate with an ATM application. CMC has indigenously developed FACTS (Fingerprint Analysis and Criminal Tracing System)-an advanced automated fingerprint identification system, using image processing and pattern recognition techniques. FACTS was initially targeted at law enforcement, but with increased concerns on security and personal identity, CMC started focusing on the banking and related sectors. B M Mehtre, DGM, R&D, CMC Ltd says, "Fingerprints of account holders are captured through the scanner in the system at the time of account opening. A template is created for each fingerprint by extracting features and stored in the debit card against the unique Customer ID. During verification, the fingerprint is captured using a fingerprint scanner attached to the ATM and 1:1 matching of the fingerprint captured is done with the templates stored in the debit card. Upon a successful match, the user is allowed to perform further transactions."

Pune based Axis technology is another Indian company which is developing biometric solutions for ATMs and kiosks in the banking sector. Says Abhay Khinvasara, CEO, Axis Technology, "Our ATMs can work with popular protocols that are being used in the financial transaction infrastructure. Axis ATMs will also work with any type of authentication required be it PIN or biometric based. The ATMs are equipped with a high quality fingerprint sensor ideally suited for dry, moist and rough fingers and advanced image processing and pattern recognition algorithms for fingerprint verification (FBI approved).There are also intelligent and dynamic security settings and other biometrics like Iris, face or even layered biometrics, which can be integrated into it."

Benefits of Biometric Supported ATMs

- Provides strong authentication
- Can be used instead of a PIN
- Hidden costs of ATM card management like card personalisation, delivery, management, re-issuance, PIN generation, help-desk, and re-issuance can be avoided
- Ideal for Indian rural masses
- It is accurate
- Flexible account access allows clients to access their accounts at their convenience
- Low operational cost of the ATMs will ultimately reduce TCO

With ATMs supported by biometric solutions, banks having a presence across the country are leveraging on this technology. The ATMs are networked and connected to a centralised computer (Switch), which controls the ATMs. The use of biometrics identification is possible at an ATM. The information can be stored at a bank branch. ATMs are so prevalent and you have so many people using ATMs that it becomes easy to use biometrics as a replacement for an ATM PIN. The typical ATM has two input devices (a card reader and keypad) and four output devices (display screen, cash dispenser, receipt printer, and speaker). Invisible to the client is a communications mechanism that links the ATM directly to an ATM host network. The ATM functions much like a PC, it comes with an operating system (usually OS/2) and application software for the user interface and communications.

While most ATMs use magnetic strip cards and personal identification numbers (PINs) to identify account holders, other systems may use smart cards with fingerprint validation. The ATM forwards information read from the client's card and the client's request to a host processor, which routes the request to the concerned financial institution.

If the cardholder is requesting cash, the host processor signals for an electronic funds transfer (EFT) from the customer's bank account to the host processor's account. Once the funds have been transferred, the ATM receives an approval code authorising it to dispense cash. This communication, verification, and authorisation can be delivered in several ways. Leased line, dial-up or wireless data links may be used to connect to a host system, depending on the cost and reliability of the infrastructure. The host systems can reside at a client's institution or be part of an EFT network. The EFT network supports the fingerprint authentication. Point-of-sale services that use biometric solutions are also possible.

Shekar says, "The FSS Biometric ATM Solution consists of a central server which holds a repository of customer fingerprints. It also customises the Switch to enable authorisation of a customer's biometric data and interfaces with ATMs enabled with biometric devices as per FSS specifications.

The central server solution is platform independent, it uses Java and can run on Unix and Oracle/ Microsoft SQL Server, customisation to BASE24 Switch (of which FSS is the distributor) is done using TAL. Biometric application and devices from Secugen are used for customer interface and application development."

Axis Technology on the other hand, has developed an innovative new product called the Biometric Retrofit Kit for ATMs. This kit converts a regular ATM to one that authenticates users based on biometrics-fingerprint or iris. This is an affordably priced kit tgat has generated interest among financial institutions.

Recent Initiatives

Deploying ATMs for rural masses depends largely on banks stepping forward to take the requisite initiatives. The recent directive from the government on financial inclusion ("banking for the common man") is a key driver for the growth of such solutions in India. Banks are quite aware of the untapped potential in the rural sector. The telecom industry is witnessing a blistering growth pace, and so is the Internet. The National Rural Employment Guarantee Program that guarantees employment and payment in the rural sector requires robust solutions. Using thumbprint and voice guidance in ATMs reduces literacy requirements to a considerable extent. However, the technology is not restricted to rural masses. FSS is in discussions with Andhra Bank for deploying the BAIS. Several other public sector and private sector banks have shown interest too. Says Shekar, "FSS would like to work with ATM and POS vendors to provide innovative and cost effective solutions to banks and customers." FSS is striving to modularise and 'ruggedise' the solution to perform online functions across a wide variety of delivery channels and payment systems. Apart from these banks, some other banks such as ICICI Bank are planning to introduce biometric authenticated ATMs in rural India.

CMC has been working with Institute for Development and Research in Banking Technology (IDRBT) on a pilot project in rural banking. Biometric (Fingerprints) smart cards, which consist of fingerprint data and financial data, will be issued to the rural banking customers for carrying out financial transactions. Elaborates Mehtre, "For building and developing various applications, CMC has a biometric technology group at its Research and Development Centre in Hyderabad. The team evaluates the latest technologies emerging in the biometrics area. This helps CMC's solutions to be competitive and cost effective. CMC has been working with Bank of India for introducing biometric ATMs. CMC has demonstrated its Biometrics ATM solution on the eve of inauguration of mobile ATMs for the bank."

SAVING THE REGIONAL RURAL BANKS

Recent moves by the Union Finance Ministry are likely to weaken RRBs and lead to the bleeding of financial resources from the countryside.

According to the United Progressive Alliance's Common Minimum Programme, the revival of agricultural credit is one of the important priorities of the Central government. There is no doubt that there has been some improvement in this regard since July 2004; certainly the downward movement in terms of access to institutional credit has been stopped and in several States reversed.

However, some current moves of the Finance Ministry and the Reserve Bank of India (RBI) are likely to worsen the situation and once again contribute to the bleeding of financial resources from the countryside. These moves relate to the Regional Rural Banks (RRBs), which are public financial institutions set up three decades ago to serve specifically rural needs.

These banks (which are popularly known as Gramin Banks) were set up in 1975 with the explicit objective of bridging the credit gap in rural areas, which it was hoped would thereby also check the outflow of rural deposits to urban areas, reduce regional imbalances and increase rural employment generation.

It is obvious, in the circumstances, that RRBs require special conditions given the fact that they are meant to cater exclusively to rural needs with much higher transaction costs and greater difficulties in lending and loan recovery. In the early phase, this was accepted in policy circles. However, more than a decade of financial liberalisation has sought to create a "level playing field" between RRBs and credit cooperatives, which are relatively weak financial institutions by their very nature, and commercial banks operating on market principles. Regulatory regimes, capital adequacy norms and other compliance with rules has been imposed in exactly the same way on the RRBs as on commercial banks.

Despite this, the RRBs' performance in respect of some important indicators was certainly better than that of commercial banks or even cooperatives. As of March 31, 2004, the credit-deposit ratio of all the RRBs taken together was more than 46 per cent, and the recovery of loans was 74 per cent. Despite the widespread perception that most RRBs are struggling with losses owing to bad loans in fact most RRBs have been profitable - out of 196 RRBs, 165 earned profit and only 31 incurred losses, and the group as a whole showed a net profit of Rs.754 crores in 2003-04. Non-Performing Assets (or bad loans) amounted to only 16 per cent of gross advances in 2003-04.

Further, priority sectors have accounted for over 70 per cent of RRBs' lending, with loans specifically to agriculture amounting to 46 per cent. RRBs have also performed better in terms of providing loans to small and retail traders and petty non-farm rural activities. In recent years, they have taken a leading role in financing Self-Help Groups (SHGs) and other micro-credit institutions and linking such groups with the formal credit sector.

Given these priorities and the past performance, RRBs should really be strengthened and provided with more resources with which they can undertake more of these important activities. And most certainly they should be kept apart from a profit-oriented corporate motivation that would reduce their capacity to provide much needed financial services to the rural areas, including to agriculture. Ideally, the best use of the resources raised by RRBs through deposits would be through extensive cross-subsidisation. This, in turn, really requires an apex body that would cover and oversee all the RRBs, something like a National Rural Bank of India (NRBI).

Instead, the focus has been on integrating the RRBs with private commercial banks that are "sponsor banks". Currently, there are 28 such sponsor banks, which have essentially sought to introduce corporate culture into the functioning of RRBs, with associated decline in attention to priority sector lending, especially to small producers in agriculture and non-agriculture.

In fact, the reduced attention to serving rural needs has been evident in the way the RRBs themselves have responded to the changed incentives emanating from the government and the RBI. From September 1992 onwards, the RRBs were allowed to finance non-target groups to the extent not exceeding 40 per cent of their incremental lending, and this limit was enhanced to 60 per cent in 1994. Because of this, the RRBs diversified into a range of non-priority sector advances, including jewel and deposit-linked loans, consumer loans and home loans.

The RRBs adopted new innovations for credit delivery with lower risk of default such as SHG-linked lending, non-priority sector collateralised lending, and so on. As a proportion of total advances, priority sector lending dipped from around 70 per cent in 1990 to 57 per cent in 2001. Even among the categories that were eligible as priority sector, the attempt was to minimise credit risk and make easy loans. Between 1996 and 2003, while short-term agricultural credit under the priority sector increased at about 29 per cent per annum, term loans declined by 2.6 per cent a year. Over the same period, the number of rural branches of RRBs declined by 459, even as the number of urban and semi-urban branches increased. The share of outstanding credit of RRBs going to rural customers declined from 78 per cent to 71 per cent.

So, already financial liberalisation measures and the changed messages from the RBI had led to pressures on the RRBs to move away from their basic purposes. The recent moves of the RBI are even more worrisome, since they have involved a reduction in the number of RRBs through amalgamation and even raise the possibility of merger with some of the commercial sponsor banks. In fact, the Government of India has already requested the National Bank for Agriculture and Rural Development (NABARD) to look into the implications of reducing the number of RRBs from 196 to only 62. There are already seven proposals for amalgamation from various commercial banks such as the Bank of Baroda, the Central Bank of India, the Punjab National Bank and so on.

Such a plan would have serious implications. It would mean that there would be no possibility of national level or even State-level RRB, with related impact on the possibility of cross-subsidisation. It would allow the sponsor banks to continue to siphon off deposits to urban borrowers. Essentially, the dominantly rural character of the RRB or Gramin Bank would effectively disappear.

In addition, a recent notification of the RBI (December 27, 2005) announcing a special package for the RRBs, has effectively allowed them to diversify their activities away from agricultural lending and lending for productive activities in the rural areas, to a range of other activities. While there are measures for increasing access to resources by allowing sponsor banks to provide lines of credit to the RRBs and allowing access to inter-RRB term money and borrowing, the RRBs are also being allowed to enter into ready forward transactions in government securities.

Requests from RRBs for opening of currency chests would be considered by the RBI, on a case-by-case basis, taking into account their financial position, compliance with Statutory Liquidity Ratio (SLR)/Cash Reserve Ratio (CRR)/inspection findings, the general position of management, grading, and so on.

In addition, the statement reveals that the RBI is in the process of reviewing the existing norms for conduct of various types of foreign exchange transactions by the RRBs with a view to allowing them to undertake non-trade related current account transactions pertaining to release of foreign exchange for certain specified purposes such as private visits, business travel, medical treatment, overseas education, visa fees and so on.

It is obvious that such opportunities would only encourage RRBs to move further away from the core concerns for which they were set up, and which remain vital for the urgent revitalisation of crop lending and viability of agriculture to which the government is explicitly committed.

Instead of these policies, a focussed programme for making the RRBs more viable and more able to concentrate on their social and developmental functions must be put in place. The number of rural branches should be increased rather than reduced; they should be encouraged to develop more sophisticated methods of credit delivery to meet the changing needs of farming; and most of all, there should be greater coordination between district planning authorities, panchayati raj institutions and the banks operating in rural areas. Only then will the RRBs fulfil the promise that is so essential for rural development.

ACCELERATING RURAL FINANCING PROCESS BY BANKS IN INDIA

The goal of Union Government to double the flow of farm credit in three years [2004-05 to 2006-07]was achieved in two years. Actual flow of credit during the year 2006-07 is expected to exceed the target of Rs.1,750,000 million set for the year by Rs. 150,000 million. During April to December 2006, around 5,337,000 new farmers, as against target of five million, were linked with the institutional credit system. For the year 2007-08, target of farm credit disbursement has been fixed at Rs.2,250,000 million[28.6% over target of 2006-07] and an addition of five million new farmer-borrowers. Performance of public sector banks in particular, alongwith their sponsored RRBs, has indeed been satisfactory in increasing flow of credit to farm sector, improving recovery and containing overdues & NPAs.

Their involvement in financing weaker sections of the society and beneficiaries under Differential Interest Rate scheme & Government sponsored programs [SJGRY &PMRY] has also improved.However,the share of institutional credit declined to 57% in 2001 as compared to 64% in 1991. Moreover, debt sourced from money lenders, the very informal agents the institutionalization of credit was designed to replace, increased in overall share of rural debt from nearly 18% in 1991 to nearly 30% in 2001. According to recent Survey, formal institutional credit provision in India now accounts for just 27% of total cultivator debt, & that this reduces to just 20% if data for the five States reporting the highest proportion of fromal rural debt are removed.

Table: Farm Credit Disbursements by Cooperative, Commercial & Regional Rural Banks [2001-02 to 2005-06] Rs. in Million

Year	Co-op. Banks	Com. Banks	RRBs	Others	Total
2001-02	235,240 [37.91]	335,870 [54.13]	48,540 [7.82]	800 [0.14]	620,450 [100]
2002-03	236,360 [34.00]	397,740 [57.18]	60,700 [8.72]	800 [0.10]	695,600 [100]
2003-04	268,750 [30.91]	524,410 [60.29]	75,810 [8.71]	840 [0.09]	869,810 [100]
2004-05	312,310 [24.92]	814,810 [65.02]	124,040 [9.91]	1,930 [0.15]	1,253,090 [100]
2005-06*	372,520 [23.65]	1,061,520 [67.41]	140,760 [8.94]	NA	1,574,800 [100]
Total	1,425,180 [28.42]	3,134,350 [62.52]	449,850 [8.97]	4,370[0 .09]	5,013,750 [100]

Moreover, nearly 90% of households reporting no debt, either formal or informal are headed by small & marginal farmers suggesting institutional -rather than self-exclusion. Intriguingly, Andhra Pradesh, the State with the highest concentration of SHGs, MFIs & banks, reports the highest proportion of rural non-institutional debt [nearly 73%] and the highest proportion of rural money lender debt [nearly 57%] for all States in India, according to All India Debt & Investment Survey, 1991 & 2001. It is in this context an attempt is made here to analyse the data on the performance of banks, more imortantly public sector banks, & appreciate the immediate need to create enabling environment that can facilitate banks to:

[i] expand outreach especially in remote locations to cover small/marginal & tenant farmers, share croppers, oral lesees, landless labourers and households residing in dryland, desert, drought prone, hilly & tribal areas of the country

[ii] understand the new & diversified demand for rural financial products & services emerging in the changed rural socio-economic scenario & meet them

[iii] introduce improvements in operational management, inter alia, HRM & Training policy for rural areas; reducing transaction costs & mitigating portfolio risk on a continuing basis and

[iv] pursue rural finance research & development tasks.

Table: Flow of Farm Credit during April to December 2005 & 2006 [Rs. In Million]

Period	Public sector Banks	Private sector Banks	Cooperat ive Banks	Regional rural Banks	Total
April-Decembe r' 05	Rs.689,9 10 [57.92%]	Rs.100,3 10 [8.42%]	Rs.289,4 70 [24.30%]	Rs.111,4 60 [9.36%]	Rs.1,191, 150 [100.%]
April-Decembe r' 06	Rs. 868,650 [58.16%] [25.91%] *	Rs.141,3 40 [9.46%] [40.90%] *	Rs.331,7 40 [22.22%] [14.60%] *	Rs.151,7 00 [10.16%] [36.10%] *	Rs.1,493, 430 [100.%] [25.38%] *

Figures in brackets indicate percentage share in the total.

Figures in bracket with * indicate percentage increase during April-December'06 over April-December'05

Farm credit disbursements progressively increased from Rs. 620,450 million in 2001-02 to Rs. 1,574,800 million in the year 2005-06 reflecting rise by 153.8%. Commercial banks & RRBs recorded phenomenal rise by 216% & 189% respectively as compared to 58% by cooperatives.While there has been progressive rise in each successive year in case of cooperatives, commercial & regional rural banks, there has been spectacular increase during 2004-05 & 2005-06 in respect of commercial banks & RRBs. The share of cooperatives in the total disbursements of short-term & long-term credit progressively declined from 37.9 per cent in 2001-02 to 23.65 per cent in 2005-06 whereas that of commercial banks recorded progressive increase from 54.13 per cent to 67.41per cent during the corresponding years.

RRBs accounted for 7.82 per cent in 2001-02 which progressively rose to 9.91 per cent in 2004-05 but declined by one percentage point in the following year. Agriculture credit flow for the banking system as a whole during 2005-06 has surged to Rs 1,804,860 million, reflecting 128 per cent of the target of Rs 1,410,000 million that was set for that year.

Agriculture credit flow target for 2006-07 had been pegged at Rs 1,750,000 million. However, for the fiscal year 2006-07, agriculture credit up to December 2006 stood at Rs 1,493,430 million which represented a 25.38 per cent increase over the achievement of Rs 1,191,150 million recorded in the same nine-month period in the previous year. Agriculture credit flow during April to December 2006 from public sector banks grew by 25.91 per cent to Rs 868,650 milion from Rs 689,910 million during the corresponding period in the previous year. In case of private sector banks, it increased by 40.90 per cent to Rs 141,340 million from Rs 100,310 million.While cooperative banks recorded increase by 14.60 per cent from Rs. 289,470 million to Rs 331,740 million during the period, the RRBs showed increase by 36.10 per cent from Rs. 111,460 million to Rs 151,700 million. Share of public sector banks in the total disbursement during April-December'06 accounted for as high as 58 per cent folowed by cooperative banks at 22 per cent where as RRBs & private sector banks had almost equal share of 10 & 9 per cent respectively.

During the seven year period from 2000-2006 public sector banks' outstanding credit to priority sectors increased by 221.9% from Rs.1,274,780 million as on 31st March, 2000 to Rs. 4,103,790 million as on 31st March'06, whereas that of private sector banks shot up by 480.2% from Rs. 183,680 million to Rs. 1,065,660 million during the corresponding period. Priority sector advances of public sector banks as group accounted for over 43% of net bank credit in four years as against the target of 40% which,however, declined from 42.8% to 40.3% in three years. In this respect, private sector banks as a group had less than that of targeted 40% during initial three years but they showed impressive performance [42.8% to 47.3%] in the following four years.

Agricultural advances of public sector banks during the period rose by 242% from Rs. 452,960 million to Rs. 1,549,000 million whereas that of private sector banks increased significantly by 799% from Rs. 40,230 million to Rs. 361,850 million during the period.

Share of agricultural advances in the net bank credit by public sector banks ranged between 14.3% & 15.7% whereas that of private sector banks varied from 8.3% to 14.2% during the period. Neither public sector banks nor private sector banks as a group could achieve targeted agricultural credit of 18% of net bank credit..

During 2005-06, all public sector banks [except State Bank of India (SBI) and State Bank of Patiala] were able to meet the priority sector target of 40 % of net bank credit in 2005-06 & only 10 public sector banks met the 18 % sub-target for agriculture. None of the private sector banks could meet sub-target for lending to agriculture.

All banks' outstanding loan to weaker sections of the society as on 31st March'06 amounted to Rs. 1,045,768.9 million with NPA amount of Rs. 88,172.6 million accounting for 8.43 per cent of outstanding loan. Only eight banks in the public & nationalized sector could achieve the stipulated target of 10% of net bank credit,whereas none of the old & new private sector banks could meet the target.

While 19 nationalised & nine public sector banks as a group had 8.17% & 8.45% NPAs, respectively, eight old & 20 new private sector banks as a group had higher percentage of NPAs at 11.3% & 9.43% respectively.

Rural & Semi-Urban branches of each of the public sector banks have been alloted Service Area comprising specified number of villages, since April, 1989. Each branch is expected to formulate Service Area Credit Plan every year for the purpose of providing credit to the rural households.

This micro level credit planning exercise should help the bank to progressively bring within its fold all eligible house holds for providing credit & related services. In the ultimate process this exercise should prove to improve quality & productivity of lending.

RBI has since the year 1994-95 has advised public sector banks to ensure 25% annual growth rate in the matter of disbursement of credit in their Service Area. Accordingly, the data presented in the above Table showed that annual growth was between 12.5% and 24.% during 2000-2001 to 2003-04.

The growth was spectacularly high at 54.5 during 2004-05 which, however, declined to 44.6% in the following year. Disbursements of credit as against targets ranged from 92.1% to 117.3% during the six year period. Achievements were higher than 100% only in the last two years. This is attributed to Finance Minister's directives to double the farm credit disbursement in three years effective from April, 2004.

Public sector banks recovery to demand under direct agricultural advance was 69.3% during the year 2001 which gradually increased during following three years. It, however, phenomenaly rose to 84.1% in the year 2005.

During the five year period the demand , loan amount to be recovered & percentage of recovery to demand have progressively increased in the successive years whereas over due amount has increased until the year 2004 & then it steeply declined by Rs.29,620 million in the following year.

As on 31st March'05 aggregate recovery of 196 RRBs was 79.8% and that of 20 State Cooperative Agricultural & Rural Development Banks [SCARDBs] was 43.7%; 727 Primary Cooperative Agricultural & Rural Development Banks [PCARDBs] at 50.6%, 31 State Cooperative Banks [SCBs] at 83.47% & 367 District Central Cooperative Banks[DCCBs] at 71.23%.

As reported under the NABARD-GTZ Rural Finance Program, at around 98 % on time repayment to the SHGs is reported to be very high.

As on March'06 the number of SHGs stood at just over two & quarter million , of which over one & a half million had outstanding bank loans. Even with this huge number of SHGs it is estimated by the Committee on Financial Inclusion that the munber of SHGs will have to be doubled to cover all the 50 million poor households in the country.

Other Programs

- Under Differential Interest Rate scheme [at 4%] loan outstanding as on 31st March'05 was of the order of Rs. 4,900 million outstanding with 389,000 borrowers accounting for 0.07% as of previous year's outstanding credit as against stipulation of one per cent.
- During the year 2005-06 banks have lent Rs. 6,440 million accompanied with Government's subsidy of Rs. 2,380 million to 755,969 beneficiaries of Swarna Jayanti Gram Rozgar Yojana & under Prime Minister's Rozgar Yojana sum of Rs. 7,610 million was provided to 131,290 beneficiaries.
- During the period from 2001-02 to 2005-06 banks provided 59,093,000 kisan credit cards to farmers to facilitate them to purchase farm inputs & other requirements. Share of commercial banks was 37% as against cooperatives & RRBs at 51%&12% respectively.
- Commercial banks, RRBs & Cooperative banks have disbursed sum of Rs. 221.4 million, Rs. 22.2 million & Rs. 70.5 million to 5,173 farmers,283farmers &2,826 farmers respectively to redeem their past debt with informal sources.during the year 2005-06.
- As on 31st March'06 commercial banks provided to NABARD sum of Rs. 313,373.4 in 11 tranches under
- Rural Infrastructure Development Fund for financing 244,651 projects in respect of creating irrigation facilities, constructing rural bridges & roads, assisting social sector & powergeneration etc.

NPA status of public sector banks revealed that during the year 2005-06 though amount of NPA under priority sector advances declined to Rs.223,740 million from Rs.233,970 million in 2004-05 share of NPA in the total NPA increased to 54.1% from 49.1%.

In respect of agricultural advances NPA amount declined by Rs.10,510 million & its share in the total NPA amount also declined by 0.2 per centage points, whereas its share in the priority sectors NPA amount declined significantly from 31% to 27.7% during the period.

As of 31st March 2005, total NPAs costituted 4.96% of total loan outstanding. NPAs under priority sectors were as high as 7.02% of its outstanding loans as against 3.87% in respect of all other loans.

Within priority sectors, agriculture NPAs accounted for 6.6% of its outstanding loans which were significantly lower than that of small scale industries [10.29%] but marginally higher than that of other priority sectors [5.64%].

Priority sector loan outstanding accounted for 34.7% of total loan outstanding where as share of priotity sector NPAs in the total NPAs was as high as 49.05%. NPAs under agriculture were 15.21% of total NPAs as against share of agricultural advances at 11.45% of total outstanding loans.

There was wide difference in respect of small scale advances with regard to its share of NPAs in the total NPAs [16.43%] as compared to 7.93% share in the total outstanding loans. Other priority sector advances had also higher percentage share of NPAs [17.42%] in the total NPAs when compared with its share [15.32%] in the total loan outstanding.

Public sector banks were able to clean their balance sheets by writing off NPAs built over a period of time in financing Government sponsored programs viz, IRDP,Agro-Service-Centers & high tech projects viz, Floriculture, Aquaculture, Mushroom Farming, Tissue Culture etc.

In case of private sector banks. while NPA amount under priority sectors has increased by Rs. 950 million in the year 2005-06 its share in the total NPA amount has significantly increased to 29.2% from 24.9% in the previous year. NPA amount under agriculture as well as its share in the total NPA amount & in the priority sectors also increased marginally.

As on 31st March'05 NPA status of 196 RRBs was Rs.28,043.5 million & that of 20 SCARDBs at Rs. 54,373.8

million, 727 PCARDBs at Rs. 40,559.1 million, 31 SCBs at Rs. 60,716 million & 367 DCCBs at Rs. 145,196 million accounting for 8.5%; 31.27%; 31.9%; 16.25% & 19.87% respectively of the loan outstanding.

Enabling Environment

In order to encourage Rural Financial Institutions to play catalytic role in lubricating the process of both fam sector development & rural rejuvenation at a time when the country has launched its 11th Five Year Plan[2007-08 to 2011-12], enabling environment needs to be created specifically in the areas of removal of urban-biased policies, sound agricultural & rural development policies, promotion of broad-based rural financial sector reforms & development of effective legal system to enforce contracts, sound interest rate policies, & appropriate legal status & prudential regulation of Rural Financial Intermediaries etc.

Financial Sectors

- Encourage & facilitate RFIs expand their outreach in rural areas, especially in remote locations in a cost-effective way & achieve sustainability of their methodolgies. Different types of RFIs can have comparable advantages in terms of sustainability, quality,& scope of products & services being offered.
- RFIs can incorporate operational solutions to reduce transaction costs & mitigate portfolio risk, such as using remote operating models & outsourcing services [mobile banking, ATMs, mobile phone & internet banking, correspondent retail outlets& agents]; accepting alternative collateral [warehouse receipts, assured contracts, third party guarantees]; and employing portfolio securitizations & loan guarantees.
- Changing rural economic scenario has opened several opportunities for investment & development and has impacted the demand for new financial products & services among rural population.

- Needs of rural clients for financial services now extend much beyond traditional, short-tern credit products. RFIs need to develop & experiment with different new products which include term loans for agriculture& investment, leasing products, credit & debit cards & overdraft lines, flexible saving products, insurance [agriculture, life, health& property], cash transaction/ remittances etc.

Investment in Agriculture

Investment pattern both in public & private sector during the period from 1999-2000 to 2004-05 has been irratic as total investment was as low as Rs. 381,760 million in 2001-02 which increased to the highest level at Rs. 478,330 million in 2003-04 but declined to Rs. 431,230 million in the following year.

Average annual investment during the six year period was Rs. 442,027 million reflecting share of public & private sector at 21.32 % & 78.68% respectively. Gross Capital Formation as percentage of total GDP ranged from 1.7 to 2.2 & that of Agricultural GDP from 8.4 to 10.2 respectively with average value of 2.0 & 9.3 respectively.

Investmant, more importantly in public sector, supported by well intentioned public policy is both essential & desirable in specific areas such as,

[i] development of irrigation [exploiting potential surface irrigation & ground water resources, generation of electricity/power to draw ground water]

[ii] intensifying soil & moisture conservation measures,

[iii] land development & reclamation

[iv] improving drainage system[iv] strengthenig flood control measures

[v] all weather road to facilitate transport

[vi] storage/warehousing facilities & cold chains

[vii] marketing infrastructure

[viii] developing sound information, communication & market intelligence system

[ix] building integrated agricultural research, extension & education system and

[x] effective soil & water testing facilities and quality control & pricing system to facilitate competitively &timely supply of farm inputs [seeds, fertilizers, pesticides, water, fuel, farm equipment & machinery etc].

Table: Public & Private Sector Investment & Share of Agriculture in GDP & Gross Capital Formation as percentage of GDP at 1990 prices [Rs. in Million]

Year	% share of Agri in GDP	Investment Public in Rs.m	Investment Private in Rs.m	Investment Total in Rs.m	GCF % of Agri. GDP	GCF % of Total GDP
1999-2000	NA	77,540 [17.8]	357190 [82.2]	434730 [100]	9.6	2.2
2000-01	24.2	70,180 [18.4]	311580 [81.6]	381760 [100]	8.4	1.9
2001-02	24,4	85,290 [18.2]	382150 [81.8]	467440 [100]	9.7	2.2
2002-03	21.9	78,490 [17.1]	380180 [82.9]	458670 [100]	10.2	2.1
2003-04	22.2	128,090 [26.8]	350240 [73.2]	478330 [100]	9.7	2.0
2004-05	20.8	125,910 [29.2]	305320 [70.8]	431230 [100]	8.7	1.7
2005-06	19.9	NA	NA	NA	NA	NA
Total		565500 [21.3]	2086660 [78.7]	2652160 [100]	9.3	2.0

Figures in bracket indicate % share of public & private sector investment to total.

Public investment has potential to substantially improve credit absorption capacity of farmers & geographical areas and ultimately stimulates private sector investment & facilitates smooth flow of bank credit for undertaking seasonal agricultural operations & investment purpose which in the ultimate process lays strong foundation of sustainable agriculture.

Creation of rural infrastructure to integrate rural development with banking & finance, particularly is a must in respect of upgrading literacy & education level & providing all weather roads, electricity which have direct impact on information & communication technology,

Farm Productivity & Returns

Productivity of crops per hectare & milk per lactation has been low as compared to other countries as well as in the world & return per hectare is not remunerative for small & marginal farmers to sustain a reasonable standard of living even in prosperous regions, leave dryland, desert & drought prone areas.

Table: Productivity of crpos /ha & milk/ lactation period in India & other countries

Country /Cro	Paddy	Wheat	Maize	S'canc	Cotton	Milk [Kg]
India	2811	2559	1481	69197	922	1000
China	6062	3759	5173	59589	2302	1476
Indonesia	4515	NA	2362	80133	NA	NA
USA	6860	2442	7975	73816	2043	7454
Canada	2558	2410	7255	NA	NA	6255
World	3730	2541	4117	61304	1581	2305

Farming even in well-endowed States where yields of crops viz,wheat, paddy, s'cane, cotton & mustard are relatively very high & farmers receive better minimum support price is not more remunerative. These States & crops are Punjab [wheat & paddy]; Tamil Nadu [S'cane]; Andhra Pradesh[Cotton] & Gujarat [Mustard]. What clearly emerges from the exercise is that under the best irrigated conditions-making it feasible to take out two seasonal crops or one full crop of sugarcane-a farmer owning one hectare of land would earn a profit of Rs. 12,000 & Rs.23,000 respectively. This would be on an average per month Rs. 2000 only. Even after factoring in net income from milk & sale of by-products such as straw[say Rs. 1000] the maximum that farmers in India's well endowned areas can earn around Rs. 3000 per month, assuming no crop losses due to natural calamities such as hailstorms, floods, pest-disease infestations & weather abberations etc.

Table: Return to better-off farmers from different crops

	Paddy Punjab	Wheat Punjab	Sugarcane Tamil Nadu	Cotton Andhra Pradesh	Mustard Gujarat
Yield Quintal/ha	58.55	42.13	1026.95	14.62	14.86
Cost in Rs. Per Quintal	480.53	515.59	67.05	1815.2	1151.34
MSP in Rs/Quintal	600	650	90	1980	1715
Return Rs/Quintal	119.47	134.41	22.95	164.8	563.66
Return Rs/hectare	6994.97	5662.69	23568.5	2409.38	8375.99

According to 1995-96 Agricultural Census out of 115.58 holdings, 61.6% & 18.7% are marginal & Small" holdings with average size of 0.40 hectare& 1.42 hectares respectively. Thus, over 80 per cent of India's farming families own less than two hectares. And only 30 per cent of Marginal & Small holdings are " wholly irrigated" & rest being either "partly irrigated or wholly unirrigated" It can safely be concluded that three-fourths of Indian farmers can earn only upto Rs. 3000 per month.Stagnating yields & rising costs make farming day by day unremunerative or non-viable.Stagnating yields & rising costs make farming day by day unremunerative or non-viable. The average farm size is becoming smaller & cost-risk-return structure of farming is becoming adverse. All this is increasingly pushing farmers into debt, leading to distress & even suicides in some cases. Even NSSO survey reveals that nearly 40 per cent of farmers would like to quit farming, if they have option.

As per the Commission for Agricultural Costs & Prices [CACP] latest data for the year 2005-06, the total cultivation costs cover & refer to actual production expenses in cash & kind incurred by the farmer plus rent paid to leased-in-land plus imputed value of family labour plus rental value of owned land plus interest on value of other owned capital assets. These numbers particularly relating to costs tend to be on the lower side & to that extent may little exaggerate the actual returns accruing to farmers. The costs of paddy in Punjab as estimated by CACP in 2005-06 were Rs. 480.53 & MSP were Rs. 600 per quintal & yield of 58.55 quintals per hectare. Thus net return from growing paddy in Punjab per quintal was Rs. 119.47 & per hectare was Rs. 6994.97 during 2005-06. Thus, it can be observed that if a farmer were to raise two crops [paddy in kharif & wheat in rabi season] he would annually earn Rs. 12,657/- [Rs. 6994.97 + Rs. 5662.69]. In case of sugarcane return per hectare would be higher at Rs. 23,568, which however is full 12- month crop unlike 120 to 150 days each for paddy, wheat, cotton & mustard.

Research institutes should, therefore, address issues viz, diversification of agriculture; availability of limited water; minimum use of chemicals; integrated pest, nutrient & water management; cost reduction & maximum return per rupee investment. Productivity of crops must necessarily be significantly stepped up at farmer's field level through provision of proven & demonstrated cost- effective & high- return technology; supply of quality inputs including water & electricity on time & at reasonable price. On lines Land Grant College of the USA integrated concept of research, extension & education may need to be operationalised by Farm Universities. Besides, India will have to embark upon farmer-friendly research in bio-technology to improve productivity, products of international quality standards & marketibility.First Green Revolution began with seed-water-fertilizer technology, second will begin with bio-technolgy Farm Input Regulatory & Development Authority needs to be established to develop & enforce strict quality standards in respect of quality, price & relable source of supply of seeds, fertilizers, pesticides, fuel/energy,water, farm equipment etc. Soil, water & input testing laboratories must be established for this purpose. Network of Agri-meteorological stations to forcast day-to-day data & information on weather must be well equipped & strengthened & weather based insurance scheme should be developed gaining experience of Food & Agriculture Organization . Besides, marketing infrastructure needs to be developed. Both these should insulate farmers against adverse impact.Insurance companies[domestic & multinationals] may need to progressively provide life & non-life insurance cover to all poor rural house-holds.

Pressure on Land

There are 1.4 million large holdings exceeding 10 hectares with an average size of 17.33 hectares of which around 11% are " wholly irrigated".There are about 10,000 farmers in Punjab alone having holdings exceeding 40 hectares. As against this, 71.18 million out of 115.58 million holdings were " Marginal" holdings of less than one hectare, with an average size of 0.40 hectare. Another 21.64 million constituted " Small" holdings of 1-2 hectares, with an average size of 1.42 hectares. Thus, over 80 per cent of India's farming families own less than two hectares. And only 30 per cent of Marginal & Small holdings are " wholly irrigated" & rest being either "partly irrigated or wholly unirrigated In the context of competing demand for land & water there is immediate need for "Land & water reforms" to guarantee the fulfillment of objectives of social equity, growth & modernization of rural economy among all rural inhabitants.

About 65% of the population deriving livelihood from farming; farm population growing by 1.84 per cent annually; the average farm size becoming smaller & cost-risk-return structure of farming becoming adverse. All this is increasingly pushing farmers into debt, leading to distress & even suicides in some cases. Even NSSO survey reveals that nearly 40 per cent of farmers would like to quit farming, if they have option. Pressure on land needs to be reduced progressively by 30 % in five years through creating significant number of self-employment opportunities in secondary & tertiary sectors of economy. Autonomous bodies viz, Khadi & Village Industries, Handloom/ Handicraft /, Coir / Silk / Tea/ Coffee & Rubber Boards etc, must bc made responsible & accountable for creating enabling environment such that progressively self-employment opportunities in these avenues absorb the released labour force from the farm sector.

Rural Banking

The concept of agricultural banking & credit should be replaced by rural banking & finance for total integrated rural development & not farm sector or for that matter any other sector in isolation. Rural house-holds expect a variety of financial sevices, not only credit, Government may consider doing away with stipulation of targets & sub-targets. Let RFIs concentrate on their Service Area to bring every household within the fold of banking & finance during 11th Five Year Plan. Financial sustainability [not alone operational viability] of RFIs is a must. Government may therefore need to reimburse the loss incurred by RFIs while providing credit at concessional inteest rate when Government is committed to the principle of social equity & removing regional imbalances.

Code of ethics not to vitiate climate of recovery of bank credit through interest waiver & loan write offs need to be evolved & meticulously implemented. It is for RFIs to consider this on its merits. The spatial spread of cooperatives across the country, especially in more remote & economically deprived areas has already identified itself with the rural households. Every sixth village has a cooperative; cooperative membership touches the lives of 480 million rural households, more than half the aggregate rural population. Seventy per cent of rural cooperative clients are marginal & sub-marginal farmers. This sharply focuses the need for its revival, restructuring & reforming through greater involvement & commitment by State Governments.

Subsidy linked Credit programs sponsored by Government agencies should have clear demarcation of role, functions & accountability between sponsorers & RFIs and should help targeted beneficiaries to fully achieve the enshrined objectives.

Banking Sector in Budget 2008

The Union Budget of India for the year 2008-2009 was announced by the Indian Finance Minister, Mr. P Chidambaram, on 29th February 2008. The policies and initiatives taken in the Union Budget of India 2008-2009 on the Indian Banking sector were in tandem with the requirements of the Indian economy.

Small and marginal farmers have been relieved of all farm loans, disbursed till March 2007 and also all loans, which are due till December 2007 and was unpaid till February 2008. These farm loan waivers would be facilitated by all the concerned Public Sector Banks and Regional Rural Banks of India. A total of Rs 60,000 crores would be waived-off under such scheme. The settlement of these loan-waivers will be offered through special type of scheme.

Further, the Public Sector Banks and Regional Rural Banks of India were also suggested, to bring within their fold, a minimum of 250 rural household accounts at every branch every year. The Indira Awas Yojana was brought under the ambit of Public Sector Banks. Loan limit up to Rs 20,000 per unit at 4% interest was fixed under differential rate of interest (DRI) scheme. The Finance Minister also advised the Indian PSU Banks to open 288 branches in minority districts of India. Further, he also asked the Indian banking industry to embrace total financial inclusion. In another landmark decision, the Finance Minister, Mr. P. Chidambaram said that the Ex-banking servicemen in India would be offered employment opportunities in the banking sector.

Another major announcement was that, the much talked-about 'Banking Cash Transaction Tax (BCTT)' would be withdrawn from the financial year 2009-2010. Experts believe the impact of the decisions and policies taken during the Union

Budget of India 2008-2009 on the Indian Banking sector would be mixed. It is expected that the Indian PSU banks will face pressure on their net interest margins due to the waiving-off of agricultural loans.

Further, the cumulative cost that will be incurred for opening up of new Regional Rural Banks in India may substantially increase thc operating cost for the banks. The inclusion of the Indira Awas Yojana houses under the differential rate of interest scheme and at 4% interest will increase the proportion of sub-PLR lending for the concerned banks. The major Public Sector Banks of India like the State Bank of India, Bank of Baroda, Punjab National Bank may see their net interest margins shrinking till the subsidy for waiver of agricultural loans is being completely released. Moreover, experts are skeptical about the long term benefit of such agricultural loan waiver as offered through the Union Budget of India 2008-2009.

RURAL CREDIT

In 2000, over seventy percent of India's population, and roughly three quarters of its poor, lived in rural areas. The main livelihood in rural India remains agriculture, an activity characterized by significant time-lags in production and a high degree of sensitivity to weather conditions.

These features of agricultural production make access to financial instruments critical to a rural household's ability to smooth income shocks and make long-term productive investments. However, as is well known lenders' inability to perfectly identify the credit-worthiness of potential borrowers and the cost of enforcing repayment places severe restrictions on rural households' access to credit. These problems are potentially more severe for the rural poor who are less able to reduce lender risk by providing collateral.

This also has implications for the geographical distribution of formal credit lenders. Anticipating insufficient profits, lenders such as commercial banks, may choose not to set up branches in relatively poor rural areas. This, in turn, by giving lenders in the informal sector monopoly power may further raise the interest rates faced by the rural poor and restrict their access to affordable credit. Banerjee (2004) provides evidence that informal interest rates in India are high and exhibit significant variation.

A belief that the welfare costs of exclusion from the banking sector, especially for the rural poor, are high has led to widespread government intervention in the banking sector of low income countries. Examples of such interventions range from interest rate ceilings on lending to the poor to State-led branch expansion in rural areas. India was home to some of the largest policy interventions aimed at providing banking for the poor.

The motivation for the Indian interventions can be traced to the All-India Credit Survey Report (1954). This report showed that four years after independence, the informal credit sector accounted for the bulk of rural lending, with moneylenders contributing close to 70 percent of the total. The average annual interest rate on these loans exceeded 20 percent. In contrast, less than one percent of the borrowing was accounted for by commercial banks.

Commercial banks remained confined to urban areas and geared towards the financing of trade and commerce activities. The survey data also showed a strong positive relationship between asset ownership and borrowing. The Report concluded that financial backwardness was a root cause of rural poverty, and that commercial banks needed to be harnessed to enhance formal credit in rural areas - both to enable poor, rural households to adopt new technologies and production processes, and to displace 'evil' moneylenders who exploited their monopoly power to charge high rates of interest.

The conclusions of this Report have guided Indian government's policy towards rural credit markets. By 1991, according to the All India debt and investment survey, the share of moneylenders in total credit had reduced to 15 percent, and the share of commercial banks soared to 29 percent. Equally striking is the fact that by 1991 the probability of having a rural household having a formal loan was only weakly correlated with the amount of land it owned. At the same time, the total number of locations with atleast one bank branch had increased from under 2,000 in 1951 to over 30,000. By the year 2000, the Indian rural banking sector accounted for the rupee equivalent of 26,768 million dollars as deposits and 10,834 million dollars as loans outstanding.

In terms of population reached, the rural sector accounted for 125 million savings accounts and 25 million borrowing accounts. A proximate reason for these changes in borrowing practices was the fact that the Indian government, and Central Bank followed an aggressive policy of state intervention in rural credit markets, often described as `social banking'. The policy instruments to achieve these objectives included the expansion of the institutional structure of formal-sector lending institutions; secondly, directed lending; and thirdly, concessional or subsidized credit. In 1969 the fourteen largest Indian commercial banks were nationalized, at which point they came under the direct control of the Indian central bank and were formally incorporated into the planning architecture of the country.

Bank nationalization was intended to allow the state to target financial backwardness as a means of promoting social objectives. A central aim was to reduce and equalize the average population per bank branch across Indian states. To achieve this the Indian central bank adopted an area approach whereby unbanked locations - census locations with no prior presence of commercial banks - were targeted. The Indian central bank, however, still needed to coerce commercial banks to expand into unbanked, rural locations. In particular, in states where unbanked locations were remote and/or unprofitable.

Under the Banking Regulation Act of 1949 commercial banks have to obtain a license from the central bank in order to open a new branch. On January 1, 1977 the Indian central bank announced that to qualify to open a branch in an already banked location a commercial bank must open four in unbanked locations. This licensing rule was frozen in 1990 when India began liberalizing the ecnomy, and was formally repealed in

1991. At this point it was deemed that future branch expansion should depend on "need, business potential and financial viability of location".

A second feature of the Indian social banking program was an emphasis on directed bank lending towards sectors deemed as priority sectors (these included agriculture and small scale industries), and within these sectors to individuals belonging to weaker sections of society.

The latter included members of the historically disadvantaged scheduled castes and scheduled tribes. In 1980 the Indian central bank formalized its directed lending policy by requiring that, by 1985, 40 percent of all bank lending go to priority sectors. Moreover, 25 percent of this lending must go to individuals belonging to the weaker sections.

While these targets remain to date, bank compliance with these targets sharply reduced after financial liberalization. The success of the Indian social banking program in expanding the presence of commercial banks in rural India is incontrovertible.

Much more debated, is the question of whether commercial banks in rural India affected the extent and type of economic activity in rural areas, and whether they affected poverty and inequality. The extent to which credit disbursements by the banking sector were based on need rather than political power is also debated. Finally, the extent to which any economic gains were due to productive investments associated with credit provision, rather than simply attributable to the redistribution of resources through the banking sector remains unclear.

Burgess and Pande (2005) use panel data for Indian states, 1961-2000 to examine whether the bank branch expansion program affected state output and poverty outcomes.

The typical problem with examining this relationship is the fact that banks are prone to open more branches in richer states. Not accounting for this fact can lead to biased estimates of the relationship between branch expansion and economic outcomes. Burgess and Pande address this problem by exploiting the fact that between 1977 and 1990 more bank branches were opened in financially less developed states. The opposite was true outside this period.

This change in the trend relationship between a state's financial development and branch openings allows them to isolate the policy-driven part of branch expansion and to use that to examine how this expansion affected the Indian economy. They show that branch expansion was associated with an increase in the shares of rural credit and savings. In keeping with earlier studies, they also find that the branch expansion increased non-agricultural, but not agricultural, output.

In companion work, Burgess, Pande and Wong (2005) used household data from the National Sample Survey to show that the simultaneous enforcement of directed bank lending requirements was associated with increased bank borrowing among the poor, in particular low caste and tribal groups. On the flip side, it is also true that commercial banking in rural India remained unprofitable.

The average default rate for commercial banks during the 1980s stood at 42 percent (as a share of all loans due for repayment). Default rates were very similar across types of borrower - a finding consistent with poor monitoring of borrowers at all levels, and the fact that large scale loan defaults were very often politically condoned.

In the end, it was the relative unprofitability of rural banking which led to the demise of social bankng in India. In 1991, at the outset of liberalization of the Indian economy, the Report of the Committee on the Financial System stated that redistributive objectives "should use the instrumentality of the fiscal rather than the credit system" and that directed credit programmes be phased out and that branch licensing policy be revoked. As a result post-1991 rural branch expansion has been limited and multiple studies suggest that access of the rural poor to the banking sector reduced.

The share of rural banks in total banks has fallen from 58 percent in 1990 to under 50 percent by 2000 and the share of total bank credit that went to rural areas declined, from 15.3

per cent in 1988 to 10.6 per cent in 2000. The policy recommendation is that this reduction in formal sector lending be filled by micro-credit institutions. Despite impressive advances by the Indian micro-credit sector it is still unclear whether they will be able to achieve a mobilization of rural savings and a credit outreach which equalled the achievements of the Indian social banking experiment in the 1970s and 1980s.

Agricultural Credit & Taxation in India

Credit institutions in India serving agricultural-sector needs developed in three phases. In the first phase, which lasted from 1947 to 1969, cooperative agencies were the primary vehicle providing credit.

In the second phase, after nationalization of banks in 1969, commercial banks were assigned a role in providing agricultural credit but were supplementary to cooperatives. In the last phase starting in 1975, regional rural banks were established to provide credit. In the 1990s, agricultural credit is provided through a multiagency approach in the form of cooperatives, commercial banks, and regional rural banks. These institutions have gradually ensured that credit reaches the most remote agricultural and rural areas.

Since the inception of central Indian economic planning in 1950, the government has favored cooperative societies as a channel for providing credit and as a means of broadening the experience of villagers in such activities as marketing, community farming, and consumer purchasing.

Credit societies were the first to be established and continue to be the most extensive and important group of cooperatives. Of the roughly 250,000 cooperatives in India in 1980, about 100,000 were primarily agricultural credit cooperatives. By the late 1980s, because regional rural banks were doing more lending, the number of agricultural credit cooperatives had decreased to 87,300. By 1988 there were 93,000 primary agricultural credit societies operating in rural areas, with a membership of 89.8 million. The societies aimed for universal membership in order that poorer members of society could join cooperatives and use their services. Total loans advanced by such societies amounted to nearly Rs36.9 billion during FY 1987. These agricultural credit societies had a share capital of about Rs10.1 billion at the end of June 1988.

Public-sector banks in India, including commercial and regional rural banks, increased their activities in the countryside after the nationalization of banks. Many bank branches were opened in rural areas. One indicator of increased availability of credit through public-sector banks was the increase in the number of accounts.

The number went from 164,000, with outstanding loans of Rs1.6 billion, to nearly 21.8 million accounts, with an outstanding balance of nearly Rs165.2 billion in March 1990. In economic terms, the growth in credit supply has been satisfactory, but the growth in deposits has not kept pace with credit supply and there has been a high rate of loan defaults. Field-level rural financial institutions have increased, however, even though there are fewer primary agricultural credit societies. The large increase in the number of branches of commercial banks in the rural areas and the expansion of regional rural banks led to the reduction.

Agricultural Taxation in India

Agricultural property and some agricultural income were being taxed in the early 1990s, but the revenue from these taxes was negligible. In the early 1950s, however, land revenue agricultural property taxes were a significant form of government income, providing just under 10 percent of the tax revenue of the central, state, and union territory governments. At the end of the 1980s, that proportion was less than 1 percent because land revenue had been fixed.

For instance, land revenue was an average of Rs28 per hectare in Kerala and Rs23 per hectare in Uttar Pradesh, the two states with the highest assessment rates. The national average was Rs16.50 per hectare. Agricultural property also was subject to stamp duties and registration fees. (All property transactions have to be made on official, stamped forms, and registration fees have to be paid to register transactions.)

No data were available in early 1993 on the proportion of these fees that came from the agricultural sector, but a taxation inquiry committee put it at approximately 20 percent. Between 1950 and 1990, only about 1.5 percent of the total taxes collected by the central, state, and union territory governments came from the agricultural sector. Overall, the impact of tax on Indian agricultural property was negligible but was a likely target for economic reform in the mid-1990s. Since the 1950s, agricultural taxation in India has been collected as a federal tax, but it has been levied only on income from plantations. All other agricultural income has been exempt from tax. The total collection from this tax was less than 1 percent of the total taxes collected by the central, state, and union territory governments in FY 1950; in the late 1980s, it had dropped below 0.3 percent.

3

DIFFICULTIES OF THE RURAL PEOPLE

The burden of indebtedness in rural India is great, and falls mainly on the households of rural working people. The exploitation of this group in the credit market is one of the most pervasive and persistent features of rural life in India, and despite major structural changes in credit institutions and forms of rural credit in the post-Independence period, Darling's statement (1925), that "the Indian peasant is born in debt, lives in debt and bequeaths debt," still remains true for the great majority of working households in the countryside. Rural households need credit for a variety of reasons.

They need it to meet short-term requirements for working capital and for long-term investment in agriculture and other income-bearing activities. Agricultural and non-agricultural activity in rural areas are typically seasonal, and households need credit to smooth out seasonal fluctuations in earnings and expenditure.

Rural households, particularly those vulnerable to what appear to others to be minor shocks with respect to income and expenditure, need credit as an insurance against risk. In a society that has no free, compulsory and universal education or health care, and very few general social security programmes, rural households need credit for different types of consumption. These include expenditure on food, housing, health and education. In the Indian context, another important purpose of borrowing is to meet expenses for a variety of social obligations and rituals.

About 75% of the Indian population lives in rural areas and about 80% of this population is dependent on agriculture for its livelihood. Agriculture accounts for about 37% of the national income. The development of the rural areas and of agriculture and its allied activities thus becomes vital for the rapid development of the economy as a whole.In this regard, India has succeeded in developing one of the largest rural banking systems in the world.

Various regulatory measures have been taken enabling the banking system to play an important role in the economic development of the rural areas. The two most prominent measures are rural commercial bank branch expansion, thus moving from class banking to mass banking and secondly, priority sector lending and the formulation of specific development programmes and action plans to facilitate credit flow to the rural sectors. Despite these measures, as per the Debt and Investment Survey, Govt. of India (1992) about 36% of the rural households are found to be outside the fold of institutional credit.

AGRICULTURAL PRODUCTIVITY

Even though India occupies the first or second position in the world in several crops in terms of area and production, it's rank in terms of productivity per hectare in the world is 52 for rice, 38 for wheat and much low in several other crops. The productivity of some crops is not only low but also remained stagnant over the years. The yield gap needs to be bridged through an integrated package of technology and agricultural policies to reap the untapped production potential, particularly, in rain-fed and other low productivity areas.

CAUSES FOR BACKWARDNESS IN VILLAGES

Zamindari System, the Legacy of the British Rule

India was under British rule for 200 years. British policies were aimed in revenue collection and not rural development. They introduced the zamindari system. The zamindars were deemed the owners of all land and they collected as much revenue as they could from the peasants. The system left the peasants very poor and the zamindars did very little to improve the conditions of the villages. After the country attained independence this system was abolished, but the conditions of the peasants is yet to transform completely.

The Bonded Labour System

It is equivalent to near slavery. Bonded labour is an indebted agricultural worker, who had borrowed from the money lender at usurious rate of interest and had to work in his farm for low wages. The system was used to permanently enslave the worker, as the worker was only able to repay a part of interest and the loan with compounded residual interest went on swelling. The agricultural labour can free himself eventually only by giving his son in bondage as a substitute. Under the 20-point economic programme, the Government India under Prime Minister Mrs.Indira Gandhi abolished bonded labour system and brought legislation to this effect in 1975. Despite the legislation the system is known to persist here and there in select areas.

Other contributory reasons are the total lack of agricultural development under foreign rule, poor communication, roads and other infrastructure development in villages, lack of education and health facilities, and the destruction of the thriving Indian cottage industries on account of competition from the cheap machine made goods imported under British rule

Progress made after the Country Attained Independence

After Independence the Country adopted planned development. The very first five year plan laid stress on agricultural development. It took a number of measures to bring more land under irrigation. Major irrigation Dams like Bakra Nangal, Hirakud, Nagarjunasagar, Tungabhadra were constructed which generated power for industrialisation of the country and water for irrigation. A number canals were build to distribute stored water over an extensive area. The Indian farmer, as a result, is now not exclusive depending on the monsoon.

Intensive cultivation of land is made possible through farm mechanisation. Tractors are being produced in the country and these are available to the farmers everywhere. Farmers are also using threshing machines, deep boring and irrigation pumps. They get supplies of high yielding improved seeds, fertilisers and other inputs. To enable them to purchase such inputs the rural credit system has been invigorated with Cooperatives, Regional Rural Banks, and Rural Branches of Commercial Banks. The recent boon to the poor Indian peasant is the micro finance system and Self Help Groups that have rendered financial support within the easy reach of all.

Land Reform legislation introduced in the country after independence include the abolition of the zamindari system, the abolition of bonded labour system, land ceiling legislation etc.. Legislation was also introduced to relieve rural indebtedness and the money lender could no longer legally collect more than reasonable interest. Untouchability was abolished and special legislation for the upliftment of scheduled cases and scheduled tribes were enacted.

Community Development Programmes, Integrated Rural Development Programme, bringing local self-government to the roots of the village through introduction of panchayat raj system ushered a new era of rural development. Development of public health care system, schemes undertaken for promoting literacy and adult education in the country, programmes for development of rural industries are other development programmes that have received the thrust of the Government's development approach.

Future Perspectives

Agriculture, with its large dependent population has to thrive and flourish, in order to secure rural prosperity. To ensure orderly and vigorous growth of agriculture policy and structural issues need to be addressed quickly. Some of the important issues that need to be addressed are -

1. Improving profitability of agriculture, through yield improvements, diversification and reform of agricultural marketing.
2. Strengthening backward linkages and expanding irrigation coverage.

3. Providing forward linkages especially for post harvest management, processing, transport, storage and market infrastructure.
4. Securing a stable long term policy on agricultural commodities trade, including the role of private sector.
5. Encouraging emergence of a market mechanism for agricultural commodities such as a commodities exchange.
6. Streamlining the cooperative credit structure for facilitating hassle free flow of credit.
7. Implementing watershed development projects in the rain-fed and dry-land areas.

Rural Banking Faces Twin Challenges

Banking in rural India is faced with the twin challenges of regulation and distribution. Regulation with respect to banking has been designed for delivery in urban India and distribution required more manpower to be deployed in rural areas. Initiatives like cheque transaction - where the electronic image and not the actual cheque is sent - have in mind the urban customer, he said. "About 500-600 million people in India still do not have bank accounts. For the rural segment, one needs to design no-frills products and deliver hard core value".The other handicap was that while Rs 1-crore business in microfinance required 30 people in terms of manpower, the same volume of business in other portfolios required only one person. Also, contract farming and supply chain integration has not gone the way they should have. Power, telecommunications, banking and transportation had reduced the urban-rural divide, he said. Besides traditional banking services, people in the rural and semi-urban areas are expressing interest in liability and investment products. He said, "Rural India is fast transforming a nation of savers into a nation of investors".

CONCLUSION

No doubt, villages are in a state of neglect and under-development, with impoverished people, as result of past legacies and defects in our planning process and investment pattern. But the potential in rural India is immense. What if every village in the country is provided with basic amenities, like drinking water, electricity, health care, educational transport, communication and other facilities, with only a smaller population of the village engaged in agriculture and the remaining in other gainful occupations? When this happens India will turn into mighty country. The purchasing power of the rural population throwing enormous demand for goods and services will boost the national economy tremendously. The day will see the reverse migration of people from the urban slums back to the villages. Rural Development is the subject to come to the forefront after the economic reforms and rural banking will serve the backbone of this development.

WHY GLOBAL BANKS ARE BANKING ON INDIA

Follow the money for a sure bet, they say -- and the world's big and small banks are doing just that in India's juggernaut economy, whose GDP now approaches $800 billion.

Citigroup said last February that it will invest more than half a billion dollars in its Indian operations in 2006; in 2005, it pumped $415 million into its operations there. Others writing expansion checks in India include HSBC, Bank of America, Standard Chartered Bank and Deutsche Bank. Besides organic growth, these banks are expanding in India by buying stakes in private banks and setting up non-bank finance companies.

That India is viewed as one of the biggest growth stories among emerging markets explains only part of the attraction for foreign banks. The country's central bank has outlined the roadmap for foreign players to grow, allowing them to set up branches in rural India and take over weak banks with an investment of up to 74% -- and promises to do more in three more years. Credit off-take has grown 25%-30% annually in recent years, with most of the new action in retail consumer lending, which tends to be happy hunting ground for foreign banks.

Not everybody in the industry is happy, of course, to see bigger room for foreign banks, which some view as not adequately embracing India's developmental agenda. India Knowledge@Wharton spoke to heads of several leading banks, experts from consulting firms and faculty members from Wharton and the Indian Institute of Management to get insights into the key drivers of the expansive sentiment in Indian banking. Mirroring India's economic bounties, India's banking industry has been on a high since the beginning of this decade, with advances growing annually at an average of 23%. The Indian banking industry is made up of 28 public sector banks, 30 foreign banks and 29 private banks, excluding cooperative banks and regional rural banks.

Advances posted the biggest jump of 31.4% to Rs. 15,13,481 crore (nearly $330 billion) between fiscal 2005 (April to March) and 2006, according to the Indian Banks Association in Mumbai. Net profits of these banks, however, grew only about 17% to Rs. 24,061 crore ($5.2 billion) over the past year. Collectively, they reported Rs. 25,79,980 crore ($561 billion) in assets in FY 2006. Those assets are expected to grow to $915 billion by 2010 representing a compounded annual growth rate of 15%, says the IBA.

According to Wharton professor of finance Krishna Ramaswamy, "The fact that there are very profitable private banks since the liberalization in such a short order -- between 1993 and 2005 -- is a testimonial to the fact that people will get very sophisticated in the banking services they demand and receive, whether at the retail or corporate level."

Fine-tuning the Roadmap

In its February 2005 roadmap, India's central bank -- the Reserve Bank of India (RBI) -- said that between March 2005 and 2009, foreign banks that were so far restricted to branch operations could also set up wholly owned subsidiaries. It also said they could buy up to 74% of a private bank, a gray area so far. The guidelines also noted that foreign bank subsidiaries with a minimum capital requirement of Rs. 300 crore ($65 million) would be treated on par with existing branches of foreign banks for branch expansion. However, foreign banks cannot grow unrestrained through local acquisitions; they can buy only weak local banks the regulator identifies. The RBI said the second phase of opening up would commence in April 2009, after "a review of the experience gained and after due consultation with all the stakeholders."

Size or the lack of it remains the key to banks' growth aspirations in India. Little wonder then that the announcement of a roadmap of banking reforms was enough to spur a series of investments. Bank of America, a small and subdued player in India, said it would pump $175 million into its Indian operations. Of that amount, $150 million is already in. The Hongkong & Shanghai Banking Corporation (HSBC) brought in $180 million with another $63 million waiting. Citigroup's planned investments this year include $75 million in Citi Financial, a non-bank finance company, or NBFCs, as they are called; that's on top of $50 million it sent that way last year. (NBFCs can perform most banking functions except accept deposits or run savings accounts.)

Deutsche Bank, too, invested $91 million in its Indian operations over the past year, of which $50 million went into an NBFC. Barclays invested $50 million. Late entrants like Dutch bank ING have been faster on the acquisition track. ING surprised the markets by acquiring a 45% stake of Bangalore-headquartered Vysya Bank, now known as ING Vysya Bank. HSBC had bought close to a 15% stake in UTI Bank and would have gladly gone on to secure a total of 21% had the banking regulator not stopped it early last year. HSBC has since brought down its stake to 4.99% as the banking regulator does not allow any bank to hold more than 5% of another bank without its clearance. HSBC is also considering setting up its own NBFC, regulatory approvals for which tend to arrive faster than those for a new bank or branch expansion.

However, foreign banks like HSBC may not any longer find it easy to float NBFCs. In November 2006, the Reserve Bank of India not only disallowed banks from holding 5% of the equity of any NBFC; it also limited any bank's credit exposure to all NBFCs to 40% of the bank's net worth. Those two measures will effectively frustrate foreign banks' perceived attempts to use NBFCs as de facto branches. Further, the banking regulator also required NBFCs to adhere to capital adequacy norms (these didn't apply to them earlier), restricting the size and structure of their loan portfolio, and a capital adequacy requirement (it didn't apply to NBFCs earlier); it also decided to regulate NBFCs promoted by the parents of foreign banks operating in India on a consolidated basis, and not as independent entities. India's NBFC industry is both large and fragmented enough for the regulator to keep a close watch. There are 436 deposit-taking NBFCs, of which 16 have asset sizes of over Rs. 500 crore ($112.5 million) and account for 49% of the aggregate deposits of the total NBFC sector. Then come another 2,615 non-deposit taking NBFCs, of which 104 have assets worth at least Rs. 100 crore each. Citigroup heads the segment of non-deposit taking NBFCs, followed by GE Capital and its associates. Ten of these 104 NBFCs account for more than 43% of the total assets of this sector; five of these 10 companies are foreign-owned.

The banking regulator's new guidelines aim at reining in the huge regulatory arbitrage that the foreign players have been enjoying. As the regulator has indicated that the banking sector would not open up before April 2009, foreign banks have been using the NBFC route to add muscle to their balance sheet and expand their activities. This is possible since under the foreign direct investment norms, any foreign player could set up an NBFC once it is cleared by the foreign investment promotion board and the RBI nod in this case is a mere formality (required only to bring in foreign capital.

Citigroup in May 2005 paid $676 million for a 9.3% stake in India's leading mortgage lender Housing Finance Development Corp., taking its total stake in that company to 13%. Others have begun circling. After spending more than a decade as an NBFC doing small retail loans, GE Capital said it wants to buy an Indian bank. Two South African banks, First Rand Bank and Standard Bank are also believed to be eying the country. And not far behind are believed to be UBS of Switzerland and Australia-based Macquarie Bank. Even ANZ, which a few years ago sold its operations in India to Standard Chartered Bank is said to be keen on coming back to India.

Early to Arrive, Slow to Grow

Citibank was late to arrive in India, going by the general benchmark for adventurous foreign banks at that time. After all, it set up shop only in 1902, while the British-owned Standard Chartered arrived 54 years earlier in 1858 (then called Chartered Bank). HSBC came a few years later, setting up shop in 1867. Foreign banks have been around in India for a more century, but stringent controls on market access and expansion restricted their growth.

Their presence has been restricted to a handful of branches and representative offices. Citibank India's CEO Sanjay Nayar says banks like his have contributed significantly to the growth and maturing of India's banking sector. "We were the first to introduce credit cards in the mid-eighties and also responsible for pioneering securitization," he says. "Increased access to consumer finance, internet banking and ATMs are other good examples."

This is a lead that he obviously does not want to lose. Nayar's bank belongs to a small universe of 30 active foreign banks in India. Collectively, they earned more than Rs. 3,068 crore ($667 million) in after-tax profits in fiscal 2005-06. Citibank, the most profitable, has 39 branches in 27 cities and covers another 50 through a distribution subsidiary. Its asset book is worth $7.3 billion and it posted an after-tax profit of Rs. 600 crore in 2005 (more than $130 million).

Standard Chartered is the largest foreign bank in India with 81 branches in 26 cities. Its asset book of $8.1 billion brought home profits of $131 million in 2005. The business landscape for these banks, however, began to change dramatically with the opening up of the consumer markets in the late eighties and nineties.

Cars, white goods, computers and entertainment electronics suddenly became more affordable as the government steadily lowered tariff levels on both domestic and imported products. The major foreign banks were quick to spot the opportunity, introducing products and services focusing on specific consumer niches like credit cards and car loans.

Private Banks and Their Fortunes

Just as banks including Citibank, Standard Chartered and HSBC began to get a hold on the growing middle class in these niches, two large private Indian banks -- ICICI Bank and HDFC Bank -- arrived on the scene in mid-1990s. They grew rapidly by copying the foreign banks' products, improving and considerably scaling up offerings like mortgages, car loans and credit cards. By comparison, Indian state-owned banks are huge with a market share of 78% of deposits and 73% of advances, but have been losing ground.

Interestingly, in the early 1990s, India's state-owned banks commanded shares of around 85% for both deposits and advances. But privately owned banks have since then snatched away 7% of deposits and 12% of loans and advances from the public sector; foreign banks haven't scored as many gains in the past 15 years.

Private banks today boast market shares of 19% in deposits and more than 20% in loans and advances; foreign banks come next with shares of 5% and 7%, respectively. "Foreign banks have ceded territory to the new private banks in the last decade," says K.V. Kamath, CEO of ICICI Bank, the country's largest private sector bank with an asset base of Rs. 2,51,389 crore ($55 billion). "Foreign banks have not been able to seize the opportunity in India. They were not willing to commit capital to the country," he says. "They are now looking for acquisitions of those players who have built scale of operations; it's only natural that the regulator has laid down a roadmap for acquisitions."

The road ahead for foreign banks is clear from the above scenario: Join the private banks' party with strategic stakes, as they wait for more policy latitude to fire their own growth aspirations. The promise lies in those market segments that now account for small shares. Retail lending represents only about 20% of the Indian banking industry's advances and less than 7% of India's GDP of $775 billion, lower than Thailand (18%), Malaysia (33%) and South Korea (55%). India's demographics with its young, consuming class that represent good opportunities are now high in the sights of the foreign banks. A report from Boston Consulting Group in 2005 on opportunities for foreign banks in India outlined the opportunities.

It said 60 million new households should be added to India's bankable segment in three years The report highlighted the fact that only around $35 billion in assets -- less than 6% of GDP -- were being managed "professionally," (meaning the organized banking and financial services industry and excluding the informal sector made up of largely local money lenders). And with more than $180 billion in long term fixed deposits in banks and low penetration in the pension market, the opportunity for sustained double-digit growth is attractive.

Outside the metros, a huge market is in waiting, says Wharton's Ramaswamy. "There is still a very large informal finance sector in India which provides working capital to small businesses," he says, adding, "They are really financial institutions on a modest scale, and they fill the gap." But as banking penetration increases in rural India, Ramaswamy expects the interest rates -- often usurious - extracted by local moneylenders to dramatically fall. "The customers will get sophisticated and learn that they could perhaps get better rates in the organized sector," he says.

Globalization Will Stay

Boston Consulting Group director and banking industry analyst Janmejaya Sinha sees "the most dramatic impact of globalization" on remote servicing in India of banks' back-office processes. He notes that "the huge improvements in telecommunications and computing technology combined with vast variations in factor costs across the world and tight immigration laws will lead to large shifts in work that doesn't a require customer interface."

He says the beginning of this trend is evident mostly in outsourcing of voice-based services. "This is a tide that cannot be turned back," he says. "This will lead to huge improvements in the efficiency of the financial services industry's operations

-- both in cost and quality --and lead to a further integration of the global financial industry."

Tarashankar Bhattacharya, managing director of India's largest bank, the State Bank of India, says he welcomes foreign banks so long as he has a level playing field with them. One of his chief complaints here is while Indian banks have to lend a minimum of 40% of their assets to government-specified "priority sectors" such as agriculture and small scale industries, that requirement is lower at 32% for foreign banks operating in India. Banks don't relish priority sector lending because they come with low profit margins and a high incidence of delinquencies.

Bhattacharya's lament is shared by CEOs of most state owned banks in India. They complain that they are constantly reined in from competing effectively. They cannot, for instance, pay market-linked salaries. Except in rare cases, they are unable to create or hold onto the best talent. They cannot acquire other banks without lengthy and often unsuccessful bureaucratic wrangling.

And, as Bhattacharya says, they cannot lend or invest in the booming stock markets as they please. Nor can they raise much needed capital easily. All this, government-owned bankers privately admit, is because they continue to be viewed as instruments of social policy, rather than as commercial institutions by their principal owner, the government. And yes, along with the rest of Indian industry, they cannot downsize at will. The RBI appears to recognize this. The regulator says a calibrated approach is necessary in the absence of a safety net and labor law reforms. It takes some pride in the fact that India has never faced significant financial sector turmoil like other emerging markets. It wants to ensure consolidation in the domestic sector first before allowing foreign banks a freer entry. The RBI also wants the large public sector banks to merge with each other to create big banks.

Many private banks have taken the cue, albeit with gentle nudges, and have grown with acquisitions. But the big state-owned banks are yet to follow. In September 2005, Indian finance minister P. Chidambaram made a strong pitch for mergers and acquisitions amongst public sector banks. He was speaking at the centennial celebrations of the Bank of India, another large bank.

"A country as large as India cannot be content with one large bank (referring to the State Bank)," he said. "Bank of India should lead the way in creating a giant bank which will take on the world's best and biggest." No deal has materialized since. But the State Bank, which typically sets the ideological agenda for the rest of the banking industry, now openly says that thinking global is critical to domestic success. Last year, State Bank's then chairman A. K. Purwar stated that the bank's goal was to be in the top 50 globally by 2008; it currently holds the 71st ranking in terms of Tier 1 capital (a yardstick used by the Bank for International Settlements in Basel, Switzerland).

State Bank's strategy to get higher up the global pecking order is through acquisitions primarily. The State Bank of India hasn't had much traction in acquiring other Indian banks, but it has made significant strides internationally. It kicked off that effort in February 2005 when it paid $10 million for a 51% stake in Indian Ocean International Bank, the fourth largest in Mauritius.

Purwar then said the bank's targets were medium sized banks with assets of $50 million to $200 million each. In the past year, State Bank bought two other banks -- Indonesia's PT Bank IndoMonex and Kenya's Giro Commercial Bank. It is now actively scouting for other acquisitions in Asia and Africa. State Bank's current chairman O. P. Bhatt, however, has said his bank would not acquire small banks any more.

"We would buy reasonably big banks if there is a strategic fit," he says. Citibank's Nayar says globalization forces local banks in emerging-market countries to adopt international best practices in order to stay competitive. These areas include risk management techniques, technology upgrades, more efficient capital allocation tools, focus on marketing and sales and other such areas resulting in improved operating and financial leverage. 'But it is not entirely a one-way street," he says.

"There are also areas where international banks are adapting and learning from local best practices, particularly in areas like SME (small and medium enterprises) lending and agri-financing. The main impact is higher efficiency levels in the banking system in terms of more optimal capital allocation, better profitability, prudent risk management and greater competition, which ultimately benefits the end customer through new products and services at affordable prices."

All Roads Lead to Consolidation

Nayar sees consolidation within the banking industry as imperative. "Commoditization of the traditional banking products and the need to invest in technology, marketing and product innovation has made size and scale critical success factors in this industry," he says. "Consolidation is imminent, and foreign banks with their large capital and product expertise can play a significant role in this process." Hrishikes Bhattacharyya, professor of finance and banking at the Indian Institute of Management in Kolkata, doesn't think that's such a good idea.

"The Indian financial system is not yet very strong to take on stiff foreign competition," he says. "There is still not a level playing field between Indian banks and foreign banks; the latter does not have developmental obligations like 40% lending to the priority sector where returns are low." Foreign banks are not required to direct more than 32% of their net credit to the "priority sectors" identified by the RBI, which include agriculture, small-scale industries and exports.

ICICI's Kamath concedes that over the years foreign banks have contributed to the development of the Indian banking industry in areas like product knowledge and risk management services, but doesn't see any new gains on the horizon. "Frankly, we have nothing to learn from them [now]," he says. "Both in terms of products and technology, we are ahead of them."

Citibank's Nayar says the RBI's approach to opening up the banking sector to foreign investors is well calibrated, but would like quicker branch permissions and access to some government and public sector business. "Foreign banks continue to face constraints in these areas and this significantly impacts their ability to grow their footprint, customer base and restricts access to savings deposits," he adds.

Kamath doesn't buy the contention of the foreign banks' lobby that they don't enjoy enough growth freedom. He in fact sees the current regulatory regime offering them "sufficient flexibility," and points out that the central bank has stated its resolve to be liberal in granting branch licenses. "The only major restriction for them is on the acquisition of existing banks, and that too will be revisited in the second stage of the roadmap that the RBI has set out (beginning March 2009)," he says.

"Essentially, the question is not one of the country's openness but of whether foreign banks are willing to commit capital and enter the Indian market for the long haul." Nayar points out that India isn't alone in opening up the banking sector as globalization advances, and that foreign investors are focused on the opportunities these throw up in many developing countries. "The RBI has a well-calibrated approach for opening up of the banking sector to foreign investors," he says of the central bank's phased and cautious approach. "Countries like Korea, Russia and Brazil have opened up their banking sectors significantly." India's banking industry has so far avoided a major financial crisis, unlike those in other developing countries, and that deserves a hand, says Nayar. "Indian banking has been relatively well managed and, more importantly, well regulated," he says. "Most of the other emerging economies have seen at least one period of significant turmoil in the last decade or so -- the Asian financial crisis in the late 1990s, the Latin American meltdown in 2001-02, and Mexico in the early 1990s."

Much now depends on how the RBI picks up the threads three years hence in 2009 when it reviews the progress achieved in the current opening-up phase. Boston Consulting Group's Sinha says the best course of action is to allow foreign banks entry into India up to a level that can be fixed in a variety of ways.

"The Australians have a four-pillar policy where their biggest four banks cannot buy each other or be ought by foreigners" In India, says Sinha, this could the State Bank of India, the Life Insurance Corporation of India (an insurer and not a commercial bank) and three other players who in turn would have consolidated with some smaller players Together they would control between 60 and 70% of total banking assets. This way, he says, all the constituents would be satisfied.

Development Economics and Public Policy Cluster

The macroeconomic crisis of 1991 forced India to address problems of unviability and inefficiency across a number of sectors of the economy, including the financial sector. In India, the government owns the majority of the formal banking sector which consists of Commercial Banks, Co-operative Banks (both rural and urban) and Regional rural Banks. The existence of large number of loss-making units with the extensive state rural banking system gave cause for particular concern.

The study by Thankom Arun with Paul Mosley (Sheffield University) and Samuel Maimbo (World Bank) examines the ability of the Indian rural financial sector to meet the credit needs of lower income groups, and, in future, those who are currently financially excluded.

The major objective of this research is to analyse key constraints and challenges to better financial access for the rural poor such as examining the need for better institutions, and new products and technology, to bridge the gaps between the supply of, and demand, for providing financial services for the rural poor. The study examines the factors which has prevented the formal financial institutions from reaching out to the poor. Also the study explores the factors constraining the outreach and sustainability of micro finance institutions in India, including capacity constraints, financial sustainability and the legal and regulatory framework. As part of the study, the team members participated in a World Bank Mission on Improving Access to Rural Finance in India, and, visited New Delhi, Mumbai, Hyderabad and Lucknow. The mission met with senior officials from the Government, the Reserve Bank, the National bank of Agricultural and Rural Development (NABARD), Public and Private financial institutions, and, micro finance practitioners and self help groups.

The emerging conclusions of the study orient towards the key themes of (1) lack of financial viability across much of the Indian rural credit system (2) continuing financial exclusion of many poor people and (3) the need of poor people for flexible, easy to access financial services which protect against risk. The poorer people are, the greater the damage that is done by any decline in assets or income and the greater the need for financial services of a type which will protect the household's livelihood rather than promote it at the cost, perhaps, of greater financial and possibly physical vulnerability.

4

POLICIES AND THEIR IMPLEMENTATION IN INDIA

This chapter deals with rural banking and credit policy in contemporary India and with the effect of the current policy of financial liberalization on the credit portfolios of rural workers. It examines, first, the major directions of rural banking and credit policy and indicators of performance of this activity in India since 1969, the year in which 14 major commercial banks were nationalized. Secondly, it attempts to describe and analyse features of indebtedness of rural households, particularly rural worker households, in a south Indian village during different periods of national banking policy. Thirdly, it attempts to evaluate the potential of a new policy alternative microcredit projects controlled by non-government organizations - as a solution for problems of rural indebtedness.

Problems of rural credit

The burden of indebtedness in rural India is great, and falls mainly on the households of rural working people. The exploitation of this group in the credit market is one of the most pervasive and persistent features of rural life in India, and despite major structural changes in credit institutions and forms of rural credit in the post-Independence period, Darling's statement (1925), that "the Indian peasant is born in debt, lives in debt and dies in debt," still remains true for the great majority of working households in the countryside.

Rural households need credit for a variety of reasons. They need it to meet short-term requirements for working capital and for long-term investment in agriculture and other income-bearing activities. Agricultural and non-agricultural activity in rural areas are typically seasonal, and households need credit to smooth out seasonal fluctuations in earnings and expenditure.

Rural households, particularly those vulnerable to what appear to others to be minor shocks with respect to income and expenditure, need credit as an insurance against risk. In a society that has no free, compulsory and universal education or health care, and very few general social security programmes, rural households need credit for different types of consumption. These include expenditure on food, housing, health and education. In the Indian context, another important purpose of borrowing is to meet expenses for a variety of social obligations and rituals.

If these credit needs of the poor are to be met, rural households need access to credit institutions that provide them a range of financial services, provide credit at reasonable rates of interest and provide loans that are unencumbered by extra-economic provisions and obligations.

Historically, there have been four major problems with respect to providing credit to the Indian countryside. First, the supply of formal sector credit to the countryside as a whole has been inadequate.1 Secondly, rural credit markets in India themselves have been very imperfect and fragmented. Thirdly, as the foregoing suggests, the distribution of formal sector credit has been unequal, particularly with respect to region and class, caste and gender.

Fourthly, the major source of credit to rural households, particularly income poor working households, has been informal sector loans which are usually advanced at very high rates of interest. Further, the terms and conditions attached to these loans have given rise to an elaborate structure of coercion-economic and extra-economic - in the countryside.

That these factors constitute what may be called the "problem of rural credit" has been well recognized in official evaluations and scholarship since the end of the nineteenth century. Given the issues involved, the declared objectives of public policy with regard to rural credit in the post-Independence period were, in the words of the Governor of the Reserve Bank of India, "to ensure that sufficient and timely credit, at reasonable rates of interest, is made available to as large a segment of the rural population as possible" (Rangarajan, 1996, p. 288).

The policy instruments to achieve these objectives were to be, first, the expansion of the institutional structure of formal-sector lending institutions; secondly, directed lending; and thirdly, concessional or subsidized credit (ibid.). Public policy was thus aimed not only at meeting rural credit needs but also at pushing out the informal sector and the exploitation to which it subjected borrowers (Chavan, 2001, pp.5-7 passim). Rural credit policy in India envisaged the provision of a range of credit services, including long-term and short-term credit and large-scale and small-scale loans to rural households.

Three Phases of Rural Banking Policy since 1969

The period of our study three phases in banking policy for the Indian countryside. The first was the period following the nationalization of India's 14 major commercial banks in 1969. This was also the early phase of the green revolution in India. During this period, nationalized banks attempted to mop up new rural liquidity. The declared objectives of the new policy, known as "social and development banking", were the following:

- to provide banking services in previously unbanked or under-banked rural areas;
- to provide substantial credit to specific activities including agriculture and cottage industries; and
- to provide credit to certain disadvantaged groups such as, for example, Dalit households.

The Government of India and the Reserve Bank of India (RBI) issued, from time to time, specific directives regarding "social and development banking". These included setting targets for the expansion of rural branches, imposing ceilings on interest rates, and setting guidelines for the sectoral allocation of credit. Given the new farming practices associated with the green revolution, the first post-nationalization phase of expansion in rural banking saw growth in credit advances for agriculture. Specifically, a target of 40 per cent of advances for the priority sectors, namely agriculture and allied activities, and smallscale and cottage industries, was set for commercial banks. In addition, a decision was taken in 1972 to introduce regional rural banks, institutions that would specialize in social and development banking for rural areas was examined in 1993 by Binswanger, Khandker and Rosenzweig (Narayana, 2000). Advances to the countryside increased substantially, although they were, as was the green revolution itself, biased in respect of regions, crops and classes.

In the second phase, which began in the late 1970s and early 1980s, the rhetoric of land reform was finally discarded by the ruling classes themselves, and the two major instruments of official anti-poverty policy were developed: loans-cum-subsidy schemes targeted at the rural poor and state-sponsored rural employment schemes.

Thus began a period of directed credit, during which credit was directed towards the so-called weaker sectors. The most important new scheme of this phase was the Integrated Rural Development Programme (IRDP), a scheme for the creation of productive incomebearing assets among the poor through the allocation of subsidized credit. Initiated as a pilot project in 1978-79, it was extended to all rural blocks of the country in 1980.3 Much has been written on the failure of IRDP to create long-term income-bearing assets for asset-poor rural households. Among the many reasons for this failure were the absence of agrarian reform and decentralized institutions of democratic government, the inadequacy of public infrastructure and public provisioning of support services and the persistence of employment4-insecurity and poverty in rural society. Nevertheless, the IRDP strategy did lead to a significant transfer of funds to the rural poor.

The second phase also involved an expansion and consolidation of the institutional infrastructure for rural banking. "Even ardent critics of India's growth strategy," wrote a noted scholar of India's banking system, "would admit that what the country achieved in the area of financial sector development before the present reform process began, particularly after bank nationalization, was unparalleled in the financial history of any other nation in the world" (Shetty, 1997, p 253). According to Shetty, there was, after bank nationalization, "an unprecedented growth of commercial banking in terms of both geographical spread and functional reach".

The third phase was that of liberalization, particularly after 1991. The policy objectives of this phase were encapsulated in the Report of the Committee on the Financial System chaired by M. Narasimham. In its very first paragraph, the report called for "a vibrant and competitive financial system...to sustain the ongoing reform in the structural aspects of the real economy" (RBI 1991). The Committee said that redistributive objectives "should use the instrumentality of the fiscal rather than the credit system" and accordingly proposed that "directed credit programmes should be phased out." It also recommended that interest rates be deregulated, that capital adequacy norms be changed (to "compete with banks globally"), that branch licensing policy be revoked, that a new institutional structure that is "market driven and based on profitability" be created, and that the part played by private Indian and foreign banks be enlarged. In short, the Narasimham Committee recommended that banking policy be guided more by the market than by regulations set by the public authority.

Let us make it clear that, before the 1990s, the banking system was open to much criticism, including in periodic evaluations by banking commissions particularly of its bureaucratic failures and its insensitivity to the social and economic context in which it functioned. The reforms proposed in 1991, however were not an attempt to bring rural banking closer to the poor, but to throw the entire structure of social and development banking overboard. Shetty shows how the present strategy fails to take account of the structural features of the Indian economy. First, the strategy aims for the "most premature and operationally infeasible goal...of globalization" for the financial sector in India, a goal that has not been set even by industrialized countries. This goal has resulted in the costly and "forced application of capital adequacy and other supervisory norms." Secondly, a monetarist approach guides the new policy. This has meant "primacy to the control of money supply" and monetary targeting at the cost of neglecting the "size and distribution of bank credit". Thirdly, the "uncritical acceptance of the free-market philosophy has blinded the government to the needs of a genuine reform of the financial system" (Shetty, 1997, pp.254-263).

The third phase inevitably saw a reduction in rural banking in general and in priority sector lending and preferential lending to the poor in particular. The new policies also contributed to other distortions in the financial system (Shetty, 1997).

Record of Progress of Rural Banking

This section documents changes in rural banking at the national level with respect to five indicators: total deposits mobilized and credit advanced in rural areas; the share of priority sectors in total advances; credit advanced to agriculture and allied activities; and the scale of credit disbursed through the IRDP.

Rural Bank Offices: Deposits and Credit

The impact of bank nationalization on the growth of scheduled commercial banks in rural areas is clear: the share of rural bank offices in total bank offices jumped from 17.6 per cent in 1969 to 36 per cent in 1972. The share rose steadily thereafter, and attained a peak of 58.2 per cent in March 1990. From 1990 onwards, there was a gradual decline in the share of rural bank offices, and the share fell below 50 per cent in 1998 and thereafter. In fact, the absolute number of bank offices fell in the 1990s: 2,706 rural bank offices were closed between March 1994 and March 2000, most in 1995 and 1996.

The period after nationalization was characterized by an expansion of bank credit to rural areas. The proportion of credit disbursed to rural areas tripled in the 1970s, and continued to rise in the 1980s. After 1988, however, the share of total bank credit that went to rural areas declined, from 15.3 per cent in

1987 and 1988 to 10.6 per cent in March 2000. Rural deposits also grew rapidly after nationalization; their share of aggregate deposits doubled in the 1970s, from 6.3 per cent in 1969 to 12.6 per cent in 1980 and continued to grow, although at a slower pace, in the 1980s. Once again, the peak was reached in 1990, when rural deposits accounted for 15.5 per cent of aggregate deposits.

The pace of deposit mobilization in rural areas fell in the 1990s. Given the pattern of growth of gross bank credit and aggregate deposits, it is not surprising that the credit-deposit ratio in rural areas rose after 1969. The ratio peaked at 68.6 per cent in 1984 and remained above 60 per cent until 1990. From 1985 to 1988 the share of the rural sector in gross bank credit was higher than its share of total deposits, and in these years, the rural credit-deposit ratio exceeded the all India credit-deposit ratio. In the 1990s, the credit -deposit ratio fell sharply, coming down almost to the level of 1969. The credit -deposit ratio fell after 1984 at the national level as well. In the metropolitan areas, however, the decline has been reversed significantly in recent years; the data thus reveal a relative shift of credit from rural, semi-urban and urban areas to metropolitan areas.

The time-periods chosen were determined by the availability of data. A relatively sharp increase in the number of rural and semi-urban bank offices and in the credit disbursed by them took place in the period 1973 to 1981. This expansion slowed down in the period 1981 to 1991, and declined sharply in the next period, 1991-1999. The same trends were true of total commercial bank credit to agriculture.

Credit to "Priority Sectors"

One of the objectives of banking policy after nationalization was to expand the flow of credit to agriculture and small industries, or what were termed "priority sectors". The share of these sectors in the total advances of scheduled commercial banks rose from 14 per cent in 1969 to 21 per cent in 1972 and then went up to 33 per cent in 1980. The RBI set a target of 40 per cent for priority sector lending and by the mid-1980s this target was met. From 1985 to 1990, in fact, the target was over -achieved, that is, more than 40 per cent of total advances went to those sectors. From 1991 to 1996, the share of priority sector advances fell, in line with the recommendations of the Narasimham Committee. From 1990/91 to 1996/97, loan accounts to agriculture fell by 5 million (Narayana, 2000). While 52 per cent of bank credit in rural areas went towards agriculture in 1985, the proportion fell to 38 per cent in 1998 (Nair, 1999).

At first glance, the direction in priority sector lending appears to have been reversed over the last four years. This is, however, a reversal by redefinition. In the late 1990s, priority sector lending was redefined to include advances to newly-created infrastructure funds, to non-banking finance companies for on-lending to the very snall-scale sector, and to the food processing industry. Loans to Pepsi, Kelloggs, Hindustan Lever and ConAgra now count as priority sector advances, according to the Finance Minister's budget speech in 1999 (Business Standard, March 1, 1999). When data for scheduled commercial banks are disaggregated by type of bank (public sector banks, regional rural banks, private banks and foreign banks), we find that there was no lending to rural areas or agriculture from foreign banks. Further, foreign banks failed to meet the priority sector targets through the 1980s (although these targets for foreign banks were lower than for other banks in India) (Ramachandran and Swaminathan, 1992).

Loans to Agriculture

The term loans issued by scheduled commercial banks to agriculture between 1980/81 and 1997/98. In real terms, advances rose from 1983/84 to 1990/91, fell in the first four years after 1991, and showed some recovery in 1995/96. It is instructive here to look at the distribution of advances to cultivators by size classes of land holdings. The smallest cultivators i.e., those with land holdings of less than 2.5 acres, were the worst affected by the post-1991 decline in credit to agriculture. The cutback in advances to small cultivators persists: in 1997/98, in real terms, aggregate credit to small cultivators was less than the amount advanced in 1984/85. By contrast, advances to cultivators with more than five acres of land (the largest category) have risen in the last few years and are higher in real terms than before liberalization.

Loans under the Integrated Rural Development Programme

Indicators of IRDP, a major component of the credit-led poverty alleviation strategy of the 1980s. First, the number of families assisted annually with IRDP loans rose from 2.7 million in 1980/81 to 3.9 million in 1984/85 and 4.2 million in 1987/88. Although the programme slackened after that, the number of beneficiaries in 1990/91 remained above the level of the early 1980s. After 1991, there was a steep decline in the number of IRDP beneficiaries; only 1.2 million families were assisted in 1998/99.

Indexing the number of families assisted in 1982/83 at 100, means that the number assisted in 1998/99 was a mere 36.7. The term credit disbursed by banks under IRDP followed a similar trajectory. With 1982/83 indexed at 100, total term credit mobilized for IRDP peaked at 113 in 1987/88 and went down to 46 in 1998/99. To sum up, the period after the nationalization of banks was one of expansion of rural banking, both in terms of deposit mobilization and in terms of credit advances. The spread of banking in rural areas began in the 1970s and was strengthened in the 1980s. The trend was reversed after the introduction of policies of financial liberalization in 1991. This analysis is consistent with S. L. Shetty's observation that "every banking indicator has shown deterioration after the reform process began in 1991-92" (Shetty, 1997, p 265). The extension of private commercial banking in India - including attempts to denationalize banks - is likely to exacerbate this reversal.

Official sources of large-scale data on banking do not touch upon many critical features of the credit system. First, they do not report the total flow of credit to specific sections of rural households, such as the rural poor, the landless, or women within such households. Secondly, they provide no information on the share of the formal and informal sectors in the debt portfolios of rural households. Thirdly, banking statistics tell us nothing about the variety of loan transactions entered into by rural households, the terms of such transactions, and, more generally, the burden of indebtedness on different classes of rural household. Such information can be collected at the village level; village surveys also help provide insights into the local-level socio-economic relations that mediate credit transactions.

Study Area and Database

Gokilapuram village is in Theni district, in the south-west of the state of Tamil Nadu, in the area known as the Cumbum Valley, a distinct geographical and agroeconomic region within the district. The Valley is shaped like an inverted triangle with rounded apex, wedged between the Cardamom Hills, whose watershed marks the western and south western wall of the Valley (and the border between Tamil Nadu and Kerala) and the High Wavy and Erasakkanayakanur Hills in the east and south-east. It is an area of much natural beauty and whose specific agroeconomic features include loamy and sandy soils of comparatively high fertility and with assured surface and groundwater irrigation over large parts of the region.

The Valley stands out in Tamil Nadu as a vanguard agrarian region. Paddy and some sugarcane are grown on surface-irrigated land (irrigated by the Periyar system) and coconut, banana, grapes and vegetables are the main crops on groundwater-irrigated land. The cultivation of these crops is characterized by advanced levels of agricultural techniques by the standards of Tamil Nadu. The agriculture of the Valley draws on a numerically preponderant, largely settled force of hired workers. This paper reports results from a census -type socio -economic survey of 650 households in Gokilapuram Village in 1999, covering 908 households and compares them with some results from previous surveys, in 1977 and 1985.

The Data Set used in this Paper

As a proxy for the class of landless households whose income comes mainly from the earnings of its members from hired labour we have separated for this paper two sets of households from the rest. The first set consists of those households that are landless and whose entire income derives from hired labour on agricultural or non-agricultural tasks (we shall call these households "landless labour households with no other sources of income" or "Set 1 households").

The second set consists of landless households whose members are hired labourers, but also gain income (however small) from self-employment, salaries or remittances (these households are called "landless labour households with other sources of income" or "Set 2 households"). Incomes in Set 2 other than wages from hired labour generally come from dairying, artisan or service castes' earnings, small salaried jobs (as watchmen or subordinate government employees) and small remittances from the children of the household.

For 1977, we use data for landless households whose major income came from earnings from hired labour in agriculture. This set consists of 257 households; from the sample survey of 1985, we use the category of households with no ownership holdings of land for comparisons with our data for 1999 and 1977 presented a detailed analysis of their socio-economic characteristics (Ramachandran, 1990).

The surveys thus provide data on the level of indebtedness of each household (a measure of the stock of debt) at the time the household was surveyed. Data on loans were collected in similar questionnaires under the following heads: principal, collateral, principal outstanding, rate of interest, interest unpaid, source of loan and purpose of loan. Where individual loans had special terms and conditions attached to them, investigators made separate notes on them. While the three data sets do not represent precisely equivalent categories at the three time periods, they are close enough for comparative use.

Main Results from the Field Data

As it turned out, the reference period for each survey represented a specific phase of credit policy in the countryside. The first survey was conducted eight years after the nationalization of banks in 1969, and gives us a picture of credit policy during the high tide of the green revolution in the village. The volume of short-term and term-loans coming into the village increased; the flow, however, mainly benefited those who had land on which to introduce the new technology and who were creditworthy, that is, mainly the rural rich (Ramachandran, 1990).

The second survey was conducted at the high point of the implementation of the IRDP in the village. Although coverage of the village poor by the scheme was not complete, loans-cum-subsidies were advanced among the poor on an extensive scale, one that no previous or subsequent credit-based scheme achieved (Swaminathan, 1986; Ramachandran, 1990). The third survey was conducted in 1999, eight years after economic policy was explicitly reoriented in the direction of liberalization.

To simplify, the three surveys represent conditions in the village during the green revolution phase (1977), the IRDP phase (1985) and the liberalization phase (1999) of credit policy towards the rural poor.

Sources of Loans

About 68 per cent of landless labour households in 1999 were debtor households. This proportion has declined sharply since 19805; the reason for this is the fact that landless worker households no longer have the same access to loans from the formal sector as they did in 1985. The average size of loan among debtor landless hired labour households was Rs 4,556 (Rs 3,494 for Set 1 households and Rs 5,218 for Set 2 households respectively).

In respect of outstanding debt, only 11.8 per cent of landless labour households had loans outstanding from the formal sector. Scholars have criticized the All India Debt and Investment Surveys, a major source of data on household indebtedness, for underestimating the extent of indebtedness of households, and for overestimating the share of the formal sector in the total principal borrowed by rural households (Chavan, 2001).

Nevertheless, it is interesting that even data from another official source, the Rural Labour Enquiry (RLE), indicate that the share of the formal sector in the debt portfolio of rural households has fallen in recent years after rising steadily for over two decades. According to the Rural Labour Enquiry, the amount borrowed from the formal sector as a proportion of all borrowings in the debt portfolios of landless agricultural labour households in Tamil Nadu was 0.4 per cent in 1964/65 and 5 per cent in 1974/75 (Ramachandran, 1990). The proportion rose to 24.2 per cent in 1983/84, rose further to 32.9 per cent in 1987/88, and fell to 23.3 per cent in 1993/94 (RLE, 1990, 1997).

The low share of formal sector loans in the debt portfolios of landless labour households is mirrored in the low share of advances to landless workers by commercial banks. We studied the advances registers of the two main commercial banks (both public sector banks) in Uthamapalayam, the taluk centre, in order to derive a summary measure of their advances to the poor. We first looked at the total amount of credit advanced by a bank. We then separated out any advances for which assetless rural workers did not qualify: these included crop loans, terms loans for the development of crop land and plantation land, loans for agricultural machinery that required the hypothecation of land holdings, loans to provide working capital to merchants and loans advanced against the deposit of gold ornaments. The balance of advances - typically, loans for the purchase of milch cattle and draught animals and loans for small-scale self-employment - were loans to which a landless rural labour household had, in theory, access. We then calculated the proportion of such advances to all advances. We visited both banks in mid-July and data refer to total advances as on July 11, 2000 and July 18, 2000. In the branch of the State Bank of India, India's major commercial bank, the advances to which a landless labour family could possibly have had access as a proportion of all advances was a mere 8.4 per cent. In the other bank - the Lead Bank for the district - the proportion was 1.9 per cent.

To summarize, one of the stated objectives of earlier credit policy - whatever its achievements - was to provide preferential access to the poor to credit from the formal sector for production and self-employment. Current policy has reversed that objective. The share of loans from the formal sector in the debt profiles of landless labour households in 1999 was very low and fell steeply between 1985 and 1999. The reversal is clear also from the pattern of advances from local branches of nationalized commercial banks and, in particular, from the minuscule share of total advances to which landless labour households had access.

Purposes of Loans

Data on the purpose for which a household took each loan typically record the proximate reason for taking each loan. Respondent were asked why they took a particular loan, but the replies must be read with care. First, the respondent may have borrowed money for one purpose and used it for quite another. Secondly, the particular purpose stated may be somewhat fortuitous; the respondent may have borrowed money to buy food today because she incurred unexpected medical expenditure yesterday. Bhaduri (1982) examines the fungibility of cash and its implications for separating consumption credit from productive credit.

The rural poor always need consumption credit, particularly in situations where social security systems are either non-existent or ill-developed: they need credit for food and household subsistence, to meet social and ritual commitments, to pay for educational and medical expenses, to build and repair dwellings and for other purposes. The rural poor also need loans for productive purposes; to finance agriculture, to buy and maintain incomebearing assets, and to finance other small means of employment. The major source of formal-sector loans, commercial banks, do not lend money for other than income-bearing uses. Individual loans from the formal sector are generally larger than loans from the informal sector. Fluctuations in the share of loans borrowed for productive purposes in all loans in the debt portfolios of the poor generally reflect changes in the provision of formal credit to the poor; they do not necessarily reflect changes in the demand for consumption loans.

In Gokilapuram in 1999, the share of loans borrowed by landless labour households for consumption was very high, higher in fact than in previous surveys. In 1999, only 22.6 per cent of the principal borrowed by landless hired labour households was taken for directly productive activities (agriculture, livestock and other businesses). The sharp decline between 1985 and 1999 in the share of loans taken for agriculture, livestock and other businesses reflects the reduction in access to formal credit over the period.

Landless Labour Households vs. all Households

Although data on indebtedness of households other than hired labour households are not yet available, estimates of the indebtedness of all village households have been made by Chavan (2000). The proportion of indebted households in the village as a whole (66 per cent) was similar to the proportion of indebted labour households (68 per cent). Similarly, the average size of loan for all households (Rs 27,383) was greater than the average size of loan for labour households by about a factor of 6. This reflects, among other things, the greater access of non-labour households to formal sector credit, since the size of a formal sector loan to landed households is typically much larger than an informal sector loan to a landless household. The share of the formal sector in the total principal borrowed by all households was 40 per cent, while the correspondin g share for landless labour households was 22.4 per cent. With respect to thc purposes for which loans were taken, 42 per cent of the total principal borrowed by all households in the village were taken for productive purposes; the corresponding share for landless labour households was 23 per cent.

Informalization, Rates of Interest

The 1990s have not just been a period when the share of informal sector loans in the debt portfolios of the poor increased sharply; they have also been a period over which the process of informalization of the credit market intensified. A formal sector loan is one where the terms and conditions of the loan are regulated by the public authority. An informal loan is subject to no such regulation: it is a personalized transaction, dependent on the specific relation of power between borrower and lender. Over the study period, the personalized nature of transactions in the informal sector intensified. There are two trends in moneylending as an occupation in the village. First, the number and proportion of persons living off moneylending or whose major occupation is moneylending has expanded. Secondly, moneylending as a part-time occupation or secondary source of income has spread in the village. These trends are supported by the evidence on the composition of lenders within the informal sector. The principal borrowed from different informal sector sources as a proportion of the total principal borrowed from the informal sector by landless labour households. The most striking feature of the table is the sharp rise in the share of moneylenders in informal-sector advances, from 27.2 per cent in 1977 to 41.9 per cent in 1999. The traditional dependence of landless labour households on landlords for credit clearly became weaker; the share of landlords in informal sector advances to landless labour households fell from 23.1 per cent in 1977 to 2.4 per cent in 1999. The data also indicate that moneylending as a part-time occupation has spread in the village.

New sources of usurious loans have appeared in the village. These are moneylending associations (or sangams) whose size varies from about 5 or 6 to 25 subscribers. The members of the group generally belong to the same caste (although in one case the sangam consists of workers on grape fields) and each member pays a fixed amount at regular intervals (say once a week) in to a common fund. This fund is then given out as loans, generally at 60 per cent rates of interest per year. The significance of the sangams should not, however, be exaggerated. Loans taken from sangams constituted about 7 per cent of the total principal borrowed by landless labour households.

The incidence of a type of loan called the kanthu loan has increased sharply since the first survey in 1977. As example of a kanthu loan, a moneylender gives B a nominal loan of one thousand rupees. It is not actually a loan of Rs 1,000, since B is given only Rs 850. B has to repay the moneylender Rs 100 on an appointed day every week for ten consecutive weeks. The distinctive feature of the kanthu loan is that it is time-bound and at the end of the specified time period, the principal and interest are repaid. Kanthu loans otherwise vary greatly with the amount advanced, the periodicity of repayment and the amount to be repaid each time. Some kanthu loans have to be repaid every day; we do not know of any such loan for which the time given for each instalment of repayment was greater than a week.

Every borrower is screened by the lender for his or her creditworthiness and lenders have a sharp-eyed assessment of the borrower's income and wage-earning capacity when they lend money. As a consequence, there has been a proliferation of different types of loans with respect to the terms and conditions attached to each loan. In 1977, a major feature of the labour market in the village was the mediation of the system of wage labour by an elaborate system of labour service; this system had important implications for creditor-borrower relations as well (see Ramachandran, 1990). The system of labour service has now declined. Concurrently, transactions in the informal sector of credit have become more commercialized: a lender lends primarily to gain an income or property through loans, not to be able to extract unpaid labour or to reinforce traditional patronclient relations between himself and the borrower.

A consequence of the commercialization of transactions in the informal sector is that lenders got tougher and tougher with respect to monitoring and enforcing repayment (although physical violence is not a routine method of enforcement). Those who manage sangams generally get a person close to the borrower to sign on as a surety and many moneylenders regularly issue promissory notes with each loan. Much time is invested by moneylenders and their henchmen in enforcing repayment (and much scorn poured by them on fellow-lenders who are poor enforcers). In nearby Gudalur (a small town where the major occupation is agriculture), some moneylenders enforce repayment by announcing the names of debtors over loudspeakers fitted on jeeps that are driven through the village; the strategy is that public disgrace (and the fear of public disgrace) will force defaulters back in line. The last resort of many borrowers is flight; those defaulters who flee (individually or with their families) generally go to the industrial town of Tiruppur and its environs in Coimbatore district. They go there to seek work as casual manual workers in wretched working and living conditions rather than having their lives and property uprooted and stripped by their creditors at home.

As already mentioned, agricultural labourers have little - and reduced - access to formal sector loans and the determination of the terms of loans in the informal sector loans have become more individual-specific. These changes have had two consequences on the level of nominal interest rates in the informal sector. First, the general level of interest rates is higher than before and a larger share of loans is borrowed at very high rates of interest. The second consequence is that the interest rates that lenders charge, while being high, vary from household to household, and from individual to individual.

In 1999, of the total principal borrowed by landless labour households, 64 per cent was borrowed at nominal rates of interest of 36 per cent per year and above. Forty three per cent of the total principal was borrowed at rates of interest of 60 per cent per year and above. If only loans from the informal sector are considered, 56 per cent of the principal borrowed by landless hired labour households was at interest rates of 60 per cent a year or more (Chavan, 2001). As expected, for all village households, a significant share of loans (41.5 per cent) were at low interest rates (1-24 per cent per annum), and only 15 per cent of loans were taken at interest rates of 60 per cent per annum or above. This finding is consistent with the general feature of rural credit reported that the share of formal credit advanced to households with less than 2.5 acres of land is declining over time. Formal credit typically was disbursed at interest rates that were below 15 per cent per annum.

The share of principal borrowed by landless labour households at rates of interest higher than 36 per cent has doubled between 1977 and 1999 and the share of principal borrowed at rates of interest higher than 60 per cent has risen sharply between 1985 and 1999.11 It is clear that interest rates in the informal sector rose even during the phase of expansion of subsidized formal credit (1977 to 1985). With the post-1991 withdrawal of the formal sector from lending operations for the rural poor, usury has intensified.12 In the 1990s, some scholars expected that the formal sector would be a civilising influence on rates of interest in the informal sector of credit (Athreya et. al., 1990), p 269). Their understanding was based on a belief that the formal sector would serve as a countervailing force to the informal sector in the credit market. Events have clearly belied that expectation.

Ideally, a comparison of interest rates over time should be based on real interest rates. The computation of real interest rates, that is, nominal interest rates adjusted for expected inflation, is a complex task, as the expected rate of inflation will vary with the duration of a loan. To simplify, a common inflation rate could be applied to all loans reported in a given year. However, given the relatively low and stable rates of inflation around our three survey years (4 per cent per annum in 1977-80, 6 per cent per annum in 1983-85 and 5 per cent per annum in 1997-99) nominal rates of interest are not very different from the real rates of interest.

Is NGO-controlled Microcredit the Alternative?

It is clear from the preceding sections that neo-liberal banking reform amounts, in theory and practice, to a reversal of the public policy objectives of extending the reach of rural credit, providing cheap and timely credit to rural households (particularly economically vulnerable households), overcoming the historical problems of imperfect and fragmented rural credit markets, and displacing the informal sector from its powerful position in rural credit markets. As we have seen, there was a large-scale retreat by the formal sector from the Indian countryside in the post-1991 period. From official policy statements, it appears that the Government envisages only one policy instrument to fill the gap left by the formal credit sector in the countryside: the establishment of microcredit projects in rural India.

Why Microcredit?

In official statements, the move to hand over banking functions in rural areas to NGOs is motivated by weaknesses in the banking system itself, most notably the "twin problems of non-viability and poor recovery performance" of existing rural credit institutions (Rangarajan, 1996, p. 68). The failure of financial institutions to deal with income-poor borrowers in an imaginative and sustainable way and the inaccessibility of these institutions to the poor are stated to be major disadvantages of the existing system.

Microcredit institutions are seen as being able to rectify these weaknesses; according to the Governor of the RBI, "the main advantage to the banks of their links with the SHGs [selfhelp groups] and NGOs is the externalization of a part of the work items of the credit cycle, viz., assessment of credit needs, appraisal, disbursal, supervision and repayment, reduction in the formal paper work involved and a consequent reduction in the transaction costs" (ibid., p. 70).

Thus, microcredit is the favoured alternative to the present system because, first, it is assumed that the transaction costs of banks and other financial institutions can be lowered significantly if these costs are passed on to NGOs or self-help groups,13 and secondly, because NGOs are expected to perform better than formal sector credit institutions in respect of the recovery of loans.

Defining Microcredit

The terms microcredit and micro-finance have risen spectacularly to fame in the development profession and in development literature in the last decade and a half. The Declaration of the Micro-Credit Summit held in Washington, D. C. in 1997 defined microcredit programmes as those "extending small loans to poor people for selfemployment projects that generate income, allowing them to care for themselves and their families". The Declaration also stated that, "in most cases, microcredit projects offer a combination of services and resources to their clients in addition to credit for selfemployment. These often include savings facilities, training, networking and peer support" (Micro-Credit Summit, 1997). In India, the Task Force on Supportive and Regulatory Framework for Micro-Finance in India (NABARD, 2000) defined micro-finance as the "provision of thrift, credit and other financial services and products of very small amounts to the poor in rural, semi-urban or urban areas enabling them to raise their income levels and improve living standards." The Reserve Bank of India uses the same definition (RBI 1999a).

While microcredit loans are generally advanced for self-employment projects, they are sometimes advanced for consumption as well. A distinction between consumption and production is, of course, difficult to draw, both on account of the fungibility of cash and because of the organic links between consumption and production.

Thus it is not entirely accurate to classify an educational loan or a loan taken to meet medical expenses as purely a consumption loan; medical care and education contribute to productivity as well.

Nevertheless, the advocates of microcredit do consider it necessary for microcredit institutions to get borrowers to make the transition from consumption loans to production loans (or loans for income-bearing projects) (Rangarajan, 1997, p. 71).

The characteristic features of microcredit operations, then, are small loans to poor households in rural and urban areas for income generation through self-employment. Microcredit institutions may also provide facilities for savings and other financial services. Microcredit, as discussed in the international literature, is associated with certain other recurring empirical features.

First, microcredit involves loans without collateral. In the absence of specific policy intervention, landless and asset-poor households are deemed not to be creditworthy by formal sector lending institutions, sinc e they cannot provide collateral that is deemed to be appropriate. In his opening speech at the Micro-Credit Summit, Mohammed Yunus, founder of Grameen Bank, Bangladesh, said that by means of microcredit, "we are celebrating the freeing of credit of the bondage of collateral" (Yunus, 1997).

Secondly, NGO-controlled microcredit loans are generally advanced to individuals who are members of groups. Organizations such as BRAC and Grameen Bank in Bangladesh lend through groups. The NABARD task force identifies three ways of banking with the poor: by means of conventional bank lending, by linking self -help groups with bank lending, and by banks lending to microcredit and micro-finance institutions for on-lending to groups or individuals. The Task Force goes on to say that the second and third methods "are characterized by low transactions costs and high repayments" (NABARD, 2000). The group (or "self-help group") is, in fact, viewed as standing in the place of collateral (Hashemi and Morshed, 1997, p 217). The presence of a group has been called a form of "social collateral" (Johnson and Rogaly 1997). The formation of groups, it is argued, has the double advantage of lowering transactions costs and improving repayment.

Thirdly, and following from the previous paragraph, microcredit is viewed as a way of promoting market-led growth, or, in the words of Mohammed Yunus, of "privatizing the economy" (Yunus 1997). This objective was stated in another way by World Bank President James Wolfensohn in his speech to the Micro-Credit Summit: "Microcredit programmes have brought the vibrancy of the market economy to the poorest villages and peoples of the world" (Micro-Credit Summit, 1997).

Fourthly, this target group are generally only those below a line of absolute poverty as determined by national estimates. Consequently, beneficiaries of microcredit projects constitute a fraction of those in need of credit.

Fifthly, while all definitions concur on microcredit as the provision of "small loans", the scale or "smallness" of loans varies and has to be identified empirically. Loans from the Grameen Bank had an upper limit of 5,000 Taka or around USD 100 (Hossain, 1993). In a sample survey conducted in 1985, however, Hossain found that the loans averaged Tk 3,040 (Tk 3,279 for men and Tk 2,843 for women). The scale is similar in other developing countries; the average loan size was USD 88 in Mexico and USD 157 in Pakistan (Johnson and Rogaly, 1997, pp. 88-89). The NABARD Task Force estimated the credit requirement per family as Rs 6,000 in rural areas and Rs 9,000 in urban areas (respectively USD 128 and 191) but recommended that the average loan given to members of self-help groups (or SHGs) be around Rs. 1,000 (NABARD 2000).14 The Microcredit

Cell of the RBI, however, has proposed a ceiling of Rs 25,000 for micro-finance, and suggests that the ceiling may be raised, say to Rs 40,000, for borrowers with a track record of regular repayment over two to three years (RBI 1999a).

Finally, while these are the general characteristics of microcredit, a great deal of discussion of the "microcredit alternative" has been on the institutional mechanisms for the delivery of microcredit. A very important component of the argument in favour of a largescale microcredit effort is that commercial banks cannot and should not directly be responsible for disbursing microcredit loans (because of transactions costs that are allegedly very high and poor recovery).

The Microcredit Cell of the RBI, for instance, states clearly that, "NGOs have widespread appeal as micro-finance delivery vehicles" (RBI 1999a). In the Plan of Action of the Microcredit Summit, the responsibility for achieving the goals of the Summit was placed clearly on "the thousands of existing microcredit NGOs, cooperatives, credit unions, grassroots groups, and poverty banks that at present comprise the microcredit movement" (Micro-Credit Summit, 1997). Thus "microcredit" as commonly used means credit provided mainly by the private sector, including NGOs, where the private sector not only controls disbursement but also determines the terms and conditions attached to each loan.

To summarize, microcredit is usually associated with:

- very small loans,
- no collateral,
- borrowers from among the rural and urban poor,
- loans for income-generation through market-based self-employment,
- the formation of borrower groups, and
- privatization, generally through the mechanism of NGO control over disbursement and the determination of the terms and conditions attached to each loan.

In India, as we have noted, microcredit has been described as the way to go with respect to rural banking for the poor.

However, NGO-controlled microcredit is not yet as widespread and does not represent as general a policy towards rural credit in India as in Bangladesh, for instance.

NGO-controlled Microcredit: an Evaluation

It is clear that, by its very nature, NGO-controlled microcredit does not offer a solution for the problems of rural credit listed in the introductory section of this paper. It is not an instrument for mobilising large-scale funds for scientific and technical change in the countryside, and it does not and cannot supplant the informal sector or overcome the historical imperfections and fragmentation of rural credit markets. NGO-controlled microcredit projects in India cannot hope to achieve the spread and reach of the rural banking system. There are also problems of accountability involved here: NGO-controlled microcredit organizations are not accountable to public scrutiny or to local governments. Being essentially private, market-oriented organizations, their only formal responsibility is to their donors. But what of the more limited claim made for NGO-controlled microcredit? Do NGOcontrolled microcredit institutions incur lower transactions costs than formal-sector financial institutions and is their record with respect to the repayment of loans superior to that of formal-sector financial institutions? We examine the evidence below.

Transactions Costs

To begin with, it should come as little surprise - despite suggestions to the contrary - that the administrative costs of NGOs (and such costs are, of course, the major component of total transactions costs) are relatively higher than those of commercial banks. NGOs cannot match the economies of scale of a comprehensive system of banking (in the case of India, perhaps the best network of rural banks in the less developed world).

For the period 1988-92, the costs of administration of the Grameen Bank constituted 12.3 per cent of the bank's total portfolio, and the costs of administration of BRAC constituted 40 per cent of its total portfolio (Hulme and Mosley, 1996, cited in Chavan and Ramakumar, 2000). An important finding from the work of Hulme and Mosley is that, in a cross-country study of rural credit institutions, the lowest costs of administration, 8.1 per cent of the total portfolio, were incurred by Regional Rural Banks in India. Secondly, the costs of administration of NGO-controlled microcredit have actually risen when NGO activity is scaled up. As the Grameen Bank expanded its activities, administrative costs rose from 8.6 per cent of liabilities in 1988 to 18.1 per cent of liabilities in 1992 (Hossain 1988, cited in Chavan and Ramakumar, 2000).

Thirdly, repayment rates in NGO-controlled microcredit projects are related directly to the level of administrative costs and mobilization efforts (Rahman, 1999 and Bhat and Tang, 1998, cited in Chavan and Ramakumar, 2000). Organizations such as the Grameen Bank need large numbers of employees for regular monitoring and assessment, to conduct weekly visits and meetings and to collect dues. Mahabub Hossain notes that, in the case of the Grameen Bank, "the paperwork and the staff time for servicing a given amount of loan are higher than for a normal rural credit programme," and that "the benefits of this intensive credit programme...need to be evaluated against the high costs of operation" (Hossain, 1993, pp. 119-120).

How do NGO-controlled microcredit projects finance their high-cost operations? The evidence on this seems clear. They do so by turning to donors for funds or by raising interest rates to levels higher than those offered by the banking system or by doing both. In his review of the performance of the Grameen Bank in 1984-86, Mahabub Hossain found that although the Annual Reports of the bank reported a small profit, his scrutiny of the account books showed that "the credit operations of the bank involve losses that are compensated for by profits from deposits in other banks of a substantial amount of lowcost funds available from international donors" (Hossain, p. 120). It is acknowledged widely that interest rates charged by microcredit organizations are higher than the corresponding rates charged by commercial banks or other financial institutions.

Real interest rates in 1992 varied from 15 per cent per annum in Bangladesh for Grameen Bank to 45 per cent in

Bolivia for loans advanced by BancoSol, and 60 per cent in Indonesia for loans advanced by BKK (Hulme and Mosley, 1998, cited in Chavan and Ramakumar, 2000). In Bangladesh, the interest rate charged by Grameen Bank was around 8 percentage points higher than the market rate (Rahman, 1999 cited in Chavan and Ramakumar, 22 2000).15 In fact, the literature notes that, in the era of financial liberalization, NGOs too are "free to charge whatever interest rates they wish in order to cover the (at present very considerable) costs of institution building, supervision, experimentation and insurance" (Mosley, 1999, p 377).

Thus the transfer of the task of serving the credit needs of rural borrowers from the banking system to NGO-controlled microcredit projects does not reduce transactions costs but, in effect, transfers transactions costs - higher transactions costs - to donors as well as borrowers.

Repayments and Overdue Loans

A record of near 100 per cent repayment is a major success of NGO-controlled microcredit. Repayment rates are reported to be over 95 per cent in many microcredit programmes (Hossain, 1988, Hulme and Mosley, 1998, cited in Chavan and Ramakumar 2000, Johnson and Rogaly, 1997).

This achievement, however, is not costless. A system based on the quick repayment of very small loans does not allow for funds to go into income-bearing activities that have a gestation period of any significance. Only projects with very quick rates of return and high rates of return relative to the tiny investment can meet existing repayment schedules. The first payment on a microcredit loan is generally to be made a very short time after the loan is given. It has been argued that this can put the poorest out of the pale of microcredit, since the ability to pay the first few instalments depends on the initial resource base of the borrower (Zaman, 1997, p. 247).16

The repayment record of NGO-controlled microcredit projects slackens as the size of loan rises and as the frequency of borrowing rises. To take the example of the Grameen Bank once again. the default rate was 0.4 per cent among first-time borrowers, 1.2 per cent among second-time borrowers, 6.6 per cent among third-time borrowers and 9.5 per cent among fourth-time borrowers (Hossain, 1988, cited in Chavan and Ramakumar, 2000). Further, when the pressure to repay is as overbearing as it often is, borrowers have to borrow from moneylenders in order to repay NGO-advanced loans (Rahman, 1999, cited in Chavan and Ramakumar, 2000).

High repayment is dependent on high transactions costs. As already mentioned, NGOs invest heavily in supervising, monitoring and enforcing loan repayments. When the activities of NGO-controlled microcredit projects are scaled up, the relative burden of administrative costs tends to increase.

Dealing with Overdues: an Indian Example

Adequate data are not available for a comparative study of the problem of overdues in commercial and cooperative banks on the one hand and independent microcredit agencies on the other. Nevertheless, two recent analyses published by the Reserve Bank of India (Ghosh, 2001 and RBI, 2001a) permit some observations on the issue of overdues with particular reference to the performance of one of India's most distinguished microcredit and self-employment organizations, the Self Employed Women's Association (SEWA). SEWA, based in Ahmedabad, is an organization of working women, and has long been involved in disbursing microcredit. It has established a bank, the SEWA Bank, which now operates in five districts of Gujarat and advances around 90 million rupees annually. Most of the working capital of the Bank comes from members' savings. A borrower's repayment record is used, in lieu of collateral, to assess her creditworthiness. A recent study of the financial performance of SEWA Bank has found that, at present, "overdues are the major area of concern".

In the financial years 1996/97, 1997/98 and 1998/99, Non-Performing Advances (NPAs or overdues) amounted to 28 per cent, 20 per cent and 27 per cent respectively of total loans and advances (Ghosh, 2001,Table 1). For roughly the same period, 1995/96, 1996/97 and 1997/98, the RBI estimates that gross NPAs as a share of the total advances of all public-sector banks together amounted to 17.3 per cent, 18 per cent and 16 per cent (RBI, 2001a). If only Priority Sector advances of public -sector banks are considered, the ratio of NPAs to total advances was 27 per cent, 26 per cent and 23 per cent in each of the three reference years.

The data thus show that the proportion of overdues to total advances of an independent microcredit bank was actually marginally higher than the corresponding ratio for public-sector banks. Scaling-up NGO-controlled microcredit, it appears, can generate problems similar to those faced by traditional banking institutions. The corrective measures being taken by SEWA Bank to address the problem of overdue loans involve greater supervision and monitoring (Ghosh, 2001). For example, daily targets for collection are being set and monitored, leaders from all areas are being called for weekly meetings, a special team of field workers has been created to regularly visit borrowers, and so on (Ghosh, 2001).

In short, higher and better repayment requires more staff and closer monitoring. This is as true, of course, for commercial banks as it is for SEWA Bank. In fact, it may well be argued that one reason for the unsatisfactory performance of rural banks in India (both in terms of advances and in terms of recovery) is under-staffing in rural bank branches. In an early assessment of the performance of banks after nationalization, Shetty pointed out that rural and semi-urban bank branches are "generally starved of staff inputs and hence have not fared well in business". For instance, in 1974, rural areas accounted for 36 per cent of bank branches but only 10 per cent of bank employees (Shetty, 1978, p. 1417).

Small-scale Credit and Rural Banks

As mentioned in an earlier section of this paper, rural credit policy in India needs to offer a range of services and types of loan to rural households. While small-scale, shortterm loans - or microcredit - constitute only one among the many services that the public authority should provide, schemes that provide such loans to rural working households do nevertheless serve as a kind of palliative reform in the countryside. For all the weaknesses in its implementation, IRDP played an important role in the 1980s in that it gave new access to millions of rural households to the formal banking system and increased levels of purchasing power in rural India significantly. Small-scale credit schemes have also been the basis for useful and socially progressive experiments in social mobilization. It is clear that the Indian banking system - cooperative banks and commercial banks - failed on many fronts to fulfil its commitment to the people of rural India in respect of social and development banking. The banking system, we believe, can and must improve its functioning by working with local governments and local voluntary organizations.

Some of the transactions costs of loans, costs for banks as well as for borrowers, can be lowered when banks work in an innovative way with panchayats and self-help groups. Small-scale rural credit is indeed necessary, but rural credit policy should build on the strengths of the banking system in this regard. This issue has now been officially recognized in an official report as well. The Expert Committee on Rural Credit set up by NABARD in its report states that "commercial banks cannot be allowed to withdraw from rural credit" and that cooperative credit institutions need to be strengthened to meet the huge unmet needs of rural credit in India (NABARD, 2001). This paper argues that, despite assertions to the contrary, NGO-controlled microcredit organizations do not incur lower transactions costs than banks (they are able to transfer these costs to others).

Banks have many advantages over private microcredit organizations as providers of small-scale loans. They have advantages of scale; the banking system in India has a reach and spread that NGO-controlled microcredit cannot begin to match; banks can cross-subsidize loans; banks are better placed to provide specialized training to their employees in development banking; banks are in a better position to coordinate banking activity with development administrations, local governments and self-help groups; and banks are better able than private microcredit organizations to offer a wide range of financial services to borrowers.

For the state to withdraw from the field and hand over small-scale credit to NGOcontrolled microcredit organizations is, in effect, to undermine and weaken a major national asset, the widespread rural banking system.

CONCLUSIONS

Credit policy that attempts to deal with the enormity of the problem of rural indebtedness in India must provide a range of credit services to the countryside, and on a scale that the problem demands. This paper attempted to describe and evaluate rural credit policy in India over the last three decades and to examine its effects on rural workers at the level of a single village.

Three broad phases of banking policy with regard to the Indian countryside can be observed: an early green revolution phase that followed the nationalization of major commercial banks; IRDP phase of credit-based poverty alleviation initiatives; and the most recent phase of liberalization and market-guided banking policy. The first two phases witnessed a significant expansion and consolidation of banking infrastructure in rural areas and, correspondingly, a rise in rural deposit mobilization and advances to rural areas. While the first phase concentrated on the expansion of credit to cultivators, particularly landlords and rich peasants in selected areas, the second phase included credit-based schemes for landless and asset-poor households. The flow of formal sector credit to the rural areas, and specifically to the rural poor, peaked in the late 1980s. The liberalization phase of banking policy has seen a sharp withdrawal of formal banking instruments and credit supply from rural areas.

The village data show that changes in national banking policy have had a rapid, drastic and potentially disastrous effect on the debt portfolios of landless labour households. Rural credit markets in India abhor a vacuum: with the withdrawal of formal sector credit for the village poor, the informal sector has rushed in to fill the space. The village data discussed here refer, to the class of landless labourers. We are thus not in a position to examine the distribution of formal credit in the village as a whole nor can we comment on changes in the distribution across classes after the initiation of financial reforms.

The share of the formal sector in the principal borrowed by landless labour households increased from 17 per cent in the green revolution phase to 80 per cent in the IRDP phase and fell to 22 per cent in the liberalization phase. The share of production and business-related loans in the proximate purposes for which all loans were taken by landless labour households was 23.8 per cent in 1977, rose to 44.2 per cent in 1985 and fell sharply to 22.6 per cent in 1999.

The 1999 survey showed new forms of informalization of the credit market, a proliferation of moneylending as a whole-time or part-time occupation, and new trends in the personalization of individual loans. Usury increased over the 22-year period covered by our survey: in 1977, 32.3 per cent of the total principal borrowed by landless labour households was borrowed at nominal rates of interest of 36 per cent and above; the corresponding figures for 1985 and 1999 are 50.3 per cent and 64 per cent.

Twenty four per cent of total principal borrowed in the 1985 survey was at rates of interest of 60 per cent and above; the share rose to 43 per cent in 1999. Every indicator of indebtedness that has been used thus shows that the exploitation of the rural poor in the credit market has intensified in the phase of financial liberalization. Current policy has, in practice, seen a retreat of formal-sector banking from the countryside. The major policy recommendation designed to fill this gap is the establishment of microcredit projects. The main institutional mechanism envisaged for the disbursal of microcredit are non-government organizations. An NGO typically is expected to disburse loans and collect repayments; crucially, they are also expected to set the terms and conditions attached to each loan they disburse.

Microcredit, by its very nature, cannot attempt to meet the full range of the demand for credit in the countryside. NGO-controlled microcredit is, however, expected to incur lower transactions costs and achieve a better repayment record than the formal banking sector in respect of small-scale, short-term loans. The international evidence, however, does not justify this expectation. There are no indications that the transaction costs of NGO-controlled microcredit are lower than those of rural public -sector banks; on the contrary, the evidence shows that NGO-controlled microcredit are able to transfer their transactions costs - which are generally higher than those incurred by banks - to donors and borrowers. The relatively high rates of repayment achieved by NGO-controlled microcredit is dependent on relatively high transactions costs.

NGO-controlled microcredit projects in India cannot hope to achieve the spread and reach of the rural banking system. There are also problems of accountability involved here:

NGO-controlled microcredit organizations are not accountable to public scrutiny or to local governments. Being essentially private, market-oriented organizations, their only formal responsibility is to their donors.

In the first section of this paper, we attempted to show that access to low-interest, timely credit and freedom from extra-economic coercion in the credit market is an essential component of the income and livelihood security and the general freedom of the rural poor.

In any enlightened policy of rural credit, there is certainly a place for small-scale, shortterm loans, and for a more sensitive approach to rural lending. Banks would do well to work with local governments and self -help groups in this regard. Our view in this paper is that banks have advantages in respect of small-scale rural credit that NGOs lack. The objective of rural credit policy in respect of small-scale loans to the poor in India should be to build on the strengths of the rural banking system, not to undermine or weaken this important national asset.

5

RURAL BANKING: BRIDGING THE GAP

The vulnerability of the Indian economy to the performance of the agricultural sector despite other macroeconomic indicators and sectors gaining in strength is well known. For example, the Indian economy grew at an estimated 3.7 per cent in 2002-03 against 5.6 per cent during 2001-2. This was largely because of the negative growth of 4.4 per cent in the agriculture sector. Just prior to the current swing into election campaigning, policy pronouncements of the Government were largely agriculture and rural centric. The constitution of a Farmers Commission is one among them. Rural credit is emerging as a focal issue and this can be gleaned from the fact that the Government earmarked Rs 15,000 crore in the Interim Budget to revitalise the co-operative structure. The Tenth Plan (2002-2007) has set an ambitious average GDP growth of 8 per cent per annum.

To achieve this, it is important to revitalise and revamp not only the agricultural sector but also rural financial institutions. An annual average growth of 7 per cent from this sector alone in the next five years is crucial for achieving the GDP target. The Task Force on Rural Credit for the Tenth Plan has projected institutional credit flow to agriculture and allied activities at Rs 7,36,570 crore for 2002-2007, which is more than treble (320 per cent) the credit flow (Rs 2,29,853 crore) during the Ninth Plan (1997-2002).

This article will do a broad review of the state of rural banking and credit in the country, compare this with urban areas, assess the banking divide, point out candidate institutions for strengthening in the light of the challenges in an era of reforms, and finally draw a roadmap consisting of policy and institutional reform components.

CURRENT TRENDS IN RURAL BANKING AND CREDIT

First let's look at some broad banking data. The 2001 Census figures brought out an alarming picture about the usage of banking services among Indian households in urban and rural areas despite the wide banking network in the country. The following table reinforces the conclusions about the low level of banking usage among Indian Households in general (35.5%) and Rural Households in particular (30.1%) and also reflects the latent demand for general banking needs in rural as well urban segments.

The absolute numbers of bank branches has seen an increase in urban areas, while there has been decline in the rural areas.

CREDIT AS AN INDICATOR OF ECONOMIC ACTIVITY

The Credit/Deposit Ratio

As per statutory requirements, Banks need to maintain Cash Reserve Ratio (CRR) and Statutory Liquidity Ratio (SLR) to the extent of 4.5% and 25% of their deposits respectively. Accordingly, for every hundred rupees of the bank deposits, around Rs.30 is preempted under SLR and CRR obligations. The banks can lend the remaining amount i.e Rs.70.

The CD ratio can be 70% at most, but that often is not reached. In fact, post the onset of financial reforms, credit driven economic activity at rural and semi-urban branches has plummeted to the levels prevalent during the period of nationalization of banks.

The banking profile (as on 31-3-2003) reflects a low Credit/Deposit (CD) ratio of 42% and 35% at rural and semi-urban centres respectively compared with 69.5% of urban centers (inclusive of metro centers) and 59.3% at national level. The ratios at metro and top 100 urban centers are as high as 83%

and 74% respectively. At the time of nationalization, June 1969, the credit indicators of banks' rural and semi-urban branches were 37.2% and 39.7% respectively and they peaked to 57.7% and 49.1% at the end of June 1981.

Post the onset of financial reforms, the exclusive CD ratios at rural and semi-urban branches have almost plummeted to the levels prevalent during the period of nationalization of banks. In a developing country like India, the availability of credit is major input for any activity. From the table of CD ratios, it will be noted that CD ratio in urban India is very high beyond 60%, when compared to rural/semi-urban sector. This indicates that the rural/semi-urban branches are being used for mobilization of savings, but not for deployment of credit. Low CD ratios also indicate that Banks are not playing major role in credit expansion in particular segment/sector.

This situation matches up with the debt profile of rural households which still reflects inadequate institutional credit flow.

These trends broadly indicate that despite the widespread banking network in place, there is a continued migration of rural/semi-urban savings (to the minimum extent of Rs.1,32,295 crores) to urban/metro centers, thereby causing a banking divide a la digital/rural-urban divide. In order to obviate the regional or urban/rural imbalances, the minimum benchmark CD ratio of 60% should be envisaged in all districts of the country. That will assist broad-based and equitable credit expansion thereby contributing enhanced economic activity. The reason urban India is reflecting enhanced economic activity post-reforms is the availability and expansion of credit for housing and consumption purposes.

Agricultural Credit

An equally important concern that needs attention is the flow of institutional credit to agriculture. The growth of commercial banks' lending to agriculture and allied activities witnessed a substantial decline in the 1990s as compared with the 1980s. Agriculture's share in scheduled commercial banks' total outstanding credit as on 31-3-02 was only Rs.64,008 crores or 9.8 per cent. Even if we include loans for food manufacturing and processing (rice, sugar, edible oil, tea, fruits and vegetable processing), this share works out to Rs. 84,750.22 crores or 12.90 per cent, way below the stipulated target of 18 per cent. The total agricultural lending by commercial banks(as on 31-3-2002) is now lower than even their outstandings in "personal loans" (Rs.82,518 crores in 17.59 millions of accounts) portfolio comprising loans for housing, consumer durables, and so on.

Similarly, post reforms, the banking system has mobilized more deposits from farmers and extended less credit to declining number of farmers as illustrated here under:

Many scheduled commercial banks are shying away from agriculture and priority sector lending. For example, the commercial banks have an excess investments portfolio beyond the required limits of 25 percent. The table below illustrates the declining penetration in rural banking post-reforms, compared to an excess investments of scheduled commercial banks in treasury securities (gilts).

Furthermore, scheduled commercial banks are resorting to the soft window option of investing in the Rural Infrastructure Development Fund (RIDF) of NABARD. Contributions to the corpus of RIDF are received by NABARD by way of deposits from Scheduled Commercial Banks against their shortfall in priority sector/agricultural lending during the preceding year. The outstandings at the end of March 2003 stood at Rs. 12,159.23 crores.

Government's Response to the Rural Credit Scenario

While the current situation may not look promising for rural credit, it isn't that governments have been inactive all the way. In fact, in the early 1970s itself the Central Government observed that despite a wide banking network and developmental initiatives in the first 25 years since Independence, a critical gap still existed in meeting the credit needs of the rural poor. To find a solution, the Government appointed a working group on rural credit, the Narasimhan Committee, in July 1975. The committee observed that the cost structure of commercial banks, the attitude of bank employees and the lack of a professional approach in the co-operative credit system were the main stumbling blocks to rural credit. The committee also observed that the deposits collected by banks from rural areas were not totally deployed there. The panel, therefore, recommended the creation of a new set of regionally-oriented rural banks which would combine a co-operative's local feel and a commercial bank's business acumen.

Regional Rural Banks Emerge

The Government accepted these recommendations and, accordingly, the ordinance of Regional Rural Banks, 1975 was promulgated on September 26, 1975. This was replaced by the Regional Rural Banks Act, 1976 on February 9, 1976. The mandate of these rural financial institutions were to: take banking to the doorsteps of the rural masses, particularly in areas without banking facilities; make available cheaper institutional credit to the weaker sections of society, who were to be the only clients of these banks; mobilise rural savings and canalise them for supporting productive activities in rural areas; generate employment opportunities in the rural areas; and bring down the cost of providing credit in rural areas.

With partnerships with the Central Government (50 per cent), State governments (15 per cent) and commercial banks (35 per cent), the number of RRBs rose from just six in 1975 to 196 by 1987, covering 476 districts. They financed only the weaker sections of the rural community - small and marginal farmers, agricultural labourers, small traders, and so on. Along with commercial banks, RRBs participated enthusiastically in poverty alleviation schemes (IRDP, for example) and disadvantaged area (drought-prone regions and deserts) development programmes. They quickly became an important and integral part of the rural credit system. However, their financial viability was initially overstretched by policy rigidities coupled with a low capital base in an environment of inadequate infrastructure and deeper social and economic disparities.

After the financial sector reforms, several measures to improve the viability of RRBs were initiated. More importantly, re-capitalisation to cleanse their balance sheets was taken up in 1993-94. Other important reform measures included deregulation of interest rates on advances as well as deposits; permission to lend to others outside target groups; provision for rationalization of branch network - relocation and merger of loss-making branches; introduction of prudential norms on income-recognition, asset classification and provisioning; preparation of development action plans and signing of memorandum of understanding with sponsor bank for sustained viability in a planned manner; provision of greater role space and larger operational responsibilities to sponsor banks in the management of RRBs; encouragement to function as self-help promoting institutions and financing of self-help groups and introduction of Kisan Credit Cards to simplify provision of production credit to their clients.

Regional Rural Banks Today

At the end of fiscal 2002-3, there were 196 RRBs spread over 23 States/Union Territories and with a network of 14,350 branches, accounting for 44.5 per cent of the total rural network of all scheduled commercial banks (including RRBs). The rural and semi-urban branches of RRBs constitute 98 per cent of their network. Their deposits and advances as on March 31, 2003, were Rs 49,078 crore and Rs 22,028 crore respectively. Thus, RRBs have done well in mobilising rural deposits and infusing the thrift habit in their clients.

Out of 196 RRBs, the number of profit making banks stood at 167 in 2001-2002 as compared with 170 in 2000-2001. The combined Net Profit of RRBs for the year 2001-2002 aggregated Rs.608 crores as against the combined net profit of Rs.601 crores in the previous year. The aggregate accumulated losses of RRBs declined from Rs.2752.59 crores as on 31 March 2001 to Rs 2694.06 crores as on 31 March 2002.

As a result of the various reform measures, the RRBs showed substantial turn-around in their performance. The RRBs also displayed qualitative improvement in their NPA management and gross NPAs as percentage of gross advances stood at 16% as on 31-3-2002, down from 32.8 at March-end 1998. Similarly, the recovery performance of the RRBs steadily improved with the percentage of recovery to demand raised at 71% as on 30th June 2001 form 61.2 % at end-June 1998(41.2 % at end -June1993).

The bulk of the loans from RRBs have been to priority sectors, which accounted for over 70 per cent of the total. Agriculture alone took up 46 per cent of the priority sector advances. The involvement of RRBs in providing credit support to small and retail trade and other non-farm rural activities is better than that of co-operatives and commercial banks. As on March 31, 2002, the outreach of RRBs in terms of number of deposits and advances was 50.02 million and 11.94 million respectively. Clientele for loans and deposits in the rural sector are low-value, but large volume. RRBs have served this clientele in a more productive and efficient manner vis-à-vis other Banks. Per-employee, 885 accounts are handled by RRBs against the national average of 464 accounts per employee in the banking industry.

RRBs have also taken a lead role in financing of Self Help Groups(SHGs) mostly comprising of women leading to their economic and social empowerment. The share of RRBs in SHG-Bank linkage programme is equally commendable as under:

Comparison of RRBs with State Cooperative Banks

A note here about state government-run cooperative banks on how they compare with RRBs. Both rural financial institutions are in same rural credit market but with different ownership and management patterns. India's cooperative banks were instituted in the fifties, also to meet the rural credit requirements each district of the country. They are managed by the respective state governments under Cooperative Act. There are basically three- tier cooperative structures in most of the states. Primary Agricultural Cooperatives at grass-root level, District Cooperative Bank at District level and State Cooperative Banks at State Level with each supporting the lower one.

The co-operative credit system has come under increasing pressure from the emerging competitive scenario of low interest rate regime. Cooperative Banks have also continued to suffer from several weaknesses that do not augur well for building-up their ability to compete with banking structure in the emerging liberalized environment. In part they have not been successful due to excessive political interference in their management. It may be noted that the elected boards of 478 cooperative banks out of 1186 were superseded for a variety of reasons including political interference.

RRBs on the other hand are the result of a Parliamentary Act and they are managed by the sponsor bank (which has the experience of running a big bank) with an equity stake of 35%. The Central Government and the local State Government hold 50% and 15% equity stake in RRBs. The board of RRB constitutes the officials of NABARD and RBI. Each RRB, like Cooperatives is confined to single or two districts of the country. RRBs were sought to be a blend of cooperatives and commercial banks. State governments have no/limited role in the management of the bank.

Challenges for Rural and Agricultural Credit in the Post Reforms Era

The agriculture sector to a large extent was excluded from general economic reforms initiated in 1991. However, the reforms introduced in industry, finance, banking and other sectors over the last decade have had considerable impact on the agricultural sector. The financial sector reforms have created a level playing field between rural financial institutions (RRBs and Cooperatives) and other scheduled commercial banks in treatment and in compliance of regulatory norms, without any reforms in agricultural sector.

Without any reforms in the agricultural sector, the financial sector reforms have created a level playing field between rural financial institutions (RRBs and Cooperatives) and other scheduled commercial banks in treatment and in compliance of regulatory norms.

In the meantime, the agriculture sector is emerging as part of the new economic order arising out of globalisation and implementation of the Agreement on Agriculture (AoA) under the World Trade Organisation (WTO). If some agreement is reached at the WTO negotiations, the agriculture sector in the country would be poised for a radical transformation. To withstand the global competition, enhanced productivity and sustainability of the sector has become imperative.

With the demand for food increasing at more than 2 per cent per annum, the financial, land and water resources in the rural sector have come under severe strain. At the same time, agriculture is a matter of livelihood and food security, with nearly 650 million people depending on it. In this context, productivity augmentation in agriculture and other allied sectors, expansion of rural credit, poverty eradication, infrastructure and development and export competitiveness of agricultural products have assumed high priority in the nation's development agenda. It is in this context that the Rs 50,000-crore outlay has also been proposed by the Government to be implemented by NABARD.

The Rural Non-Farm Sector (RNFS) has emerged as key area of focus for creating employment in the rural sector and to enable migration from over-stretched farm sector. The future strategy of rural institutions would have to include strengthening the credit delivery system for increasing RNFS employment. Development of entrepreneurs' skills, enhanced credit flow to women and other weaker sections, supporting tiny, cottage and village industries, and coverage of wide variety of service sector activities would require larger and wider role of rural financial institutions in RNFS sector.

The agricultural credit provided by cooperative banks, commercial banks, RRBs and other agencies reached Rs.70810 crores during 2002-03, a growth over 14.3% over the previous year. Public Sector investments in agriculture had increased from Rs.3919 crore during 2000-01 to Rs.4794 crore during 2001-2002, breaking the earlier declining trend.

The private sector investments in agriculture and allied sectors increased from Rs.14,605 crores during 1995-96 to Rs.24,257 crore during 2000-2001 at current prices. The proportion of such capital formation financed by institutional credit increased from 59.6 to 71.5 per cent during the period between 1995-96 and 2000-01.

While all this is true, if Indian agriculture sector has to achieve sustainable growth and enhanced productivity in order to meet Tenth Plan growth targets and also at the same time to meet the emerging challenges of the WTO regime, the investments from public sector and private sector need to be increased substantially and, simultaneously, the proportions of institutional credit to capital formation should also increase rapidly. This calls for bold and innovative measures from policy makers.

The recent directions of GOI/RBI with regard to interest waiver as a part of debt relief measures and the realignment of interest rates (at 9%) on agricultural loans upto Rs.50000/- on par with commercial banks have further aggravated the viability pressures on RRBs. It is estimated that these directions on interest rate alignment would alone entail a shortfall of Rs.300-500 crores in interest income for RRBs from 2003 onwards.

The growing role of MicroFinance through women's Self Help Groups (SHGs) for unique processes of socio-economic engineering is also important. So far, the SHG movement in the country is mostly south-centric (constituting a 64% share) and in other regions of India, it is yet to take off. The NABARD goal of reaching MicroFinance services to one third of the rural poor of the country, i.e. about 100 million rural poor through one million SHGs by the year 2006-2007 poses many challenges for rural financial institutions like RRBs, who are already actively involved in SHG-Bank linkage programme. The regional spread of the SHG movement is as under:

The Current Banking Divide

RRBs and other rural financial institutions were created to exclusively serve the rural sector wherein many infrastructural deficiencies still prevail whereas commercial banks have the comfort of operating in Metro/Urban environments with obvious infrastructural advantages. However, a level playing field has been created between weak rural financial institutions and mighty commercial banks with regard to regulatory regime/practices/norms though both are operating in divergent and unequal economic backyards. The support extended to UTI, IDBI, IFC, and few other nationalized banks and institutions exceeded more than Rs.25,000 crores since 1991. And yet, fresh capital infusion in rural financial institutions is not even more than Rs 3,000 crores since 1991.

The majority of the country's population, more so marginal and disadvantaged sections of society, inhabit the villages. The country argued against comparable playing fields in agriculturalal trade during WTO negotiations and called for special dispensation for agriculture-dependent developing countries. The same argument would be equally valid against creating one playing field among the institutions serving the developed urban and the less developed rural markets within the country. Hence the regulatory norms of banking/enabling support systems need to be adequately redesigned to be more rural-centric and flexible so as to ensure the viability of rural financial institutions for an effective rural credit delivery system. All rural financial institutions need special dispensation suited to their local potential and challenges.

Post economic reforms, many urban-centric financial intermediaries have run into rough weather and received large doses of fiscal support from the government of India to sustain their viability. The cases in point are UTI, IDBI, IFC, and a few other nationalized banks and the support extended to these institutions/banks exceeded more than Rs.25,000 crores since 1991. It is to be noted that these institutions/banks had come under pressure even though they were mostly operating in economically attractive urban-centric backyards. And yet, fresh capital infusion in rural financial institutions is no more than Rs.3,000 crores since 1991 despite the fact that they are largely catering to the banking requirements of 75% of the population.

Where do we go from here - the Roadmap

Against this background and growing signs of weaknesses in the cooperative banking system and the dwindling role of commercial banks in rural credit, RRBs have ipso facto emerged as the only surviving rural financial institutions with a professional management culture to meet the small-value and large-volume rural credit needs and can be easily converted into dynamic vehicles for bridging the banking divide to some extent. Therefore, the time has come for revitalising/revamping the structure of RRBs to enable them to play a critical role in the achievement of the developmental targets in rural sector under the Tenth Five Year Plan and to emerge as strong players in rural credit in order to meet the pressures arising in the agricultural sector.

In this context, the following initiatives are suggested:

Capital Structure and Management

RRBs need to be provided with adequate capital support to enable them to have a net capital adequacy ratio (CAR) of 5 per cent. The issue of capital infusion by the owners assumes critical importance and needs immediate attention to enlarge the scope of RRB operations. The share of sponsoring institutions in the capital structure of RRBs also needs to be enlarged to make them majority shareholders. By acquiring the majority shareholding in RRBs, the sponsor banks/institutions can convert them into vibrant and professional subsidiaries and area-specific special business units (SBUs). In the long run, they may converge all their agricultural and rural activities under the umbrella of these SBUs. Even co-operative banks can be merged with these SBUs at later stages.

Norms on Non-performing Rural Assets

NPA Norms

NPAs (Non-performing Assets) and IRAC (Income Recognition and Asset Classification) norms have been made applicable to the Indian banking industry after the 1991 economic reforms, to bring it on par with international banking trends. All loans given by banks need to be classified under these norms depending upon the servicing of the loan by the beneficiary. Mostly, the servicing of the loan means payment of a) quarterly interest and/or b) stipulated periodical installments of the principal.

If a loan is not serviced within the stipulated period (90 days), the loan becomes an NPA in banking parlance. For the first one year, the NPA is called sub-standard asset. From the second year onwards, the NPA is called doubtful asset. For NPAs of different categories, the banks have to make certain provisions in financial statements from their gross profit. For example, 10% of the substandard assets is to be provided each year and the percentage increases in the case of doubtful assets, ultimately leading to full provision after few years.

Currently norms for NPAs are made equally applicable to all financial institutions, both urban and rural. But cash flows in rural areas are dependent upon harvests which happen once in six months and servicing of loans depends upon good harvests reaped in a year in two crops. There is always uncertainty with regard to marketing as a result. What is needed is relaxation in the applicability of such stringent international norms to the rural financial sector as it suffers from many infrastructural and socio-economic deficiencies. Such relaxation may improve the health of rural financial institutions apart from facilitating the adequate flow of rural credit. I.e, IRAC/NPA norms need to be different for lending to the rural sector.

NABARD

NABARD has evolved over the past two decades into a strong and rural-sensitive developmental institution with complete grass-root level understanding of the complexities of the agricultural and rural sectors. The apex rural development bank has become a major shareholder in the proposed Agricultural Insurance Corporation of India Ltd, which includes General Insurance Corporation and four public sector insurance companies, to extend crop insurance cover to all farmers. Similarly, NABARD has played a pioneering role in setting up and operationalising the National Commodity and Derivatives Exchange (NCDX) with equity participation in association with other national level institutions such as ICICI Bank, LIC and NSE (National Stock Exchange).

NABARD may also acquire an equity stake in the grassroot level rural financial institutions such as RRBs from the Central Government and State governments to enable them to play a more direct and proactive role in rural credit. NABARD should thus become an apex development bank in the rural and agricultural sectors with direct equity participation in RRBs along with sponsoring institutions. With district development managers (DDMs) in most of the districts and also on the boards of all RRBs and co-operatives, NABARD is now fully equipped organisationally and expertise-wise to emerge as a strong player in the rural credit system. A case in point is the promotion of self-help group (SHG) movements by Nabard, which reflects its immense capability in capacity building and nurturing the rural credit delivery system. Similarly, the RBI, during the past two decades, has passed on the mantle of rural planning and credit to NABARD, its own subsidiary. Post-reforms and post-liberalisation of trade and foreign exchange, the RBI is donning the role of super regulator of the monetary and financial system. With increasing complexity of macro-economic management, the RBI needs to confine itself to a regulatory role for all financial institutions, including the rural ones. The supervisory role of rural financial institutions needs to be restored to the RBI for effective monitoring and control.

Bring Down the Cost of Rural Credit

A different dispensation under CRR and SLR would make available more resources for rural credit deployment. The rate of interest paid on CRR balances held by these rural institutions might also be 100 basis points above what is paid to commercial banks. Similarly, the Central Government and all State governments need to park their rural developmental funds with RRBs to ensure cheaper flow of demand deposits. These simple measures, without any cross-subsidisation, would bring down the cost of credit to the rural/agricultural sector.

Raising the Bar

At the same time, the stipulated 18 per cent benchmark for lending to agriculture needs to be hiked to 25 per cent commensurate with the contribution of this sector to GDP. Similarly, the minimum benchmark credit-deposit ratio of 60 per cent needs to be insisted upon for each bank/RRB in every rural district of the country to ensure adequate credit flow to the rural and semi-urban sectors.

Human Resources

Much of the RRB staff was recruited during the initial stages and there has been a ban on fresh recruitment since 1992. The staff is getting older whereas the complexities and demands of rural banking now call for more dynamism and youthful talent. Rural banking has emerged as a niche, wherein special skills and sensitivity are required. Therefore, the imposed ban on fresh recruitment should be reviewed at the earliest to enhance and diversify the business of RRBs. Also, RRBs should be permitted to recruit specialists in the technology and agriculture fields. Similarly, grants/soft loans may be provided for technology so as to enable RRBs to compete with commercial/ private banks that invest heavily in technology projects. The technology induction in rural banking would facilitate handling low-value, high-volume business effectively in a more cost-effective manner.

CONCLUSION

To sum up, the mandate for the Regional Rural Banks still is largely relevant. Even 27 years since being instituted, the socio-economic conditions of the majority of the rural population continue to be a cause of concern for policy makers of the country, especially in the post-reforms, WTO-mandated era. We still have more than 200 million people in rural areas who live below the poverty line and for whom banking access is still not a reality and, despite a wide banking network the critical gap in rural credit still exists.

Therefore, the requirement for a strong and flexible structure for rural financial institutions like RRBs in rural and semi-urban segments cannot not be overemphasized. Financial sector reforms without social and rural sensitivity would only aggravate the complexities of agrarian sector reforms, which are yet to take shape. The proposed Farmers Commission and the Vyas Committee constituted by the RBI need to look into these issues comprehensively to strengthen the rural credit-delivery mechanism.

6

COMMERCIAL BANKS & RURAL BANKING—ROLE OF RURAL BRANCHES

The New Responsibility Suddenly Unfolding

When 14 banks were nationalised in 1969 and earlier social control of banks was promulgated in 1967 with the objective of providing a thrust to rural banking, the banks were not geared for discharging the new responsibilities. These banks so far were urban oriented.

The employees were graduates and post graduates selected from the cities. Lending to agriculture is a task about which they had no prior experience or awareness. Banks had therefore to be geared for the task through extensive preparation straight from the scratch.

This was also the early phase of the green revolution in India, a new found prosperity entering the Indian villagesa. This was the ideal period for nationalized banks to mop up new untapped rural liquidity. The declared objectives of the new policy, known as "social and development banking", were the following

- to provide banking services in previously unbanked or under-banked rural areas;
- to provide substantial credit to specific activities including agriculture and cottage industries; and
- to provide credit to certain disadvantaged groups such as, for example, Dalit households.

The Government of India and the Reserve Bank of India (RBI) issued, from time to time, specific directives regarding "social and development banking". These included setting targets for the expansion of rural branches, imposing ceilings on interest rates, and setting guidelines for the sectoral allocation of credit.

Lead Bank Schme & District Level Consultative Committee

To support the public sector banks and other institutions in rural banking the Government of India and RBI evolved these two Institutions of Lead Bank and District Consultative Committee.

The Lead Bank Scheme was evolved and introduce by the Reserve Bank of India towards the end of 1969 to provide an appropriate organization framework for ensuring co-operation and co-ordination by various financial institutions with the concerned Governmental agencies in assisting developmental efforts. These efforts were to be undertaken on an area basis, with the district as the unit to ensure that the credit requirement of the rural economy were addressed adequately.

The Lead Bank Scheme envisages assignment of lead roles to individual banks (both in public sector and private sector) for the districts allotted to them. A bank having a relatively large network of branches in the rural areas of the given district and endowed with adequate financial and manpower resources has generally been entrusted with the lead responsibility for the district. Accordingly, all the districts in the country (excepting the metropolitan cities) have been allotted to various banks.

The lead bank acts as a consortium leader for coordinating the efforts of all credit institutions in the allotted districts to increase the flow of credit to agriculture, small scale industries and other economic activities included in the priority sector in the rural and semi-urban areas, with the district being basic areal unit. This scheme gave a tremendous boost to rural branches and government-sponsored programmes such as poverty-alleviation, self-employment, and crop-production.

Under this Lead Bank Scheme, the lead bank have been preparing District Credit Plans since 1973. The Reserve Bank of India gave these Credit Plans a uniform and systematic shape in 1980-82. These District Credit Plans take stock of the followings:-

- Government's various programmes on poverty alleviation;
- Long-term/ short-term trend in credit disbursements by financial institutions for each of the farm and non-farm sector programmes on poverty alleviation;
- Credit-based / non-credit-based promotional programmes for rural industrie and service sector on a district location basis;

The lead bank is the convener of the District Consultative Committee meetings to be presided over by the District Collector, and participated by all officials representing the development wing of the Collectorate, along with representatives of each bank in the area (designated as district coordinators by the non-lead banks in the district). Common problems faced by Banks in funancing developmental projects were discussed and sorted out in these meetings. This focussed better liaison between the local government machinery and the banks operating in the district. Targets under District Credit Plan were allocated to individual banks according to their representation in the district. The Lead Bank also compiled the District Survey Report giving all information about the district, which were relevant and useful for the banks operating there. It surveyed unbanked centres in the district and identified centres with potential for opening new branches. These centres were allotted to the Banks in the district, priority being given to the Lead Bank and the all India/regional banks having sizeable representation in the District.

The banks as an initial venture recruited agricultural graduates and designated them as Technical Officers (Agriculture). Head office of the banks issued Manuals explaining operational guidelines and procedures for rural advances. Credit Schmes were drafted and circulated. Training programmes were conducted and Field level programmes (Agricultural Workshops) were initiated. Officers were given categorical assurances that if they acted bonafide they will not be held responsible even if there were to be unexpected losses occuring or things going wrong otherwise, on account of factors beyond their realm.

Opening Rural Branches by Banks

RBI controlled branch licensing. It settled every year with each bank its branch expansion plan and decided the number of new branches to be opened by the bank and its composition (rural, semi-urban, urban and metropolitan). Initially the banks were to complete their quota of opening rural and semi-urban branchs and only thereafter this the licences for Urban and Metropolitan Centers were normally issued to them. As the centres for opening rural branches are identified by the Task Force of the Lead Bank and allotted to different banks, the process of opening a large number of rural branches in quick succession became smooth and easier. Thus while in 1969 there were 1443 rural branches representing 17.6% of the total bank branches in the country, the number of rural branches in 1995 increased to 35008 forming 56.2% of the branch network of all banks. After the onset of the banking reforms uneconomic/non-viable rural branches were merged with other bigger units, complying ceretain norms as per guidelines issued bt thr RBI. Consequently the number of rural branchs as at the year 2000 decreaed to 32673 covering 48.7% of the total branches.

Performance under Rural Banking of Commercial Banks

Aggregate deposits of rural branches of all commercial banks, which was a meagre Rs.306 Crores (6.3%) in 1969 (brfore nationalisation) swelled to Rs.120,539 Crores (14.7%) in the year 2000. In terms of rural credit the comparative figures as at 1969, and 2000 are Rs.115 Crores (3.3%) and Rs.48753 Crores (10.6%) respectively.

Banks were under obligation to extend credit to priority sectors to an extent of 40% of their aggregate outstanding credit. As part of the overall PS-Credit, they are also to extend 18% of their aggregate credit to direct agriculture & indirect agricutlure category of borrowers. Performance of individual banks in achieving priority sector targets were reviewed regularly at quarterly intervals by the Finance Ministry & RBI. In the intial years of nationalisation the thrust was on "social & Developmental banking", the objectiveds of which are-

- to provide banking services in previously unbanked or under-banked rural areas;
- to provide substantial credit to specific activities including agriculture and cottage industries; and
- to provide credit to certain disadvantaged groups such as, for example, scheduled caste/scheduled tribe beneficiaries.

Financing Anti-poverty Programmes

Subsequently in the Eighties financing anti-poverty programmes (loans-cum-subsidy schemes) exclusively for the benefit of the weakest amongst the weaker sector beneficiaries amongst rural poor gained momentum. Thus began a period of directed credit, during which credit was directed towards the so-called weaker sectors. The most important new scheme of this phase was the Integrated Rural Development Programme (IRDP), a scheme for the creation of productive income bearing assets among the poor through the allocation of subsidized credit. Initiated as a pilot project in 1978-79, it was extended to all rural blocks of the country in 1980. Despite certain weaknesses in the programme in its implementation, IRDP played an important role in the 1980s in that it gave new access to millions of rural households to the formal banking system and increased levels of purchasing power in rural India significantly.

There are various other rural development schemes in many of which Banks have a significant role to play. Some of them are listed below:

- Jawahar Gram Samridhi Yojana
- Swarnjayanti Gram Swarozgar Yojana (SGSY)
- Jawahar Rozgar Yojana

- Employment Assurance Scheme (EAS)
- Indira Awaas Yojana
- Ganga Kalyan Yojana
- Supply of Improved Toolkits to Rural Artisans (SITRA)
- Rural Sanitation Programme
- Accelerated Rural Water Supply Programme (ARWSP)
- Drought Prone Areas Programme (DPAP)
- Desert Development Programme (DDP)
- Integrated Wastelands Development Programme (IWDP)
- Rural Water Supply Programme
- Million Wells Scheme
- National Watershed Development
- Pradhan Mantri Gramodaya Yojana (PMGY)
- Scheme for Land Development
- Pradhan Mantri Gram Sadak Yojana (PMGSY)
- Training of Rural Youth for Self-Employment (TRYSEM)
- Agricultural and Rural Debt Relief Scheme
- Food for Work Programme
- Self Help Groups
- Sampoorna Grameen Rozgar Yojana (SGRY)

20-Point Economic Programme

The programme was initiated by the Prime Minister Mrs.Indira Gandhi during July 1975 after decalring emergency in the country. It is a package of twenty measures for the quick social and economic upliftment of the poor. The programme was popular and brought about good results in realms of releasing bonded labours, steps against rural-indebtedness, providing subsidised foodgrains through fair price shops etc. However after the emergency, the new Government did not pursue it further.

A recent innovation is the institution of Micro-credit and SHGs. The subject has been dealt with elaborately in separate pages. These Institutions bears the potential for bringing productive credit within the easy reach ofthe poorestof the poor & transforming our villages into vibrant and self-reliant activity & growth centres.

Rural presence of commercial banks has come to stay. These rural branchs have proved to be viable and stable growth centres. In fact these branches have a role in ushering the green revolution and later the white revolution in the country. Precisely the "every-where presence" is one of the unique strengths of the state-owned and the old private sector banks, as against the new private and foreign banks. More appropraitely it is also a distinguishing factor that makes the banking network of our country as one of the widest in its spread globally.

As agriculture becomes more and more of a commercial venture in contrast to being a mere "way of life" as it turned out to be earlier, as infrastructure development, social, educational and economic resurgence reaches the villages, as villages boom with all diverse economic enterprises, and not merely being confined predominantly to agriculture and animal husbandry, these branches are sure to turn into robust and thriving business centres providing multiple service facilities to pose as an equal rival to the overcrowded branches of the urban centres. This process has started already.

AGRICTULURE FINANCE & COOPERATIVE BANKS

The cooperative movement in the country originated as a measure against rural poverty, aggravated by chronic indebtedness of the farmers and practice of usuary at its worst by the money lenders.

Agrarian disturbances in 1875 in the Deccan against the money lenders necessitated the enactment of Taccavi Legislation by the government and also led to the concept of the cooperative approach. The Northern India Taccavi Loan Act ,1875, the Land Improvement Loans Act, 1883, the Agriculturist Loans Act, 1884 etc. were all enacted to facilitate the availability of credit to farmers.

In 1892, Sir Federick Nicholson recommended the establishment of rural cooperative credit societies on German pattern. The Famine Commission (1901) recommended introduction of cooperatives in the country.

In 1904, the Cooperative Credit Societies Act was enacted by the imperial government to facilitate organisation of credit cooperatives and confer upon them special privileges and facilities, the scope of which was subsequently enlarged by the more comprehensive Cooperative Societies Act of 1912. Under the Government of India Act, 1919, the subject of Cooperation was transferred to the then Provinces, which were authorized to enact their own cooperative laws. Under the Government of India Act, 1935, cooperatives remained a provincial subject.

EVOLUTION OF COOPERATIVES IN INDIA

"The cooperative movement in India owes its origin to agriculture and allied sectors. Towards the end of the 19th century, the problems of rural indebtedness and the consequent conditions of farmers created an environment for the chit funds and cooperative societies. The farmers generally found the cooperative movement an attractive mechanism for pooling their meagre resources for solving common problems relating to credit, supplies of inputs and marketing of agricultural produce. The experience gained in the working of cooperatives led to the enactment of Cooperative Credit Societies Act, 1904. Subsequently, a more comprehensive legislation called the Cooperative Societies Act was enacted. This Act, inter alia, provided for the creation of the post of registrar of cooperative societies and registration of cooperative societies for various purposes and audit. Under the Montague-Chelmsford Reforms of 1919, cooperation became a provincial subject and the provinces were authorised to make their own cooperative laws. Under the Government of India Act, 1935, cooperatives were treated as a provincial subject. The item "Cooperative Societies" is a State Subject under entry No.32 of the State List of the Constitution of India.

"In order to cover Cooperative Societies with membership from more than one province, the Government of India enacted the Multi-Unit Cooperative Societies Act, 1942. This Act was an enabling legislative instrument dealing with incorporation and winding up of cooperative societies having jurisdiction in more than one province. With the emergence of national federations of cooperative societies in various functional areas and to obviate the plethora of different laws governing the same types of societies, a need was felt for a comprehensive Central legislation to consolidate the laws governing such cooperative societies. Therefore, the Multi-State Cooperative Societies Act, 1984 was enacted by Parliament under Entry No. 44 of the Union List of the Constitution of India.

"After India attained Independence in August, 1947, cooperatives assumed a great significance in poverty removal and faster socio-economic growth. With the advent of the planning process, cooperatives became an integral part of the Five Year Plans. As a result, they emerged as a distinct segment in our national economy. In the First Five Year Plan, it was specifically stated that the success of the Plan would be judged, among other things, by the extent it was implemented through cooperative organisations.

"The All-India Rural Credit Survey Committee Report, 1954 recommended an integrated approach to cooperative credit and emphasised the need for viable credit cooperative societies by expanding their area of operation, encouraging rural savings and diversifying business. The Committee also recommended for Government participation in the share capital of the cooperatives.

"In view of these recommendations, different States drew up various schemes foı the cooperative movement for organising large-size societies and provision of State partnership and assistance. During 1960s, further efforts were made to consolidate the cooperative societies by their re-organisation. Consequently, the number of primary agricultural cooperative credit societies was reduced from around two lakh to 92,000.

The Process of Evolution of the Movement

"In 1958 the National Development Council (NDC) had recommended a national policy on cooperatives. Jawaharlal

Nehru had a strong faith in the cooperative movement. While opening an international seminar on cooperative leadership in South-East Asia he had said " But my outlook at present is not the outlook of spreading the cooperative movement gradually, progressively, as it has done.

My outlook is to convulse India with the Cooperative Movement or rather with cooperation to make it, broadly speaking, the basic activity of India, in every village as well as elsewhere; and finally, indeed, to make the cooperative approach the common thinking of India...Therefore, the whole future of India really depends on the success of this approach of ours to these vast numbers, hundreds of millions of people".

"The cooperative sector has been playing a distinct and significant role in the country's process of socio-economic development. There has been a substantial growth of this sector in diverse areas of the economy during the past few decades. The number of all types of cooperatives increased from 1.81 lakh in 1950-51 to 4.53 lakh in 1996-97. The total membership of cooperative societies increased from 1.55 crore to 20.45 crore during the same period. The cooperatives have been operating in various areas of the economy such as credit, production, processing, marketing, input distribution, housing, dairying and textiles. In some of the areas of their activities like dairying, urban banking and housing, sugar and handlooms, the cooperatives have achieved success to an extent but there are larger areas where they have not been so successful.

The failure of cooperatives in the country is mainly attributable to: dormant membership and lack of active participation of members in the management of cooperatives. Mounting overdues in cooperative credit institution, lack of mobilisation of internal resources and over-dependence on Government assistance, lack of professional management. bureaucratic control and interference in the management, political interference and over-politicalisation have proved harmful to their growth. Predominance of vested interests resulting in non-percolation of benefits to a common member, particularly to the class of persons for whom such cooperatives were basically formed, has also retarded the development of cooperatives. These are the areas which need to be attended to by evolving suitable legislative and policy support."

NATIONAL POLICY ON COOPERATIVES

Coperatives in India entered the realm of providing institutional financing to agriculture much before the other agencies. Institutional financing system for agriculture commenced with the adoption of the Co- operative Societies Act in 1904. Adequate institutional finance for agriculture, however, received proper attention for the first time in 1951-52, when the All India Rural Credit Survey Committee (AIRCSC) recommended the concept of "Integrated Scheme of Rural Credit", which focussed on strengthening and development of co- operative credit institutions at all levels. This was about 18 years before commercial banks ventured into the realm. The cooperatives, despite certain drawbacks continues to be the main provider of agricultural finance.

Functional Structure of Coperatives in India

There are two separate categories of cooperative Institutions, Cooperative Banks for providing short-term (including medium term) credit and Land Development Banks for providing long term loans. Coperative banks (providing short term credit) have a three tier structure with the State Coperative Banks (SCBs) in each State at the Apex Level, Central Cooperative Banks(CCBs) at the District Level and primary agricultural cooperative societies(PACs) at the village level.

Land Development Banks (also called Agricultrual Development Banks, or Land Mortgage Banks in certain states) are specialised institutions providing long term credit to agriculturists. They are organised since 1929. In general LDBs have a two-tier structure, Central Land Development Banks at the State Level, and primary land development bank at the district or lower level. However in some states in place of the primary land development banks, the branches of the Central Land Development Banks are functioning.

Cooperative Banking Structure has a unique position in the rural credit delivery system of India. The cooperative banking sector especially with their existence of about a century has made significant strides in the field of rural credit.

Since then, the co-operative credit institutions, both in the short and the long term structures continued to play their crucial role in dispensation of credit for agriculture and rural development. Over the years, they have remained the prime institutional agencies with their vast network, wider coverage and outreach extending to remotest part of the country. Both the short term and long term cooperative credit institutions are basically farmers' organisations primarily meant to meet their credit related requirements.

Although commercial banks since nationalisation, have entered rural areas and opened large number of branches and RRBs have also established a large network of rural branches to cater to the credit need of rural poor, cooperatives continue to enjoy a place of crucial importance in the rural credit scenario. There are some niche areas where cooperatives have no competitors and cannot be replaced. The reasons for their essential existence are as under:-

These institutions are primarily owned by the farmers, rural artisans, etc.

They have been set up with the objective of promoting thrift and mutual help.

Cooperative credit societies at the grass root level are intended not only to cater to credit requirements of the members but also to provide several other credit linked services like input supply, storage and marketing of produce, etc. Keeping in view these special features of cooperatives, time and again, their role in dispensation of credit and allied services in the rural areas has been emphasised and their relevance underlined by several Committees right from the All India Rural Credit Survey Committee in the early 50s to Expert Committee on Rural Credit (ECRC), 2000.

From a meagre credit share of 2.7 percent during the early 50's, the share of agricultural credit purveyed by cooperatives has increased to a phenomenal 45 percent by March 2001.

National Policy on Cooperatives

Department of Agriculture and Cooperation, Ministry of Agriculture, Government of India has announced National Policy on cooperatives. As outlined by them, the basic concepts of the cooperatives are as under:

- A co-operative is an autonomous association of persons united voluntarily to meet their common economic, social and cultural needs and aspirations through a jointly-owned and democratically-controlled enterprise".
- Co-operatives are based on the principles of self-help, self-responsibility, democracy, equality and solidarity. In the tradition of their founders, co-operative members believe in the ethical values of honesty, openness, social responsibility and caring for others."

Cooperative Principles

1st Principle: Voluntary and Open Membership: Cooperatives are voluntary organisations, open to all persons able to use their service and willing to accept the responsibilities of membership, without gender, social, racial, political or religious discrimination.

2nd Principle: Democratic Member Control : Cooperatives are democratic organisations controlled by their members, who actively participate in setting their policies and making decisions. Men and women serving as elected representatives are accountable to the membership. In primary cooperatives, members have equal voting rights (one member, one vote) and cooperatives at other levels are also organised in a democratic manner.

3rd Principle: Member Economic Participation: Members contribute equitably to, and democratically control, the capital of their cooperative. At least, part of that capital is usually the common property of the cooperative. Members usually receive limited compensation, if any, on capital subscribed as a condition of membership. Members allocate surpluses for any or all of the following purposes : developing their cooperative, possibly by setting up reserves, part of which at least would be indivisible;

benefiting members in proportion to their transactions with the cooperative; and supporting other activities approved by the membership.

4th Principle: Autonomy and Independence: Cooperatives are autonomous, self-help organisations controlled by their members. If they enter into agreements with other organisations, including governments, or raise capital from external sources, they do so on terms that ensure democratic control by their members and maintain their cooperative autonomy.

5th Principle: Education, Training and Information: Cooperatives provide education and training for their members, elected representatives, managers, and employees so that they can contribute effectively to the development of their cooperatives. They inform the general public - particularly young people and opinion leaders - about the nature and benefits of cooperative.

6th Principle : Cooperation among Cooperatives: Cooperatives serve their members most effectively and strengthen the cooperative movement by working together through local, national, regional and international structures.

7th Principle: Concern for Community : Cooperatives work for the sustainable development of their communities through policies approved by their members.

Objectives of National Policy on Cooperatives

- Ensuring functioning of the cooperatives based on basic cooperative rules and principles.
- Revitalisation of the cooperative structure particularly, in the case of agricultural credit.
- Reduction of regional imbalances through support from Central Government / State Government particularly in the under- developed and cooperatively under-developed states / regions.
- Strengthening of cooperative education and training and Human Resource Development for professionalisation of the management of the Cooperatives.

- Greater participation of members in the management of cooperatives and promoting the concept of user members.
- Amendment / removal of provision in cooperative laws providing for the restrictive regulatory regime.
- Evolving a system of integrated cooperative structure by entrusting the federations predominantly with the role of promotion, guidance, information systems, etc. to their affiliated members and potential members.
- Evolving the system of in-built mechanism in cooperative legislation to ensure timely conduct of general body meetings, election and audit of cooperative societies.
- Ensuring that the benefits of the cooperatives endeavour to reach the poorer sections of the society and encouraging the participation of such sections and women in management of cooperatives.

Coperative Banking - Record of Progress & Performance

"From a meagre credit share of 2.7 percent during the early 50's, the share of agricultural credit purveyed by cooperatives has increased to a phenomenal 45 percent by March 2001"

Cooperative Banking Structure has a unique position in the rural credit delivery system of India. The cooperative banking sector especially with their existence of about a century has made significant strides in the field of rural credit. Since then, the co-operative credit institutions, both in the short and the long term structures continued to play their crucial role in dispensation of credit for agriculture and rural development. Over the years, they have remained the prime institutional agencies with their vast network, wider coverage and outreach extending to remotest part of the country. Both the short term and long term cooperative credit institutions are basically farmers' organisations primarily meant to meet their credit related requirements. Although commercial banks since nationalisation, have entered rural areas and opened large number of branches and RRBs have also established a large network of rural branches to cater to the credit need of rural poor, cooperatives continue to enjoy a place of crucial importance in the rural credit scenario. Some of the niche areas where cooperatives have no competitors and cannot be replaced. The reasons for their essential existence are as under:-

These institutions are primarily owned by the farmers, rural artisans, etc.

They have been set up with the objective of promoting thrift and mutual help.

Cooperative credit societies at the grass root level are intended not only to cater to credit requirements of the members but also to provide several other credit linked services like input supply, storage and marketing of produce, etc. Keeping in view these special features of cooperatives, time and again, their role in dispensation of credit and allied services in the rural areas has been emphasised and their relevance underlined by several Committees right from the All India Rural Credit Survey Committee in the early 50s to Expert Committee on Rural Credit (ECRC), 2000.

Progress & Performance - Short term Structure (SCBs & DCBs)

The short term cooperative credit structure consists of around 98843 Primary Agricultural Credit Societies, 367 District Central Cooperative Banks and 30 State Cooperative Banks functioning with 831 and 12580 branches respectively purveying agricultural credit.

Membership

Total membership of the PACS as on 31 March 2001 stood at 999 lakh of which, borrowing members at 465 lakh constituted around 47%. In 2000-2001, the borrowing members of PACS as a percentage of total members, was below the All India percentage at 47% in several states (Andhra Pradesh 24%, Himachal Pradesh 10%, Karnataka 35%, Maharashra 36%, Orissa 40%, Rajasthan 34%). The high level of overdues in these states has drastically reduced the eligibility of a large number of members for fresh borrowings and has probably hampered the growth in borrowing membership. The borrowing members as percentage to total membership was above the All India percentage in the states of Haryana(69.8%), Punjab(67.5),Tamil Nadu (56.5) and Chhatisgarh (50.9%)

The Western states of Maharashtra and Gujarat accounted for 28% of the total PACS in the country with Maharashtra alone accounting for about 21% of the PACS. The North-Eastern states, on the other hand, accounted for less than 3% of the PACS in the Country. The Central Region (U.P. & M.P.) with one-fourth of the population predominantly rural, accounted for only 12% of the total PACS. Almost 95% of the villages in the country are covered by PACS. The average coverage was 6 villages per PACS for the country as a whole, and ranged from less than 1 village in Kerala to 117 villages in Arunachal Pradesh. In Kerala, the number of PACS(1988) were more than the villages in the State (1665).

Share Capital

As at the end of 2000-2001, the share capital of the SCBs stood at Rs.695 crore including government share capital amounting to Rs.64 crore. At the DCCBs level, the paid-up share capital increased from Rs.2823 crore in 1999-2000 to Rs.3118 crore during 2000-2001, a growth of 10.5%. It cannot, however, be concluded that every DCCB has adequate share capital.

The adequacy of the share capital is judged on the basis of requirements of share capital of each DCCB vis-à-vis its lending programmes and its bad debts and other irrecoverables. The capital adequacy norms which have been made applicable to commercial banks in 1991-92 have not been introduced for cooperative banks. Being a major sector of the rural financial system, it is logical for the cooperative banks also to conform to the norms applicable to the commercial banks.

There is hence a need to strengthen the capital base of cooperative banks. It would be ideal if the cooperative banks could comply with capital adequacy norms over a period of five to six years. The Task Force (Capoor Committee), however, recognizes that the cooperative banks, as they exist now, do not have access to the capital market as in the case of commercial banks. The Task Force feels that these constraints notwithstanding, the cooperative banks may make a beginning to move in the direction of strengthening their capital base so that they could conform to the applicable norms over a period of time.

Support from State Governments

Consequent upon the acceptance of the principle of state partnership recommended by the All India Rural Credit Survey Committee in 1954, the state governments of different states began contributing towards the share capital of the cooperative credit institutions. The main idea behind state partnership was that a cooperative institution should have the necessary minimum capital right from the start to make it viable and if this minimum was lacking, the state should make good the deficit.

Though the State Governments are participating in the share capital of DCCBs/PACS/LAMPS out of the loan availed from NRC(LTO) fund of NABARD upto a limited extent, they should also contribute to the share capital from budgetory allocation to strengthen the capital base, particularly of weak banks and societies. As on 31 March 2001, the total contribution of the state governments in the share capital of the co-operative credit institutions (ST) stood at Rs.1100 crore representing an increase of 15.3% over the previous year

Resources

The composition of total resources (owned funds + deposits + borrowings) of the short term cooperative credit structure indicated that deposits constituted a major segment of the resource-base of the SCBs and DCCBs.

The PACS, however, continued to depend on borrowings from higher financing agencies. At DCCB level, the owned funds and deposits formed about 12.4% and 68.7% of the total resources, respectively. Borrowings accounted for only 18.9%. In the case of SCBs the composition of total resources was 11.0% owned funds, 65.5% deposits and 23.5% borrowings.

Deposits

Deposits of SCBs and DCCBs in the country stood at Rs32626 crore and Rs.61745 crore, as on 31 March 2001 representing an increase of 10.4% and 14.6%, respectively over the previous year. The deposits of DCCBs ranged from as high as Rs.17863 crore (Maharashtra) to a meagre Rs.18 crore (Assam). There were large regional variations in mobilisation of deposits by DCCBs. Of the total deposits of DCCBs at Rs.61745 crore, four states accounted for 57% [viz. Maharashtra(28.9%), Gujarat(10.5%), Tamil Nadu(10.4%) and Uttar Pradesh (7.2%). While DCCBs in Eastern Region accounted for a meagre share of 6.7% [viz. West Bengal(3.3%), Orissa(1.9%), Bihar(1.0%) and Jharkhand (0.5)% the SCBs in the N E Region with deposits at Rs.1130 crore as on 31 March 2001 accounted for just 3.5% of deposits of all SCBs as on that date.

Resource mobilisation continued to be a major area of weakness of the PACS. At present, most of the PACS are totally dependent on the finance provided by DCCBs. In case the DCCBs are weak, the PACS are starved of finance which affects the expansion of both the credit and non-credit functions of PACS. The majority of PACS had very little to show by way of deposit mobilisation except in a few states like Kerala and Tamil Nadu. Kerala is the only state where PACS have made such headway and a significant progress in mobilization of rural deposits as compared to other states.

The deposits of the PACS in the country stood at Rs13481 crore (provisional) as on 31 March 2001 representing a growth of about 8.2% over the previous year. The deposits of the PACS ranged from as high as Rs. 5791 crore (Kerala) to a mere Rs.0.44 crore (Jammu and Kashmir) as on 31 March 2001. Apart from Kerala, the PACS in the states of Tamil Nadu and Orissa mobilised sizeable deposits of Rs.3014 crore and Rs.2092 crore as on 31 March 2001, respectively.

Credit Outreach

Total loans issued by SCBs and DCCBs declined from Rs.37368 crore and Rs.46619 crore during 1999-2000 to Rs.34307 crore and Rs.45016 crore, respectively during 2000-2001, registering decrease of 8.2% and 3.4%, respectively. There were, however, large regional variations in credit disbursals by DCCBs in 2000-2001. Three states viz. Maharashtra (28.1%), Punjab (9.3%) and Gujarat (8.1%) accounted for 45.5% of total loaning followed by Andhra Pradesh (7.2%), Uttar Pradesh (7.2%), Haryana (6.8%), Kerala (6.7%), Karnataka (6.7%) and Tamil Nadu at (6.2%). The remaining nine states accounted for a meagre 13.7% of the total loaning by DCCBs.

Recovery Performance

The aggregate recovery of all SCBs during 2000-01 was slightly higher at 83.89 per cent as compared to 83.37 per cent during 1999-2000 and continued to register an improvement and reversed the downward trend during the earlier three years declining from 86% during 1996-97 to 84% during 1997-98 had further declined to 81% during 1998-99. The decline in recovery levels over the last few years has been arrested and this is a positive development. However, the aggregate recovery of DCCBs during 1999-2000 at 70% further declined to 67% during 2000-01 as compared to the near constant recovery levels of 70 per cent during the years 1996-97 to 1998-99

During 2000-01, the recovery performance of SCBs continued to be extremely poor in the case of banks in North East Region, Bihar and J&K as in the earlier years. The recovery percentage of Manipur SCB was lowest at 3.66% followed by J&K SCB (20%), Bihar SCB (22%), Assam SCB (22%), Tripura SCB (24%), Arunachal Pradesh SCB (27%), Nagaland SCB (28%) and Mizoram SCB (29%). During 2000-01, 19 of the 29 SCBs registered recovery levels lower than the all India average level of 84 per cent. Among DCCBs, recovery level (state average) was lower during 2000-01 as compared to 1999-2000 levels in 9 states and in the remaining 11 states the same showed marginal improvement. The DCCBs in the states of Assam, Bihar, Jharkhand and J&K continued to report poor recovery levels of 9.65%, 22.94%, 19.14% and 26.68% respectively.

Improvement in Recovery during 2000-01

The highest recovery of 99.56% has been reported by Jullunder DCCB in Punjab follwed by Rajkot DCCB (98.40%)

in Gujarat, Chennai DCCB (97.74%) in Tamil Nadu, Satara DCCB (96.76%) in Maharashtra and Pithoragarh DCCB (96.69%) in UP. At the other end the lowest recovery below 10% was reported by the following DCCBs in Bihar viz. Madhepura-Supaul (3.74%), National(Bettiah) (5.42%), Motihari (7.55%), Muzaffarpur (8.23%), Daltonganj (since delicensed- 7.79%). During 2000-01, 179 DCCBs showed improvement in recovery percentage over the 1999-2000 levels. During 2000-01, 188 DCCBs registered decline in recovery percentage over the 1998-99 levels.

Profitability

The overall profitability of the SCBs and DCCBs was better during the year 2000-2001 than in the previous year. The SCBs as a group posted net profit of Rs.204.04 crore during 2000-2001 as against net profit of Rs.141.08 crore in the previous year. During 2000-2001, 6 SCBs reported loss amounting to Rs.12.63 crore. During 1999-2000, 224 of the 367 DCCBs reported profit aggregating Rs.428.36 crore and 143 DCCBs suffered loss to the extent of Rs.511.61 crore. During the year 2000-2001, 245 DCCBs were in profit aggregating Rs.593.37 crore and 112 DCCBs were in loss amounting to Rs.514.45 crore. The improvement in the profitability position of SCBs was partly on account of the fact that they are now required to make only incremental provisions. The provisioning requirements of the SCBs and DCCBs continued to reflect on profitability figures this year also.

Non Performing Assets (NPAs)

The NPAs constituted 13.02% (SCBs) and 18.03% (DCCBs) of their total loans and advances outstanding as on 31 March 2001. The same as on 31 March 2000, the fourth year of application of prudential norms, were 10.94% (SCBs) and 17.28% (DCCBs). The aggregate NPAs were estimated at Rs.3889.28 crore (SCBs) and Rs.9370.98 crore (DCCBs) as against Rs.2813.69 crore (SCBs) and Rs.7637.60 crore (DCCBs) as on 31 March 2000. The amount provisioning made by the SCBs during 2000-01 was higher at Rs.1546.57 crore as against Rs.1330.55 crore during 1999-2000.

Accumulated Losses

Due to improved profitability during the year 2000-2001, the level of accumulated losses of SCBs came down from Rs.502 crore as on 31 March 2000 to Rs.493 crore as on 31 March 2001. Accumulated losses of SCBs constituted 0.94 per cent of the total assets as at the end of March 2001 (1.06 per cent as at the end of March 2000).

The accumulated losses at the DCCBs level as on 31 March 2001 stood at Rs.3243 crore as against Rs.2864 crore registering an increase of 13%. In all the states except of Himachal Pradesh, some of the DCCBs carried accumulated losses as on 31 March 2001. As on 31 March 2002, as many as 9 SCBs (Assam, Arunachal Pradesh, Bihar, Chandigarh, Manipur, Mizoram, Meghalaya, Nagaland and Tripura) and 139 DCCBs were not complying with the provisions of Section 11(1) of BR Act 1949(AACS). The total erosion in the value of assets as on 31 March 2002 in respect of 139 DCCBs and 9 SCBs aggregated to Rs.6073.86 crore and erosion in deposits of these banks was to the extent of Rs.1933.69 crore.

Viability of PACS

The PACS, a vital link in the ST cooperative credit structure have been financially weak. A majority of them are too small in size to be economical and viable, besides many are dormant. The PACS continue to rely heavily on external support and have not yet been able to become self-reliant in respect of resources through deposit mobilisation, share linkage and share capital affecting their growth and expansion of business activities. The PACS is the kingpin of the Cooperative Banking System. It is the edifice on which the entire superstructure of the short-term Cooperative Credit System is established. In other words, the PACS is the foundation of the Cooperative Credit Movement.

It is the PACS which deals directly with the individual farmers, provides short-term and medium-term credit, supplies agricultural inputs, distributes consumers articles and also arranges for marketing of produce of its members through a cooperative marketing society. The PACS must function as a viable unit responsive to the needs, aspirations and convenience of its members, particularly, the members of the more vulnerable sections of the society. It must function effectively as a well-managed, multi-purpose society providing a package of services including credit, supply of agricultural inputs and implements, consumer goods, marketing services, technical guidance and mobilize the savings of the rural people as deposits. The PACS, therefore, has to be developed as real service society with focus on weaker sections.

Some of the critical problems of primary level co-operative credit institutions apart from poor resource mobilisation are

- lack of diversification in business portfolio
- low volume of business
- declining trend in borrowing membership
- high level of overdues
- high cost of management
- imbalances in loan outstandings
- involvement in non/less profitable PDS business
- low interest margins
- low skilled staff
- lack of professionalisation
- weak MIS

7

COOPERATIVE BANKING—PERFORMANCE & PROGRESS-LONG-TERM STRUCTURE

Structure

As at the end of 2000-01, the long term co-operative credit structure consisted of State Cooperative Agriculture and Rural Development Banks (SCARDBs) in 20 States /Union Territories with 732 Primary Cooperative Agriculture and Rural Development Banks (PCARDBs)/ branches of SCARDBs. Of the 20 SCARDBs, nine have unitary structure with branches, twelve have federal/mixed structure with PCARDBs and their branches.

Four PCARDBs in Orissa State were liquidated during 2000-01 and twenty one PCARDBs were merged in Assam SCARDB during the year. In the states not served by the LT structure, separate sections of the State Cooperative Banks look after long term credit needs. In the North Eastern Region, only three states (Assam, Manipur & Tripura) are served by the LT Structure. Chhattisgarh SCARDB has been formed out of MPSCARDB and has started functioning from 01 November 2000 following the formation of new state of Chattisgarh.

Membership

The total membership (Ground level) of the LT structure aggregated 140.74 lakh of which, borrowing members at 98.50 lakh constituted around 69.9%.

Share Capital

In the LT structure, the average government contribution to the share capital of SCARDBs formed only 13.2% of the total as on 31 March 2001 as against 51% recommended by the ACRC. However, government contribution was higher than all India average in respect of SCARDBs of Tripura (86%), Assam (77.4%), Tamil Nadu (40.5%), Pondicherry(61.8%), Bihar (45.9%), Orissa (43.7%), Himachal Pradesh (26.5%), J&K (29.6%) and West Bengal (29.9%). The government share capital to the total share capital of SCARDBs ranged from Rs.0.03 crore (Manipur) to Rs. 15.95 crore (Bihar) and that in respect of PCARDBs from Rs. 0.33 crore (Punjab) to Rs. 24.04 crore (Haryana) as on 31 March 2001. During 2000-01, the PCARDBs in Karnataka, Kerala, Rajasthan , Orissa and West Bengal received substantial contribution of Rs.0.68 crore, Rs.1.45 crore, Rs.1.20 crore, Rs.1.60 crore and Rs.1 crore respectively as share capital.

The LT structure continued to be dependent on external financial agencies for augmenting its resources. About 79.1% and 81.9% of the total resources of the SCARDBs and PCARDBs, respectively were in the form of borrowings. The outstanding borrowings of the LT structure as on 31 March 2001 were of the order of Rs.13431 crore (SCARDBs) and Rs.8412 crore (PCARDBs) registering an increase of 8.3% and 10.0%, respectively over the previous year. Paid up capital of SCARDBs and PCARDBs as on 31 March 2001 was 21.9% and 44.2% of the Owned Funds, respectively. State Government holding in the capital base of SCARDBs and PCARDBs constituted 13.2% and 17.2%, respectively. The deposits of the SCARDBs stood at Rs.535 crore and those by the PCARDBs at Rs.235crore as on 31 March 2001. During 2000-01 SCARDBs achieved a growth rate of 9.6% in mobilisation of resources while PCARDBs could achieve growth rate of 11.2% as compared to previous year growth rate of 13.7% and 14.0% respectively.

Credit Outreach

As regards the Long-term Structure, six States viz. Uttar Pradesh (25.6%), Punjab (12.2%), Rajasthan (8.8%), Tamil Nadu (9.0%), Kerala (12.9%) and Haryana (10.8%) accounted for nearly

79.3% of the total term credit disbursements by SCARDBs. There was a steep decline in the amount of loans issued by Bihar (-66.6%), Pondicherry (-39.9%), Tripura (-34.6%) and Jammu & Kashmir SCARDBs (-33.3%) during 2000-01 as compared to 1999-2000.While Maharashtra SCARDB which had registered a steep decline in the amount of loans issued during 1999-2000 registered a substantial increase during 2000-01 from Rs. 609 crore to Rs.948 crore (55.7%), Orissa, Manipur and Assam SCARDBs could not disburse any amount during 2000-01 as in the earlier years due to their deteriorating financial position and continued default to NABARD. The loans outstanding as on 31 March 2001 stood at Rs.12596 crore (SCARDBs) and Rs.8352 crore (PCARDBs) registering a growth of 8.9% and 9.7% respectively over the previous year. The loans issued by SCARDBs as also by PCARDBs during 2000-01 increased by 2.1% and 2.5% respectively.

Recovery Performance

The aggregate recovery of SCARDBs declined from 62% in 1999-2000 to 58% during 2000-01. At the PCARDBs level, the recovery level has progressively declined from 60% in 1998-99 to 58% in 1999-2000 and further declined to 53% during 2000-01. Further, 13 SCARDBs and 464 PCARDBs had recovery level of less than 60% as on 30.6.2001. Overdues in absolute terms registered an increasing trend in both SCARDBs and PCARDBs.

The overdues as on 31 March 2001 increased by Rs.533 crore (SCARDBs) and Rs.319 crore (PCARDBs) as compared to the position as on 30 June 2000. It is a matter of serious concern that at the PCARDBs level, 41.4% of the total overdues were overdue for more than 3 years. In the case of SCARDBs the same stood at 39.7%. Overdues constituted 16.5% and 20% of the total loans and advances outstanding at the SCARDB and PCARDB levels respectively during 1999-2000.

In regard to the overdues in the long-term structure, the Capoor Committee has suggested that the SCARDBs/PCARDBs be allowed the right of foreclosure of mortgages in the case of willful defaulters. This, the committee feels should substantially improve recovery position of such institutions and pave the way for securitisation of mortgage loans to raise resources from the market at reasonable rates. The committee is also of the opinion that there is a need to evolve compromise/ settlement procedure for closing of long pending overdue loans.

One Time Settlement Scheme

Keeping in view the scheme for OTS announced for Public Sector Banks by RBI, detailed guidelines for OTS were finalized by the National Bank during 2001-02 in consultation with RBI for the co-operative banks both in the ST and LT structures. Accordingly all the banks were advised of the detailed guidelines in this regard. Most of the banks have adopted the scheme, with the approval of their competent authorities. The salient features of the scheme are as under:

- The cut off date for NPAs has been fixed as 31 March 1998 and cut-off level amount is Rs. 5 lakhs
- NPAs under all loans and advances will be covered and the scheme will be operative up to 31 March 2002 (which was subsequently extended upto 30.09.2002).
- The guidelines should be uniformly followed by the banks without discrimination.
- Wherever the state governments have formulated One-Time Settlement Scheme it would be necessary to issue instructions / orders modifying their scheme to conform to the above scheme.
- The amount recovered under the scheme should be passed on in repayments to the higher financing institutions immediately.
- No financial support from the Government, RBI or the National Bank would be available for implementation of the scheme.

Profitability

During the years 1998-99 and 1999-2000, 9 of the 19 SCARDBs earned profits. During the year 2000-2001, 10 SCARDBs reported profit and 7 SCARDBs were in loss. Further, only 284 of the 732 PCARDBs earned profits during 2000-2001 as against 284 PCARDBs (reporting banks - 733) in 1999-2000.

Non Performing Assets (NPAs)

The NPAs as on 31 March 2001 constituted 20.39% (SCARDBs) and 24.1% (PCARDBs) of their total loans and advances outstanding as on that date. The SCARDBs in Punjab and Haryana reported 'NIL' NPAs. The aggregate NPAs as on 31 March 2001 were estimated at Rs.2568.01 crore (SCARDBs) and Rs.2004.77 crore (PCARDBs).

Erosion in Assets

The accumulated losses as on 31 March 2000 stood at Rs.776 crore (12 SCARDBs) and at Rs.784 crore (PCARDBs in 9 States). As on 31 March 2001 the accumulated losses of SCARDBs (11 States) stood at Rs.891 crore and those of PCARDBs at Rs.1061 crore (10 States). As on 31 October 2001, 4 SCARDBs had defaulted to NABARD to the tune of Rs.319.36 crore. It is apprehended that due to the steadily eroding financial health, some more SCARDBs may default to NABARD in the near future.

COPERATIVE BANKING - AN ASSESSMENT & ROLE OF NABARD

NABARD has been impressing upon the State Governments the need to ensure the democratic character of cooperatives as it is an essential principle on which cooperatives have been evolved. However, notwithstanding the persuasive efforts of RBI/ NABARD, the elected Boards of Management in 10 SCBs, 4 SCARDBs, 75 DCCBs and 135 PCARDBs stood superseded as on March 2001. It is a matter of concern that a substantial number of institutions in each tier are deprived of the guidance of the elected Boards.

Audit Classification

Audit of cooperative banks is conducted by departmental auditors appointed by the State Governments. The completion of audit is, however, a slow process in cooperative banks. The co-operatives are classified into A,B,C and D categories as per audit classification norms prescribed by RBI/ NABARD and these categories correspond to achievement levels of 60% and above, 45-59%, 30-44% and less than 30% on selected financial parameters, respectively. The audit classification serves as an index for the quality of management as well as strength of the cooperatives. Information on classification of PACS is not available for an indicative macro aggregation. However, as per (NAFSCOB) data available, 3668 PACS were reported to be dormant as at the end of 2000-2001 constituting 3.7% of the total PACS in the country. Though audit is conducted for LT structure also, similar classification is not award.

Credit Deposit Ratio

The Credit-Deposit ratio (C D ratio) is a realistic indicator of the extent to which deposits raised locally are deployed in the same area in the form of loans. The low CD ratio in certain DCCBs was mainly due to their low credit absorption capacity. CD ratio also depends on growth in mobilisation of deposits, deployment of credit, infrastructural facilities etc. In recent times, however, there has been a considerable amount of discussion on the usefulness of C D ratio as a measure of allocation of funds by banks and that a few other indicators of credit deployment have been recognised.

Comparative CD ratio of SCBs, DCCBs, Commercial Banks(separately for all branches as also rural branches) and RRBs as on 31 March 2001 is indicated in the table given below. However, prima-facie comparison of the CD ratios of these institutions may lead to a erroneous conclusion as these three types of credit institutions are not comparable among themselves as they differ in their area of operation, clientele and functional mandate. Further, the credit extended by the banks also depends on the borrowings raised by the banks for lending.

Comparative CD Ratio of Rural Banking System

SCBs	DCCBs	PACS*	RRBs	CBs (rural branches)	CBs (all branches)
91.5%	88%	190.6%	41.33%	40%	68.8%

* PACS data is for 2000-01

The primaries in the cooperative structure are weak in resources and depend to a large extent on the finance provided by the higher tiers.

All India CD ratio of DCCBs as on 31 March 2001 stood at 88% as against 40% of Commercial Banks (rural branches) and 41.33 of RRBs. The DCCBs in nine states viz., A.P, Bihar, Haryana, Karnataka, Rajasthan, M.P, Orissa, Punjab and Tamil Nadu had CD ratio higher than All India average of 85%. The CD ratio was lower than the All India average in the remaining eleven states ranging from 29.1% (Uttaranchal) to 76.9% (Chhatisgarh). The CD ratio in Andhra Pradesh was high at 209.9% as the state had an integrated structure with the loans outstanding inclusive of both ST & LT wings (though the LT wing had a meagre deposit base).

Productivity Review

The cooperative banks are not well equipped with the latest technology and technologically driven product lines. Computerisation of banks appears to be the panacea for many problems faced by the industry. It directly results in increasing productivity of work-force, introduction of technology oriented and complex products, speedier operations, facilitates volume growth and better customer service.

In terms of Section 11 (1) of B.R. Act, 1949 (AACS), a DCCB and a non-scheduled SCB should have a minimum share capital of Rs.1 lakh in terms of real or exchangeable value of its paid up capital and reserves. The number of banks not complying with Section 11 (1) of the Act ibid has steadily increased especially with the introduction of prudential norms and preparation of balance sheets as per guidelines on income recognition, asset classification and provisioning as per details given below. Some of these banks have not been complying with the provision for longer periods of time. The number of non complying DCCBs as on 31 March 2002 has decreased to 139 DCCBs as compared to 142 as on 31 December 2000. However, the number of State Cooperative Banks not complying with the provisions of the said section was higher (9) as compared to 6 as on 31.12.2000.

The total erosion in the value of assets of these nine SCBs taken together was Rs.597.97 crore and erosion in deposits was to the extent of Rs.105.17 crore as on 30.03.2002. The erosion in deposits of 5 SCBs were Arunachal Pradesh (13.0%), Assam (22.3%), Bihar (19.4%), Chandigarh (4.8%), Manipur (11.7%), Meghalaya (4.1%), Mizoram (14%), Nagaland(9.7%), Tripura (1.0%). Of the 139 non-complying DCCBs, the total erosion in the value assets of aggregated to Rs. 5475.89 crore. Erosion in deposits of these DCCBs was to the extent of Rs.1828.52 crore.

Supervision Of Cooperative Banks

Under the Banking Regulation Act, 1949, the National Bank is entrusted with the statutory responsibility of periodical inspection of State Cooperative Banks (SCBs) and District Central Cooperative Banks (DCCBs).

In addition, the National Bank also conducts periodical inspection of state level cooperative institutions such as State Cooperative Agricultural and Rural Development Banks (SCARDBs), Apex Weavers Cooperative Societies, State Cooperative Marketing Federation, etc. which voluntarily opt for such inspections. The basic objective of these inspections is to assess the financial and managerial strengths of the banks to protect the interest of depositors as well as maintain sound banking systems in conformity with the banking laws and regulations.

The National Bank continued to adopt what is popularly known as CAMELSC approach in its on-site inspection of banks and it has introduced off-site surveillance system during 1998-99. During the year 2000-01, 175 banks (11 SCBs, 11 SCARDBs, 153 DCCBs) and 11 Apex institutions were inspected. These inspections revealed, inter alia, that financial and systemic weaknesses continued to exist in the functioning of these banks.

Major deficiencies observed include high level of NPAs, mounting overdues, high transaction cost coupled with lower margin, poor quality of loan appraisal, inadequate internal checks and control, lack of professionalism in their management and growing imbalances in the different tiers of cooperatives.

Board of Supervision (BoS)

The Board of Supervision (for SCBs, DCCBs and RRBs) set-up as an internal committee of the National Bank in November 1999, held two meetings during the year 2000-01. In these meetings the BoS reviewed the financial position of those weak cooperative banks whose impaired assets eroded 50% or more of their deposits. Board of Supervision recommended to RBI to initiate measures, wherever warranted and apprised the concerned State Governments about the precarious financial position of cooperative banks in their states and issued necessary warning signals to the identified banks. Cooperative Development Fund.

With a view to strengthening the cooperative credit institutions NABARD provides financial assistance to cooperative credit institutions for giving impetus to institutional development in the form of grant-in-aid, soft loan or grant-cum-soft loan for various purposes aimed at improving the performance of these institutions from Cooperative Development Fund (CDF) constituted for the purpose. Sanctions and Disbursements (Cumulative)

As on 31 March 2002, sanctions and disbursements from the Fund aggregated Rs.49.31 crore and Rs.39.22 crore respectively. The important highlights in this regard are :

- Of the total sanctions, the SCBs' share stood at 49.6% and SCARDBs' at 34.4%. Amongst the various purposes, the support to PACS for provision of infrastructure has the maximum share (23.0%), followed by computerisation (15.8%) and purchase of vehicles (13.3%).
- Six States viz., Andhra Pradesh, Tamil Nadu, Madhya Pradesh, Uttar Pradesh, Karnataka and Orissa have been sanctioned more than Rs.200.00 lakh each while four States viz., Punjab, West Bengal, Bihar and Rajasthan have been sanctioned between Rs.100.00 lakh and Rs.200.00 lakh each.
- Two States, viz., Tamil Nadu and Madhya Pradesh have utilised more than Rs.200.00 lakh each while four States viz., Uttar Pradesh, Karnataka, Orissa and West

Bengal have utilised between Rs.100.00 lakh and Rs.200.00 lakh each.

- An amount of Rs.123.53 lakh was sanctioned as grant from CDF for conducting a number of studies and seminars to facilitate successful implementation of DAP/ MoUs.
- Disbursements increased, by 25%, from Rs.3131.54 lakh as on 31 March 2001 to Rs.3921.56 lakh as on 31 March 2002.
- Awards : generated a spirit of competition.
- ACSTI/JLTCs : HRD improvements in cooperative banks.
- KCC : popularisation process.

Impact of CDF Assistance

As reported by Regional Offices and in some impact studies, the infrastructure assistance to PACS has had an overall positive impact on deposit mobilisation by PACS in the States of Madhya Pradesh, Orissa, Karnataka, Tamil Nadu, West Bengal, Uttar Pradesh, Gujarat and Andhra Pradesh. It had enabled the PACS to get a new look and thereby enhanced level of confidence of general public which helped increase in deposit accounts besides creating a sense of safety and security of savings among the clientele.

Utilisation of CDF assistance sanctioned for Computerisation is generally satisfactory inasmuch as it had helped in improving MIS, generating statutory and other returns, better maintenance of records, faster disposal/ exchange of information, etc.

Impact of CDF assistance, provided for Motor Cycles to the field Staff (LT structure only), for improving recovery performance, however, cannot be co-related to enhanced recovery. However, increased mobility on account of vehicle support had facilitated improved bank-borrower relationship which helped increase in the number of visits to borrowers, better field monitoring and supervision, etc. Recovery had improved in Madhya Pradesh SCADRB, J&KCCLDB and Nagaland SCB after vehicle support to the banks.

COPERATIVE BANKING - REFORMS

NABARD had appointed an Expert Committee headed by Prof. V S Vyas in August 2000 to review the emerging scenario in rural credit and preparation of workable comprehensive plan of action for a more effective rural credit by an expert body. The committee submitted its report on 23 July 2001. The core recommendations of the Committee are briefly indicated below:

Challenging Tasks

- Changes in rural economy may necessitate involvement of new financial agencies or groupings such as SHGs, NBFC, etc.
- Progressive integration of financial markets and autonomy to institutions and accountability necessary.
- Subsidy driven programme may do more harm than good.
- New innovations such as formation of Joint Liability Groups, freeing land lease market, contract farming, etc. need to be encouraged.
- Promote watershed development and disseminate experience gained.
- Review methods of fixing scales of finance.
- Rectify imbalance between finance for production and that for post harvest operations.
- Improve links between credit and marketing.
- Remove hurdles in taking up non crop activities and finance the same.
- FIs must prepare for a more pro-active role, shed excessive caution and explore alternative methods of providing finance, to boost private investments.
- Credit institutions need to play larger role in financing non farm activities.

Strengthening Credit Delivery System

- Act expeditiously on recommendations of Capoor Committee on revitalisation of cooperatives and place Rs.500 crore with NABARD for the purpose. State Governments be allowed to borrow from RIDF at concessional terms to meet their share.
- The Model Cooperative Act may be adopted in all states and B.R Act be made applicable to cooperatives with appropriate modifications.
- Restore health of PACS by scrapping cadre system, allow mobilisation of deposits by PACS and linking them for borrowings from higher tiers and restrict voting rights to active members, audit by professional CAs and design alternative deposit insurance schemes.
- Selective de-layering of ST cooperative credit structure.
- Integration of long term and short term structures, and to begin with strengthening of LT structure.
- After revitalisation and other reforms provide guarantee free refinance with relaxed norms for disadvantaged / under developed areas / states Continued involvement of commercial banks in rural lending.
- CBs need to offer value added services through rural branches to improve viability of these branches.
- Reduction of interest rates on RIDF deposits to deter banks from substituting agricultural advances with RIDF deposits.
- Make SAMIS returns statutory
- Ensure credit flow to disadvantaged sections and areas-amount of shortfall in lending to weaker sections be called in to RIDF and restrictions on interest rates on small loans be removed.
- Credit for ST and LT for both agriculture and non farm activities be progressively under KCC.
- The process of recapitalisation of RRBs should be completed speedily and extended to remaining banks.

- Sponsor Banks to select Chairman and provide other need based support.
- In case of patently non viable RRBs the option of liquidation be considered.
- RRBs earning profit and without any accumulated losses to adhere their CD ratio to a minimum of 60% and improve it by 5 percentage points annually and if they fail to improve CD ratio they shall deposit the shortfall into RIDF at 7% interest.
- Sponsor Banks to review system for monitoring performance of ARBs and give necessary autonomy in portfolio management and in evolving innovative credit products.
- Convert ARBs into LABs i.e. banking company and restrict setting up of LAB by private sector.
- Draft appropriate amendments to ARB Act to incorporate the recommendations of the committee.

Human Resources Development

- Attention to selection of leaders, motivating and training of personnel, incentives, etc.
- Human resources requirement study to be conducted for cooperatives and excess staff be redeployed / offered VRS, etc.
- CBs may start rural branches based on business levels.
- Cadre system of secretaries in PACS be abolished and selection of functionaries left to management.
- Cooperative CEOs be professionals and adequately empowered and ex-officio board members.
- Need to motivate and train the employees manning PACS, rural branches of CBs and ARBs.
- Computerised back and front office operations.
- Improve facilities provided to employees in rural branches Legal Environment.

- Need to improve legal environment both to increase the disbursal of rural credit and achieve better recovery.
- State Government may support the efforts of credit institutions by improving and updating land records, waive stamp duty and registration fees on loan documents, etc.
- A national consensus be built to deter political parties / other public organisations from giving call to borrowers not to repay their loans.

Planning, Supervision and Coordination

- Convene Annual Rural Credit Conference involving all stakeholders
- RBI should announce rural credit policy and review achievements, advocate revitalisation of cooperatives and extension of B.R Act to cooperatives, ensure greater involvement of CBs in rural credit, monitor lead bank performance, extend greater support to NABARD with an increase of 10% to 15% annually in its General Line of Credit to NABARD and allow access to National Industrial Credit.
- NABARD to play more active role, form a venture capital subsidy, allow preferential interest rates on its refinance to thrust sectors, make CDF more pro-active, sharpen DAP/MOU, open more DDM Offices, incorporate greater disclosure in balance sheet of cooperative banks and ARBs and publish Trends and Progress in Cooperative Banks and ARBs from March 2002.
- GOI to support revitalisation of cooperatives and ARBs, carefully select nominees to ARB board, legislate enabling measures, defer incidence of corporate income tax on NABARD by 5 years, etc.
- State Governments to take greater interest in ARBs and cooperatives, devise internal system to make the best use of District Credit Planning, promote private sector participation in rural development by creating better facilities.

- Panchayati Raj and civil society institutions can be made effective partners and helpmates to credit bodies in various pursuits, such as deposit mobilisation, awareness creation and recovery.

Joint Committee on Revitalisation support to Cooperative Credit Structure

During the consultative process on finalisation, the implementation mechanism for the recommendation of "Task Force to Study the Functioning of the Cooperative Credit System and Suggest Measures for its Strengthening" (known as Capoor Committee). In the conference of Hon'ble Chief Ministers held in New Delhi on 25 August 2001, some of the issues relating to revitalisation assistance could not be resolved and the Government of India set up a Joint Committee of the Cooperative Ministers of 8 selected states, NABARD, RBI, GOI and Ministry of Agriculture and Cooperation, Ministry of Finance as the members under the Chairmanship of Hon'ble Union Minister of State for Finance, Shri Balasaheb Vikhe Patil, to make appropriate recommendations in respect of the following issues:

- Determination / identification of sharing pattern of revitalization assistance amongst GOI, State Governments and the cooperatives;
- Funding mechanism;
- Feasibility of de-layering of cooperative credit structure especially with a view to regulating intermediation cost.

The committee has submitted its report and the summary recommendations of the Task Force in respect of Revitalisation Assistance are as under:

- The package for revitalisation of cooperative credit institutions shall consist of a four dimensional programme encompassing the financial, operational, organisational and systemic aspects of functioning of these institutions.
- The revitalisation should not be an across-the-board process and it should be confined to the potentially viable units only.

- The assistance would be provided to bring the cooperative credit institutions to 'take off' stage and enable them to stand on their own.
- The assessment of viability in each case will have to be done following the usual principles of expected volume of business over a period of time, level of income to be generated and whether a turnaround will be possible in five to seven years beyond which the assistance will not be available.
- Viability of member PACS would largely determine the viability of central cooperative banks at the district level in which the PACS federate. The banks may be taken up for revitalisation carefully on a selective basis even if the process of selection is time consuming.
- Given the priorities of the successive Five Year Plans to strengthen the food security measures through increased agricultural production and enhanced credit flow for the purpose, the central and State Governments should take the lead in the formulation of revitalisation/ revamping package for the cooperative credit institutions.
- The base-level institutions would be kept at the center-stage of the assistance programme. The higher tiers would also need additional support depending upon the position of their assets.
- Finding funds required for this purpose in a single year may be difficult for both the central and the State Governments. Since the revitalization process is quite elaborate, a longer time frame would be required for this purpose.
- The initiative should be taken only in those states which take appropriate legislative measures for ensuring elimination of duality in control in cooperative banking institutions. The State Governments should also commit their appropriate financial and administrative support.
- The share of GOI and the State Governments in S.T. structure should be 40% each and in L.T. structure it

should be 45% each. The balance amount has to be mobilized by way of contributions from the members.

- The share of GOI and the State Governments may be in the form of bonds bearing a reasonable rate of interest and these bonds may be extinguished over a period of five years (20% each year) after an initial moratorium of three years. This will not involve large outgo of funds from both GOI and State Governments as the outflows would be restricted to periodical payments of interest on the bonds.
- The bonds on behalf of PACS would be issued in favour of DCCB and interest income would go to the credit of PACS and appropriated towards clearing of dues of such PACS.
- The members' contribution could be retained at PACS level to be used for its credit business.
- A national level Committee may evolve the modalities for selection of banks.
- Certain broad conditionalities have been suggested that have to be followed in selection of banks and provision of revitalisation assistance.

The Joint Committee has submitted its report on 7th December, 2001. Recommendations of the Joint Committee are as under:

- The Joint Committee concurs with the Capoor Committee recommendation that the assistance would be provided to bring the cooperative credit institutions to "take off" stage and enable them to stand on their own.
- Parameters / items of computation of assistance amount at PACS/DCCB/ PCARDB/SCARDB levels to be identified.
- Revitalisation assistance would be computed with reference to the financial position shown in the duly audited and published Balance Sheet and Profit and Loss Accounts as on 31 March 2001.

- Amount of assistance identified at different levels in both ST and LT structure be shared by the GOI and State Governments in the proportion of 60 : 40. In case of NER states and Jammu & Kashmir, the share is 90 : 10.
- The assistance will be provided in form of Self-extinguishing bonds which will be issued by the GOI and State Governments for their own share. The interest thereon will be paid by the GOI and the State Governments out of budgetary allocations each year. The amount of bonds may be so fixed that the predetermined rate of interest the institutions receive 10% of amount of revitalisation assistance each year. These bonds will be self-extinguishing in nature and after the period of 10 years, the bonds will be extinguishing without any redemption of the principal amount.

8

THE REGIONAL RURAL BANKS

RRBs are state sponsored, regionally based and rural oriented commercial banks envisaged to combine simultaneously the desirable qualities of both co-operative banks and commercial banks. RRBs, being an important segment of the Rural Financial Institutions in the country, have carved out a special place for themselves in terms of geographical coverage, clientele outreach, business volume and contributions for development of rural economy. RRBs are focusing their attention on the attainment of sustainable viability, improved customer services, new and innovative loan products and diversified business portfolio. RRBs are at par with the scheduled commercial banks in respect of priority sector lending, investment avenues and credit discipline and transparency.

While the performance of many RRBs improved significantly, the performance of some of them remains far from being satisfactory in view of their tardy business growth and lack of operational viability.

How they are Different from Commercial Banks

Though RRBs are basically scheduled commercial Banks they differ from the commercial banks in the following respects:

- The area of operation of an RRB is limited to a particular region comprising one or more districts of a State.
- RRBs grant direct loans and advances specifically to weaker sections of the rural areas for productive purpose

They are to provide credit to agriculturists and others in the rural areas at the lower lending rate than any other agency in the rural area. To facilitate this various concessions have been provided to them by the sponsoring bank, as well as the Reserve Bank of India. These concessions take the form of lower rate of interest on refinance by RBI, refinance facilities by NABARD, lower cash ratio, lower SLR, lower rate of interest from the sponsoring banks, managerial and staff assistance from the sponsoring banks and reimbursement of expenses on staff training.

How they Came into Existence

Although the co-operative and commercial banks had an impressive record in terms of geographical coverage and disbursement of credit, it was observed that the vast majority of the poor were generally deprived of credit and other banking facilities. In order to provide access to low-cost banking facilities to the poor, a new set-up of banks, viz. RRBs, was established in the country to meet exclusively the needs of the weaker sections of the rural population, as institutions which "combine the local feel and the familiarity with rural problems which the cooperatives possess and the degree of business organization, ability to mobilize deposits, access to central money markets and modernized outlook which the commercial banks have".

The Govt. of India, in July 1975, appointed a Working Group to study in depth the problem of devising alternative agencies to provide institutional credit to the rural people in the context of steps then initiated under the 20 Point Economic Programme. The Working Group identified various weaknesses of the co-operative credit agencies and the commercial banks and felt that these institutions would not be able to fill the regional and functional gaps in the rural credit system within a reasonable period of time. The Group therefore recommended a new type of institution which combines-

- Local feel and familiarity with rural possess problems which co-operative banks.
- Degree of business organization ability to mobilise deposit, access to money market and modernised outlook which commercial banks have.

Thus, it was envisaged to combine desirable qualities of co-operative banks and commercial banks in RRB's at the same time, it was emphasised that the role of RRB's would be to supplement and not supplant the other institutional agencies already existing in the field.

The Government of India promulgated the Regional Rural Banks Ordinance on 26th September 1975, which was later replaced by the Regional Rural Bank Act 1976. The preamble to the Act states the objective to develop rural economy by providing credit and facilities for the development of agriculture, trade, commerce, industry and other productive activities in the rural areas, particularly to small and marginal farmers, agricultural labourers, artisans and small entrepreneurs.

The RRB Act empowers the Central Govt. to open the banks from time to time at places where it may consider it necessary. A Regional Rural Bank is jointly owned by the Govt. of India, the Government of concerned state and public sector bank, which sponsored it. The authorised capital of each bank is Rs. 1 crores (subsequently raised 5 Crores) with paid-up capital Rs.25 Lacs (subsequently increased to Rs.1 Crore) which is held by them in the proportion of 50, 15 and 35 per cent respectively. Each bank carries the banking business within the local limits specified by the Govt. notification.

Organisational Structure

The management of a RRB is vested in a nine-member Board of Directors headed by

Chairman who is an officer deputed by a sponsor bank but appointed by the Govt. of India.

Three directors to be nominated the Central Govt.

Two directors to be nominated by the concerned State Govt.

Three directors to be nominated by the sponsor bank.

The sponsor bank, besides subscribing to the capital and deputing one of its official as chairman, provides assistance to RRB in several ways such as financial accommodation, deputing managerial and other staff and arranging the recruitment of staff and their training.

Functions

Every RRB may undertake the following types of functions:

The granting of loans and advances particularly to small and marginal farmers and agricultural labourers individually or to a group, co-operative societies, agricultural processing societies, co-operative farming societies, etc.

The Granting of loans and advances to artisans, small entrepreneurs and small traders, businessmen, etc.

The Reserve Bank of India has brought RRBs under the ambit of priority sector lending on par with the commercial banks. They have to ensure that forty percent of their advances are accounted for the priority sector. Within the 40% priority target, 25% should go to weaker section or 10% of their total advances to go to weaker section.

From a modest beginning with 6 RRBs in 1975, as many as 196 RRBs were operating in 500 districts with a network of 14,313 branches as on 31 March, 2001 excluding satellite branches and extension counters. The branch network comprises 6 metropolitan, 348 urban, 1875 semi-urban and 12,084 rural branches. RRBs have a large branch network in the rural area, which forms nearly 37% of the total rural branch network of all scheduled commercial banks.

The rural banking system with 196 banks and 14,300 branches, employing 70,000 staff is catering to the remote villages. There are six crore account holders and the turnover is a whopping Rs. 70,000 crore. RRBs operate under the regulatory supervision of NABARD. NABARD has the responsibility of laying down the policies for RRBs, to oversee their operations, provide refinance facilities, to monitor their performance and attend to their problems.

Progress of RRBs

These banks, which at the outset adopted lower scales of compensation for their staff than their sponsor banks, were specially mandated to lend to weaker sections at rates of interest with a concessional element. They could initially manage to lend at concessional rates because of their access to subsidised refinance from their sponsor banks and NABARD. But the RRBs were crippled soon enough by several factors among which was a new compensation policy in pursuance of which they had to pay their employees on par with those of their sponsor banks. Their character as low cost institutions specially designed to serve rural areas was thus lost irretrievably. They were also adversely affected by the problems of mounting overdues and uneasy industrial relations.

Other deficiencies of RRBs are as under:

According to Narasimham Committee, RRBs have low earning capacity. They have not been able to earn much profits in view of their policy of providing low cost loans

According to RBI, recovery position of RRBs is not satisfactory. There are a large number of defaulters.

Their cost of operation has been high on account of the increase in the salary scales of the employees of these banks in line with the salary structure of the employees of commercial banks. In most cases these banks followed the same methods of operation and procedures as followed by commercial banks. Therefore these procedures have not found favour with the rural masses.

In many cases banks have not been located at the right place. For instance the sponsoring banks are also running their branches in the same areas where RRBs are operating

Reconstruction of RRBs

Government of India have to be take up reconstruction/ recapitalisation of the RRBs to sustain their viability and progress. Government of India started making recurring annual budgetary allocations for this purpose.

Impact of Restructuring Programme on RRBs

Recapitalisation and other restructuring measures have had a very positive impact on the performance of RRBs. A tremendous awareness has been created and all concerned are now alive to the reality that the future of RRBs depends upon their successfully competing with other banking organisations. For this purpose, efficiency, productivity and profitability have been given their due importance. There is now a greater awareness among the sponsor banks themselves as they have become more responsive to the problems of RRBs.

On the financial front, the performance of RRBs though actually improved in the years immediately following the first phase of recapitalisation i.e. in 1995-96 and 1996-97, it was overshadowed due to the introduction of prudential norms of Asset Classification, Income Recognition and Provisioning for the RRBs. The RRBs' financial performance came in the limelight in 1997-98 when RRBs as a group earned profit for the first time since their establishment.

During 2001-02, as many as 167 RRBs earned profit of Rs.699.92 crore as against only 32 RRBs earning profit of Rs.29 crore during 1994-95. On the other hand, the losses incurred by the loss incurring RRBs reduced from Rs.423 crore (164 RRBs) to Rs.92.05 crore (29 RRBs) during the same period.

The RRBs as a group made a profit of Rs.73 crore for the first time during 1997-98 and improved the same further to Rs.601 crore and to Rs.608 crore during the last two years i.e. 2000-01 and 2001-2002. The viability based categorisation of RRBs as on 31 March 2002 shows that out of 196 RRBs, 86 RRBs have wiped off their accumulated losses and in a way attained a sustainable viability whereas 89 other RRBs have achieved a turn around and attained a current viability status leaving only 29 RRBs which continued to incur losses.

The genuine credit needs of the borrowers are being met by RRBs in their respective area of operations. The total loans disbursed by RRBs have increased from Rs.1440 crore in 1993-94 to Rs.10571 crore in 2001-02. The total Outstanding Advances of RRBs stood at Rs.18629 crore as on 31 March 2002 as against Rs.5253 crore as on 31 March 1994.

The recovery performance of RRBs have shown a consistent improvement from around 40% in 1991-92 to 70 % during the year 2001-02. The NPAs of RRBs have also been declining in percentage terms and stood at 16% as on 31 March 2002 as against 43% as on 31 March 1996 when the norms were first made applicable to the RRBs.

Performance Highlights as at 31.03.2002 (as provided by NABARD)

The financial results of RRBs as on 31 March 2002 indicate that by and large the RRBs are on the path of recovery.

As against 170 RRBs in the previous year, 167 RRBs have earned profit during 2001-02.

121 RRBs have shown improvement in their performance either by way of increased profit or decreased loss or shifting from loss to profit.

7 RRBs have entered profit arena from loss while 11 RRBs have reduced their losses.

The aggregate accumulated losses of RRBs declined marginally from Rs.2792.59 crore in 2000-01 to Rs2694.06 crore during the year.

As against 80 RRBs as on 31 March 2001, 86 RRBs had wiped off their accumulated losses as on 31 March 2002.

The combined Net Profit of all the RRBs for the year is Rs.607.87 crore as against the combined Net Profit of Rs.600.62 crore in the previous year.

As against 170 RRBs earning a combined net profit of Rs.676.47 crore as on 31 March 2001, 167 RRBs have earned a higher combined net profit of Rs.699.93 crore during the year.

The deposits of RRBs grew on an average by 16.38 per cent.

The Outstanding Advances of RRBs at Rs.18629 crore recorded a growth rate of 17.78 per cent.

The total borrowings of RRBs at Rs. 4524 crore, registered a growth of 11.3 per cent.

The percentage of recovery to demand stood at 70.59% per cent as on 30 June 2001 as against 68.20 per cent in the previous year.

NPAs of all the RRBs have declined from 23.1 per cent as on 31 March 2001 to 16.45 per cent as on 31 March 2002.

CD Ratio increased to at the level of 42% as on 31 March 2002 as against 41 per cent as on 31 March 2001.

A viability-based review of RRBs shows that the loss-incurring RRBs are concentrated in 3 States viz Bihar, Madhya Pradesh and Orissa and in four Sponsor Banks viz UCO Bank, SBI, BOI and BOB. Their common characteristics included low productivity, high transaction costs, lower CD ratio, negative margins, low recovery rates and high NPAs.

Support Rendered by NABARD to RRBs - Institutional Development Initiatives

Regional Rural Banks are important financial institutions in the rural credit structure and they continue to receive focussed attention under the institutional development initiatives of NABARD. Some of the initiatives which have been launched by NABARD are given below:

In order to bring about an attitudinal change in the mindset of RRB employees and to improve their motivation level, NABARD has initiated a non-conventional training intervention known as Organisation Development Intervention (ODI) in 120 RRBs in collaboration with Swiss Agency for Development and Cooperation. NABARD is also supporting 147 RRBs with computers and software to develop their Management Information System.

NABARD is permitting the RRBs to relocate their loss-making branches to good business location/centres keeping in view the objective of building up sustainable rural financial institutions. Further, loss-incurring RRBs have been allowed to convert into satellite/mobile offices provided such conversion would not impair the performance of service area obligations.

For ensuring unity of command, the sponsor banks have been entrusted with full managerial and operational responsibilities. RBI and NABARD will deal with matters of regulatory and supervisory nature only, besides, monitoring the performance of RRBs. Pursuance of the monetory and credit policy for the year 2002-03 announced by RBI, RRBs are now requested to maintain their entire SLR holdings in Govt. And other approved securities only.

Micro-finance and group lending continue to be NABARD's priority area. NABARD issued guidelines for strengthening the

Self Help Group linkage programme and most of the RRBs are now participating in the programme. RRBs are also identified as Self Help Promoting Institutions (SHPI) for giving an impetus to micro finance.

NABARD deputes its senior officials to guide the Sponsor Banks in various review meetings of Sponsor Banks for RRBs on issues relating to staff matters, investment policy, turn-around strategies, etc.

NABARD through its Regional Offices is regularly monitoring the performance of RRBs on a half yearly basis and takes up the issues which need policy correction.

In order to build up the skills and expertise of the personnel of RRBs, NABARD continues to give special priority through its training institutions like BIRD, Lucknow, Regional Training Centres of National Bank at Mangalore and Bolpur. RRB officials have been trained in advanced areas of Project Management under Farm and Non-Farm sectors, Asset-Liability Management, Fund Management apart from the areas of Internal Control, MIS, Personnel Management and Industrial Relation.

Under NB-SDC-HID-VIII Project, NABARD has firmed up a detailed strategic plan on training intervention for RRBs identified under the project (120 RRBs).

In order to disseminate the best practices in RRBs, NABARD has arranged exposure visits for RRBs personnel within the country and abroad.

GOI had constituted a Working Group under the Chairmanship of Dr.K P Agrawal, ED, NABARD to review the manpower norms in RRBs. GOI has accepted the reports and issued the instructions for implementation on 22 January 2001. Accordingly the policy circular has been issued to all Sponsor Banks for implementation of the recommendations.

In order to reduce the stock of NPAs as also to improve the recovery of sticky advances, One-Time Settlement Scheme for recovery of NPAs have been introduced in RRBs. The scheme was valid up to 31 March 2002 and a sum of Rs. 208 crore have been recovered by RRBs under the scheme.

The salary and pay structure of RRBs personnel have been revised on par with their sponsor banks.

As a prudential measure aimed at better risk management and avoidance of concentration of credit risk, the existing single exposure limit of 20 % and Group exposure limit of 50% of RRBs own fund have been brought down to 15% and 40% respectively effective from 31 March 2002.

RRBs have been granted exemption from the practice of marking to market norms in respect of SLR /approved securities for a period up to 31 March 2004.

Priority sector norms applicable to RRBs have been revised. Accordingly from the year 2003-04, RRBs are required to achieve a target of 60% of their outstanding advances for Priority Sector lending as against 40% prescribed earlier. In order to supplement the resources of RRBs, NABARD refinance is now made available to RRBs for financing to farmers for purchase land for agricultural purposes, purchase of two wheelers by farmers, setting up of Agriclinics and Agribusiness Centres by Agricultural Graduates and for Rural Housing.

RRBS - RECOMMENDATIONS OF THE WORKING GROUP HEADED BY M V S CHALAPATI RAO,

Government of India has set up a Working Group under the chairmanship of Shri M.V.S.Chalapathi Rao, Managing Director, National Bank in July 2001 to examine various aspects of functioning of RRBs and to make recommendations for RRBs to become an effective instrument for development of the rural economy. Other members nominated on this ten member Working Group are senior officers/experts from RBI, select commercial banks, RRBs and NGOs

Terms of Reference of Working Group on RRBs

To review the progress in dispensation of rural credit especially through RRBs since their inception.

To examine the legal, regulatory and policy framework of RRBs with particular reference to determine their effectiveness in meeting the complete banking needs of rural households and rural economy.

To make detailed recommendations in regard to legal, regulatory, supervisory, institutional and technological dimensions for making RRBs an effective instrument for development and growth of the rural economy.

The group has submitted its report during August 2002, and has suggested amendments to several provisions of the Act.

The relevant provisions relate to Preamble of the Act, licence to RRBs, capital structure and share capital, devolution of some powers of the Finance Ministry to Reserve Bank of India, corporate governance, supervisory authority, appointment of auditors, recovery of dues and penalties. The committee has classified the RRBs (regional rural banks) into four categories. The group says, "this categorisation of RRBs into A, B, C and D should be the basis for providing flexibility in ownership options. The adoption of the concept of a "sponsor institution" has been recommended with its prescribed minimum level of shareholding at 51 per cent so as "to ensure adequate commitment as well as powers for the sponsor institution."

In the category A fall the top class RRBs, i.e. those RRBs which have no accumulated loss and which reported profits for the past three consecutive years; in category B fall those RRBs which posted profits for the past three consecutive years and their accumulated losses have not caused erosion of public deposits; in the category C are those which reported loss in one or more of the last three years and have accumulated losses that have caused erosion in the value of their assets not in excess of 10 per cent of their total deposits as on March 31, 2002 and in the category D have been put all those RRBs which have reported losses in one or more in the last three years and have accumulated loss causing erosion of the value of their assets in excess of 10 per cent of their total deposits.

After having made the classifications, the committee has suggested that category A RRBs should be allowed to access capital market. The Union Government stake in these RRBs should be reduced to 33 per cent and the State Government's stake in them too may be purchased by the sponsoring bank.

In the category B RRBs, sponsoring banks, according to the committee, must hold majority stake and thus control. Before the Union Government disinvests 17 per çent of its stake in these RRBs, the three shareholders should inject fresh capital to wipe out the past losses.

The RRB Act needs to be amended to facilitate the sponsor institution pick up the state government stake of 15 per cent (total paid up capital of an RRB is Rs. one crore). The committee argues for sponsor banks holding 35 per cent stake in RRBs to sell off to another as a part of the revamp. "In the post-capital issue scenario as well, the shareholding of the sponsor institution may continue to be at a minimum of 51 per cent though the proportionate share of the Central Government and State Government may come down," the working group adds.

These categories of RRBs may be upgraded to category A. The State Government shares in these RRBs may be purchased by sponsoring bank.

For the category C RRBs, the committee has opposed the change in the ownership pattern. The amalgamation of these RRBs with other suitable RRBs has also been suggested.

The committee has suggested liquidation of the majority of the category D RRBs, conceding that some of these perpetually losing RRBs may have to be allowed to continue in public interest.

In such cases, the Union and the State Government concerned must acquire the ownership and work out appropriate policies for their functioning. The Union and State Governments might be required to provide financial support.

The salary of those employed in the RRBs, according to the committee, should be determined by the respective boards with prior approval of the sponsoring banks and in determining so the boards should pay due regard to the standard norms relating to work performance, financial position, paying capacity and the sustainable viability of the RRB concerned.

The working group is in favour of slapping capital adequacy and licensing norms on RRBs. "The capital adequacy norms may be introduced in a phased manner... starting with 5 per cent of outstanding risk weighted assets effective April 1, 2003, to be enhanced by one percentage point every year to bring it at par with that for commercial banks," the group lays down. It wants to make licensing mandatory for RRBs under the Banking Regulation Act, 1949. As of now they draw legitimacy from the RRB Act alone.

"The existing RRBs or those created out of amalgamation of two or more existing RRBs may continue doing banking business during the pendency of consideration of their application for license by RBI and they would have to cease business if a license is refused to them." The group is in favour of RBI continuing as the regulator with a separate "Supervisory Authority" in place of NABARD to oversee functioning of RRBs.

THE LOCAL AREA BANKS

The Local Area Bank Scheme was introduced in August 1996 pursuant to the announcement of the then Finance Minister.

In his budget speech, the Finance Minister referred to the setting up of new private local banks with jurisdiction over two or three contiguous districts. He observed that this would enable the mobilization of rural savings by local institutions and make them available for investments in the local areas. The Local Area Banks (LABs) were expected to bridge the gap in credit availability and strengthen the institutional credit framework in the rural and semi-urban areas.

Following this, guidelines for setting up of LABs in the private sector were announced by the Reserve Bank of India (RBI) on 24th August 1996.

Over a period of about five and a half years, as many as 227 applications for establishment of LABs in the private sector had been received by the RBI of which 214 applications were rejected while 'in-principle' approvals for establishment of 10 LABs were issued and 3 applications are under examination. However, due to the inability of the promoters to fulfill the conditions stipulated in the 'in-principle' approvals, 4 such approvals were withdrawn.

5 banks were licensed under Section 22 of the Banking Regulation Act 1949. Of these, only 4 LABs are functioning at present. 1 application is pending.

Background of Setting up of LABS

Agriculture continues to be an important sector in our national economy even now despite the diversification, which the economy has undergone under the stimulus of five decades of planned economic development. Though the contribution of agriculture and allied activities to GDP may have declined from over 50% in the 1950's to only about 23% now, it has to be stressed that about 70% of our population still continues to be dependent on agriculture for gainful employment. Our economy is also still predominantly rural and there is imperative need for creating job opportunities outside agriculture. An expert who met us drew our attention to the fact that a special feature of China's economic policies in recent years has been the stress it has laid on generation of employment in non farm occupations in rural areas.

Rural development in general and agricultural development in particular calls for creation of outlets for provision of institutional credit for productive purposes. A conscious policy of augmenting the flow of institutional credit for agriculture has been pursued with vigour in post independent India. Recognising that cooperatives with their local knowledge and local leadership would seem to be the best agency for providing credit with mechanisms for monitoring end use of credit, Government and RBI have promoted cooperative movement on a big scale with access to special credit arrangements, some of them on concessional terms.

However, while cooperatives have made tremendous progress, they have failed to come up to the high expectations entertained of them. They are plagued by a variety of problems, - poor mobilization of local resources, ineffective leadership, poor monitoring of end use of credit and mounting overdues. The relatively dismal performance of cooperatives led the policy makers to look to commercial banks particularly the Public Sector Banks to step into the breach through their rural branches, which proliferated in the three decades following nationalisation.

Commercial banks did bring a new approach to bear on the provision of credit for agriculture with their superior material and human resources. Commercial banks, however, soon encountered problems of overdues and it was felt that their high cost structure could make them inappropriate agencies for purveying of rural credit on a dispersed basis. It was this realization which led to the setting up of Regional Rural Banks (RRBs) in 1976. These banks, in the share capital of which the Central and State Governments participated, were linked to a sponsor bank which also contributed to the extent of 35% of their share capital. These banks, which at the outset adopted lower scales of compensation for their staff than their sponsor banks, were specially mandated to lend to weaker sections at rates of interest with a concessional element.

They could initially manage to lend at concessional rates because of their access to subsidised refinance from their sponsor banks and NABARD. But the RRBs were crippled soon enough by several factors among which was a new compensation policy in pursuance of which they had to pay their employees on par with those of their sponsor banks. Their character as low cost institutions specially designed to serve rural areas was thus lost irretrievably. They were also adversely affected by the problems of mounting overdues and uneasy industrial relations.

It was presumably due to the set backs encountered in the channelisation of credit through cooperatives, rural branches of commercial banks and RRBs that the new concept of a Local Area Bank emerged. The concept was attractive in that it sought to involve local leadership in mobilization of local resources for profitable lending in a compact area. It sought to combine the kind of local knowledge presumed to be the special feature of cooperatives with the professional ethos of a commercial bank.

STRUCTURE & FUNCTIONS OF LOCAL AREA BANKS

Objective: In 1996 it was decided to allow the establishment of local banks in the private sector with the objective to bridge the gaps in credit availability and enhance the institutional credit framework in the rural and semi-urban areas and provide efficient and competitive financial intermediation services in their area of operation.

Capital: The minimum start-up capital of a LAB was fixed at Rs.5 crore. The promoters of these banks were required to bring in the entire minimum share capital up-front. It was also decided that a family among the promoter group could hold equity not exceeding 40% of the capital. The NRI contributions to the equity of the bank were not to exceed 40% of the paid-up capital. The entire initial capital subscribed by the promoters (including their friends and relatives/associates) would carry a lock in period of three years from the date of licensing of the bank. Further, the promoters' equity to the extent of 40% of the initial paid- up capital was to be locked in at least for two years beyond the aforesaid period of three years subject to review before expiry of five years from the date of licensing of the bank.

Promoters: The promoters of a LAB could be individuals, corporate entities and societies. The number of NRI promoters was not to exceed 20% of the total number of promoters.

Voting Rights: Individual shareholder voting rights were to be restricted to a ceiling of 10% of the total voting rights in terms of Section 12(2) of the Banking Regulation Act, 1949.

Area of Operation: The area of operation of an LAB was restricted to a maximum of three geographically contiguous districts. The activities of an LAB were to be focussed on local customers predominantly in rural and semi-urban areas so as to bridge the credit gap in these areas.

Scope of Activities: LABs were required to finance agriculture and allied activities, SSI, agro-industrial activities, trading activities and non-farm sector. Their lending to priority sector was to be at least 40% of the net bank credit and lending to weaker section was to be at least 25% of their priority sector lending (10% of net bank credit).

Registration, Licensing, Scheduling: The bank would be registered as a public limited company under the Companies

Act, 1956. It would be licensed under the Banking Regulation Act, 1949 and would be eligible for inclusion in the Second Schedule of the Reserve Bank of India Act, 1934.

Applicability of Statutes: The bank would be governed by the provisions of the Reserve Bank of India Act, 1934, the Banking Regulation Act, 1949 and other relevant statutes. However, in regard to liquidity requirements and interest rates, such banks would be governed by the provisions applicable to the Regional Rural Banks (RRBs) established under the Regional Rural Banks Act, 1976.

Prudential Norms: LABs would be subject to prudential norms, accounting policies and other policies as laid down by RBI. The bank would have to maintain capital adequacy at 8% of risk weighted assets and comply with the norms of income recognition, asset classification and provisioning since inception.

Licensing Procedure: As per the procedure followed in such cases the RBI granted an 'in- principle' approval for setting up a LAB which laid down the terms and conditions needed to be fulfilled by the promoters before a licence could be granted for commencement of banking business.

The RBI could, at its discretion, call for any additional information required by it or withdraw/cancel the 'in-principle' approval in the event of non compliance with the conditions laid down in the 'in -principle' approval

Status of LABs Functioning

Only four LABs are functioning at present. These are, Coastal Local Area Bank Ltd. established on 27th December 1999 with an area of operation comprising three contiguous districts viz. Krishna, Guntur and West Godavari with its head office at Vijayawada (Andhra Pradesh),

Capital Local Area Bank Ltd. established on 14th January 2000 with its area of operation comprising three districts viz. Jalandhar, Kapurthala and Hoshiarpur with its head office at Phagwara (Punjab), South Gujarat Local Area Bank Ltd., established on 3rd October 2000 with an area of operation comprising three contiguous districts viz. Navsari, Surat and Bharuch with its head office at Navsari (Gujarat),

Krishna Bhima Samruddhi Local Area Bank Ltd.established on 28th February 2001 with an area of operation comprising three contiguous districts of Mahbubnagar in Andhra Pradesh and Raichur and Gulbarga in the state of Karnataka with its head office at Mahbubnagar(Andhra Pradesh).

The licence of Vinayak Local Area Bank Ltd., Sikar (Rajastan) established on 21st October 2000 was cancelled by Reserve Bank on 16th January 2002 as major irregularities were noted in its functioning.

Branch Licensing

The LABs were allowed to open branches in only one urban centre per District and rest of the branches were allowed to be opened in the rural and semi urban centers subject to requisite clearance in respect of rural branches from the District Consultative Committee for the concerned districts.

Scheduling of LABs

The LABs could be included in the Second Schedule of the Reserve Bank of India Act, 1934 subject to the fulfillment of the eligibility criteria laid down in Section 42(6) of the said Act ibid.

Regulatory Jurisdiction

The regulatory responsibility over the LABs vests with Rural Planning and Credit Department (RPCD) of the RBI. The RPCD issues licence for these banks as per provisions of Section 22 of the Banking Regulation Act, 1949 and grants permission for opening of branches at new places of business as per the provisions of Section 23 of the Act ibid. The financial health of the LABs is monitored through off-site returns and other statements required to be submitted by these banks. The appointment of the CEO and the Chairman of the LAB requires clearance of the RBI as per the provisions of Section 10B of the Banking Regulation Act, 1949 read with Section 35B of the Act ibid. The remuneration of the CEO also requires prior approval of the RBI.

The composition of the Board of these banks is to be in accord with the provisions of Section 10A of the Banking

Regulation Act, 1949. As LABs are commercial banks in the private sector, banking policies as applicable to commercial banks are made applicable to them except where these pertain to areas of business which LABs are not permitted to undertake.

Supervision over LABs

Supervision over LABs lies with the Department of Banking Supervision (DBS). During the first year of its operation, the LAB is subjected to quarterly on-site supervisory monitoring visits. The quarterly visits cover areas such as examination of loans and investments, treasury functions, internal checks and controls so as to ensure that the affairs of the bank are not being conducted in a manner detrimental to the interests of the depositors.

Thereafter, the LAB is covered under Annual Financial Inspection (AFI) Programme of DBS. This covers areas such as management functions, functioning of Board of the bank and constitution of various committees of the Board, internal control system, internal audit and inspection, information system, deposit, advance and investment portfolio, NPAs, profitability, capital adequacy and maintenance of statutory norms as CRR and SLR.

An analysis about the functioning of LABs and about the report of the Review Group appointed by RBI in 2002 to study and make recommendations on the LAB Scheme are discussed in the next article.

Report of the Review Group for Local Area Bank Scheme

As no comprehensive review of the scheme had been made since the issuance of guidelines in 1996, the RBI appointed a Review Group in July 2002 under chairmanship of Mr.G.Ramachandran former finance secretary to study and make recommendations on the LAB Scheme.

Performances of LABs So far

As at end of 2002, the LABs have opened only 25 branches and of these only 7 were in rural areas. They are mostly operating in the already banked centers. The total volume of business handled was Rs. 153 crores as on 31st March 2002, and the bulk of the business was emanating from the district head-quarters, where the head offices of these banks were located. It is obvious that LABs have not made any impact on the local communities amongst whom they are functioning in terms of any of the significant indicators such as deposit mobilization, number of depositors, number of borrowal accounts and amounts lent, number of rural branches and number of poor people helped. LABs as now constituted and with their present capital base are unlikely to make themselves felt on the rural scene as any significant purveyors of credit in the foreseeable future.

In this context the Review Group has commented as under:

> *"In examining the working of the existing LABs, we cannot refrain from drawing attention to certain fundamental issues relating to the very concept of an LAB. We are strongly of the view that whether it is rural banking or any other segment of the financial sector, size, whether in terms of capital base or totality of operations as reflected in the balance sheets, is of critical importance. It is size which inspires and retains the confidence of depositors and borrowers alike. It is size of capital which enables a financial entity to cope with unexpected adverse trends in its business and overcome threats to its survival from any panic reaction on the part of its investors. LABs in our view fail to pass this critical test. Their initial capital being only Rs. 5 crores and the capital adequacy requirement being set at 8%, they are handicapped ab initio by the severe restrictions being imposed on their growth. They thus suffer from an inherent inability to absorb the losses which were bound to arise in the course of their business. We should remember that LABs have been mandated to lend to agriculture, priority sector and also weaker sections in the rural areas. The credit portfolio of an LAB will thus tend to be more risk prone than that of other banking institutions. In view of their size*

and location, they will not also be able to diversify and derisk their business model. Their inability to undertake other activities will also expose them to the risks of concentration. Further, since LABs depend on loan portfolio for their income and do not have diversified income stream, they have to necessarily expand their loan portfolio for generating income. This exposes them to the risk of adverse selection. It is true that none of the LABs has so far posted any non-performing assets. But this is no matter for comfort. The absence of non-performing assets is solely due to the fact that LABs are of recent origin and are not matured sufficiently. Even so, we noticed that stressed accounts are emerging in the books of one of the LABs. This LAB is also engaged in trading in securities income from which outstrips its net profit. Thus if its stressed assets become non-performing and the bank is unable to earn substantial income on its securities portfolio, there will be the worrisome prospect of the bank incurring losses. Given its narrow capital base, it will not take much time for the concerned bank to become weak and sick. There are thus fundamental weaknesses inherent in the business model of the LAB. These need to be addressed without delay. The irregularities noticed in the functioning of the existing LABs need to be dealt with quickly while initiating simultaneously measures to enable them grow on healthy lines and attain viability within a reasonable time frame. Keeping these objectives in view we make some recommendations in the following paragraphs."

The Review Group recommended a number of measures that "have to be undertaken to strengthen them and new norms of capital and capital adequacy have to be laid down if the few banks which have come into existence are to survive and grow." The summary of the recommendations of the group are as under:

Licensing of new LABs- Since the current LABs have only recently commenced functioning, some more time needs to be given to observe their performance and help given to overcome their weaknesses. We would urge that till these measures to strengthen the existing LABs are put through and the existing LABs are placed on a sound basis there should be no licensing of new LABs.

Capital base- LABs with their present capital base cannot become viable institutions. The existing LABs should be asked to reach net worth of at least Rs.25 crore over a period of five years.

Capital adequacy- LABs should also be enjoined to maintain a minimum capital adequacy of 15%. This should not be a problem for the present. A higher capital adequacy norm is being proposed because as pointed out earlier LABs carry an inherently high-risk portfolio and do not have derisking possibilities. The matrix proposed by us - a net worth of Rs. 25 crore and capital adequacy norm of 15% would enable LAB to build an asset base of about Rs.150 crore - a level at which their operations would become viable. Every one of the existing LABs should be asked to submit a suitable road map for achieving the twin objectives of higher capital base and enhanced capital adequacy norm (Para 3.18).

Trading in securities- Considering the risks involved, LABs should be prohibited from trading in Government securities and other papers during their formative years, say for a period of five years.

Engagement of agents- LABs should not be permitted to engage the services of agents and quasi agents for achieving their business outreach.

Arms length relationship- In view of the inherent weaknesses of LABs, great care has to be taken to ensure that no "Holding out" is done by the sponsoring agency and an arms length relationship is maintained with other group entities by the LAB.

Scheduling of LABs- It is too early to confer on LABs the status of a scheduled bank. Scheduling of LABs may be considered after they have reached higher capital and capital adequacy and after watching their performance for sometime.

Refinance- The absence of refinancing facility places the LABs under a serious handicap both in managing maturity mismatch and in their ability to lend at finer rates .We therefore suggest that though an LAB may not be "scheduled," it should not be denied access to refinance for its term lendings from NABARD and SIDBI.

However, as a precautionary measure we suggest that refinance should be permitted only in respect of such loans where at least one instalment repayable has been recovered by the LAB. Such a proviso would hopefully inculcate credit discipline among the LABs in the sanction of term loans and the refinance facility will not end up as a mere liquidity support.

Branch licensing- LABs should be treated on par with Cooperative Banks in the matter of opening of branches falling within their charter. Other restrictions should be waived and the opening of a branch should be subject only to the granting of a licence by the Reserve Bank of India.

Branch expansion- To enable LABs to expand their business and attain viability we recommend that after LABs have opened a certain minimum rural /semi urban branches, they could be licensed to open more urban branches. A ratio of one urban branch to 10 rural/ semi urban branches will perhaps be appropriate. While the first urban branch may be allowed to be opened at any time, the second urban branch should be permitted to be opened only after 20 rural/semi urban branches have been opened by the LAB concerned.

Regulation & Supervision- LABs need to be treated like any other commercial bank and therefore, regulation and supervision should be entrusted to the same wing of the Reserve Bank which is responsible for Regulation and Supervision of the commercial banks. The RPCD should be relieved of its responsibility of regulating LABs.

KISAN CREDIT CARD(KCC) SCHEME

Genesis

Hon'ble Union Finance Minister announced in his budget speech for 1998-99 that NABARD would formulate a Model scheme for issue of Kisan Credit Cards to farmers, on the basis of their land holdings, for uniform adoption by banks, so that the farmers may use them to readily purchase agricultural inputs such as seeds, fertilisers, pesticides, etc. and also draw cash for their production needs'.

NABARD formulated a Model Kisan Credit Card Scheme in consultation with major banks. Model Scheme circulated by RBI to commercial banks and by NABARD to Cooperative banks and RRBs in August 1998, with instructions to introduce the same in their respective area of operation.

Objectives

As a pioneering credit delivery innovation, Kisan Credit Card Scheme aims at provision of adequate and timely support from the banking system to the farmers for their cultivation needs including purchase of inputs in a flexible and cost effective manner.

Contents of Credit Card

Beneficiaries covered under the Scheme are issued with a credit card and a pass book or a credit card cum pass book incorporating the name, address, particulars of land holding, borrowing limit, validity period, a passport size photograph of holder etc., which may serve both as an identity card and facilitate recording of transactions on an ongoing basis.

Borrower is required to produce the card cum pass book whenever he/she operates the account.

Salient features of the Kisan Credit Card (KCC) Scheme

Eligible farmers to be provided with a Kisan Credit Card and a pass book or card-cum-pass book.

Revolving cash credit facility involving any number of drawals and repayments within the limit.

Limit to be fixed on the basis of operational land holding, cropping pattern and scale of finance. Entire production credit needs for full year plus ancillary activities related to crop production to be considered while fixing limit.

Sub-limits may be fixed at the discretion of banks.

Card valid for 3 years subject to annual review. As incentive for good performance, credit limits could be enhanced to take care of increase in costs, change in cropping pattern, etc.

Each drawal to be repaid within a maximum period of 12 months. Conversion/reschedulement of loans also permissible in case of damage to crops due to natural calamities.

Security, margin, rate of interest, etc. as per RBI norms.

Operations may be through issuing branch (and also PACS in the case of Cooperative Banks) through other designated branches at the discretion of bank.

Withdrawals through slips/cheques accompanied by card and passbook.

Advantages of the Kisan Credit Card Scheme

Advantages to farmers

Access to adequate and timely credit to farmers

Full year's credit requirement of the borrower taken care of.

Minimum paper work and simplification of documentation for drawal of funds from the bank.

Flexibility to draw cash and buy inputs.

Assured availability of credit at any time enabling reduced interest burden for the farmer.

Sanction of the facility for 3 years subject to annual review and satisfactory operations and provision for enhancement.

Flexibility of drawals from a branch other than the issuing branch at the discretion of the bank.

Benefits of the Scheme to the Banks

Reduction in work load for branch staff by avoidance of repeat appraisal and processing of loan papers under Kisan Credit Card Scheme.

Minimum paper work and simplification of documentation for drawal of funds from the bank.

Improvement in recycling of funds and better recovery of loans. Reduction in transaction cost to the banks.

Better Banker - Client relationships.

Refinance Support for ST(SAO) Loans disbursed under KCC Scheme

Operational Guidelines

SCBs/DCCBs and RRBs were advised operational guidelines governing provision of refinance for their ST(SAO) disbursements under the KCC Scheme vide Circular letter No. NB.PCD(OPR)/662/A137(Spl.)/99-2000 dt.26.05.99 and Circular letter No. NB.PCD(OPR)/662-A/A137(Spl.)/99-2000 dt. 26.05.99 respectively. The same are summarised below: instructions on computation of Demand, Collection and Balance (DCB) position, maintenance of Non-overdue Cover (NODC), financing of small/ marginal farmers, etc, conveyed in circular letter No.NB.PCD(OPR)/5980/A.135/90-91 dated 17 December 1990 addressed to RCS and in circular letter No.NB.PCD(OPR)/ 1271/ 334/95-96 dated 02 November 1995 addressed to RRBs will also be, mutatis mutandis, applicable for advances made under the KCC Scheme by SCBs/DCCBs and RRBs respectively. although under the KCC Scheme, production credit for SAO, advances for allied activities, non-farm activities and consumption purposes can be covered, only the production credit for SAO is eligible for refinance from NABARD under the ST(SAO) credit limits. Banks required to maintain separate details of sanctions and accounts for operations on credit limits for SAO purposes under the KCC Scheme to facilitate submission of drawal applications for obtaining refinance from NABARD in respect of eligible loans and reporting such loans in the monthly NODC statements for ST(SAO) loans and advances.

Short-term loans outstanding for financing ancillary activities relating to crop production such as maintenance of agricultural machinery/implements, electricity charges, etc. under the KCC Scheme also eligible for refinance from NABARD under ST(SAO) credit limits.

Applicable to Cooperatives only

Seasonality Discipline: In view of flexibility and discretion provided to the farmers in both drawals and repayments, it has been decided not to insist, for the present, on compliance with the seasonality discipline in respect of KCC accounts for the purpose of allowing drawals on the ST(SAO) credit limits.

Financing of Small Farmers(SF)/Marginal Farmers(MF): For compliance on financing of SF/MF, maximum outstanding under production credit for SAO reached in KCC accounts of such farmers during the year(April-March) would be reckoned as loans issued to SF/MF. Thus, for compliance in regard to coverage of SF/MF, the aggregate of maximum outstanding in KCC accounts of SF/MF as well as normal cash credit accounts together with the aggregate of crop loans issued to SF/MF under the normal loaning system, worked out as percentage to the maximum outstanding reached under all KCC (including normal Cash Credit) accounts and the total ST(SAO) loans issued during the year (April-March) will be reckoned.

Applicable to Both Cooperatives and RRBs: Computation of Demand, Collection and Balance (DCB) position: Maximum outstandings under ST(SAO) loans in KCC accounts reached during the year (July-June) be treated as demand, and outstandings in unrenewed KCC accounts may be reckoned as overdues. Percentage of overdues to demand calculated accordingly.

Maintenance of Non Overdue Cover(NODC): Outstanding in KCC accounts against PACS/Branches for financing SAO excluding amount outstanding under unrenewed KCC accounts will be reckoned as NODC for purpose of borrowings from NABARD. Thus, for purpose of working out the aggregate NODC for borrowings from NABARD for SAO, non-overdue short-term agricultural loans outstanding under normal loan accounts plus non-overdue outstanding under normal cash credit accounts and those under KCC Scheme will constitute NODC.

Coverage of Crop Loans disbursed under KCC under the Reshtriya Krishi Bima Yojna (RKBY)

GIC has agreed that the crop loans disbursed for eligible crops under the Crop Insurance Scheme will be covered under the CCIS, now under Rashtriya Krishi Bima Yojna. However, the banks are expected to maintain all back up records relating to compliance with "RKBY" and its seasonality discipline, cut-off date for submitting declarations and end use, etc. as in the case of normal crop loans.

Objectives of the Scheme : To provide insurance coverage and financial support to the farmers in the event of failure of crops as a result of natural calamities, pests and diseases.

To encourage farmers to adopt progressive farming practices, high value inputs and higher technology in agriculture. To help stabilise farm incomes, particularly in disaster years. To support and stimulate primarily production of food crops and oilseeds.

Farmers to be Covered: All farmers (both loanee and non-loanee irrespective of their size of holdings) including sharecroppers, tenant farmers growing insurable crops covered.

Sum Insured : The sum insured extends upto the value of threshold yield of the crop, with an option to cover upto 150% of average yield of the crop on payment of extra premium.

Premium Subsidy: 50% subsidy in premium allowed to Small and Marginal Farmers, to be shared equally by the Government of India and State Government/Union Territory. Premium subsidy to be phased out over a period of 5 years.

Future Agenda of the Scheme

Hon'ble Union Finance Minister in his Budget Speech for the year 2001-02 set the future agenda for the Scheme as under:

> *" The innovation of KCC is proved to be very successful. Since the year of its introduction in 1998-99, almost 110 lakh KC cards have been issued. I am asking our banks to accelerate this programme and cover all eligible agricultural farmers within the next 3 years .*
>
> *I am also asking the banks to provide a personal insurance package to the KCC holders as is often done with other credit cards to cover them against accidental death or permanent disability, upto*

maximum amount of Rs.50,000/ and Rs.25,000/- respectively. The premium burden will be shared by the card issuing institutions."

Coverage of Farmers - Future Strategy

Banks, vide our Circular letter No.NB.PCD(KCC)/29/ 2001-02 dated 10 April 2001, requested to draw up an action plan immediately in consultation with our Regional Office concerned, based on their past performance and experience in implementing the scheme, to ensure the coverage of all the eligible agricultural farmers under the KCC Scheme within the next three years i.e. by 31 March 2004.

Banks to ensure that targets fixed for 2001-02, 2002-03 and 2003-04 include new agricultural farmers likely to become eligible for their KC cards after 31 March 2001 also.

Targets fixed for issue of KC Cards be disaggregated month-wise and branch/PACS-wise to facilitate close monitoring of progress vis-a-vis target and also advised to RO concerned.

In order to ensure achievement of the targets so fixed, banks requested to follow strategies suggested by NABARD from time to time. Towards this end, banks to launch a campaign approach to accelerate pace of implementation of the Scheme. Following specific steps may be taken by the banks:

Conduct of Sensitisation/training programmes for the officers of controlling offices of banks, branch managers and field level functionaries as also district level functions for distribution of cards.

Holding Banker-Farmers' Meets, as part of the Kharif 2001 campaign, in each block to identify the ground level constraints in the smooth implementation of the Scheme and to initiate remedial measures therefor.

Use of VVV Clubs fora for propagation of the scheme.

Placement of hoardings/banners etc. at prominent places, such as branch premises, Panchayat buildings, Mandis, etc.

Use of audio-video media, bringing out KCC literature in local language to create better awareness about KCC Scheme among farmers. Issue of plastic/laminated cards to serve as Identity Cards.

Monitoring of progress in implementation of the Scheme in Board meetings as also through various state/ district and block level fora with the participation of Government functionaries, bankers, farmers etc.

Personal Accident Insurance Scheme -Salient Features

Designated insurance company will nominate one office at district level to function as nodal office for co-ordinating implementation of personal accident insurance scheme for KCC holders in the district. Nominated office of insurance company to issue a Master Insurance Policy to each DCCB/RRB covering all its KCC holders.

Premium payable Rs.15/- for a one year policy while Rs.45- for a 3-year policy. Insurance coverage available under Policy only from date of receipt of premium at insurance company.

Banks to ensure to incorporate name of Nominee in Kisan Credit Card-cum-Pass Book.

Simplified claim settlement procedure evolved under Scheme whereby an Enquiry-cum-Verification Committee comprising Branch Manager of implementing bank, Lead Bank Officer and representative of insurance company to certify nature of accident causing disability/death and recommend settlement of insurance claims.

Scheme covers risk of KCC holders against death or permanent disability resulting from accidents caused by external, violent and visible means, as under:

Death due to accident (within 12 months of the accident) caused by outward, violent and visible means -- Rs.50,000/

Permanent total disability -- Rs.50,000/-

Loss of two limbs or two eyes or one limb and one eye -- Rs.50,000/-

Loss of one limb or one eye -- Rs.25,000/-

(cover subject to certain exclusions as per Annexure-A to Master Policy document)

Major Steps taken by NABARD

A Brochure on KCC Scheme highlighting the salient features, advantages and other relevant information about the Scheme was brought out by Head Office and ROs were asked to circulate the brochure to State govt. departments, Commercial Banks, Cooperative Banks, RRBs and other concerned agencies/ officers so as to generate wider awareness about the Scheme.

Floor limit of Rs.5000/- for issue of KC Cards stands withdrawn.

Studies on KCC Scheme have been entrusted to BIRD and NABARD Staff College to facilitate feed back on the ground level issues/problems so that changes, where necessary, could be considered. Studies on the implementation of the Scheme undertaken by NABARD periodically.

Agency-wise KC Cards issued upto 31 March 2003 (since inception) (No. of cards)

Year	Cooperative Banks	RRBs	Commercial Banks	Total
1998-99	155353	6421	445451	607225
1999-00	3594869	173301	1365911	5134081
2000-01	5614445	648324	2389588	8652357
2001-02	5435859	833629	3071046	9340534
2002-03	4578923	963950	2067219*	7610092
Total	19379449	2625625	9339215	31344289

(*) data for commercial banks upto 31 December 2002.

On the lines of instructions of RBI to Commercial Banks, Cooperative Banks and RRBs have been advised that they may, at their discretion, pay interest at a rate based on their perception and other relevant factors on the minimum credit balances in the cash credit accounts under the Kisan Credit Cards of farmers during the period from 10th to the last day of each calendar month.

NABARD has prepared a Model Scheme for providing financial assistance for publicity campaign activities of Cooperative Banks under KCC Scheme under CDF with a view to speed up the pace of implementation of KCC Scheme.

Progress in implementation of the Scheme

Since launching in August 1998, around 2.38 crore Kisan Credit Cards issued upto 31 March 2002 by Cooperative Banks, Regional Rural Banks and Commercial Banks put together. Scheme implemented in all States and Union Territories (except Chandigarh, Daman & Diu and Dadra & Nagar Haveli) with all Cooperative Banks, RRBs and Commercial Banks participating. Agency-wise/State-wise progress in issue of cards by all banks during 2001-02 and since inception of Scheme.

9

MICRO FINANCE IN INDIA— AN OVERVIEW

Research studies conducted by NABARD during the early eighties showed that despite having an extremely wide network of rural bank branches which implemented specific poverty alleviation programmes that sought creation of self-employment opportunities through bank credit for almost two decades, a very large number of the poorest of the poor continued to remain outside the fold of the formal banking system.

These studies gave signals that the existing banking policies, systems and procedures, and deposit and loan products were perhaps not most suited to meet the immediate needs of the very poor. What they really needed was a better access to these services and products, rather than cheap subsidised credit.

Unique Features of Credit needs of Rural Poor

The priority of the rural poor was for consumption credit, savings, production credit and insurance, in that order. Consumption needs included credit for short periods for emergent needs.

The dividing line between consumption credit and production credit for the poor was gossamery. Consumption requirements were met by the informal sources at exploitative interest rates, as the poor borrowers were unable to offer to the banks any security for the small consumption loans.

Main constraint faced by banks in extending credit in small doses to poor borrowers was the high transaction cost in financing large numbers in small quantities.

The same constraint applied to provision of other financial services like small savings, where very small savers scattered in the rural areas were to be harnessed.

The Alternate Model - Micro Finance & its Easy Accessibility

Against this background, a need was felt for alternative policies, systems and procedures, savings and loan products, other complementary services, and new delivery mechanisms, which would fulfill the requirements of the poorest, especially of the women members of such households. The emphasis therefore was on improving the access of the poor to microFinance (mF) rather than just micro-credit. As a village based network of bank branches already existed, it focused not on creating alternate organisations, but on finding ways and means to improve the access of the poor to existing banking network.

The rural and semi-urban banking network in India includes about 33,000 branches of scheduled commercial banks, 14,500 branches of Regional Rural Banks and 92,000 Primary Agricultural Cooperative Societies. Many research studies, done in-house as well as sponsored to professional institutions, and some action research projects funded out of the Research and Development Fund of NABARD, led it to develop the Self Help Group [SHG] - Bank linkage model as the core strategy that could be used by the banking system in India for increasing their outreach to the poorest of the poor who were hitherto getting by-passed by them. The strategy involved forming small, cohesive and participative groups of the poor, encouraging them to pool their thrift regularly and using the pooled thrift to make small interest bearing loans to members, and in the process learning the nuances of financial discipline. Subsequently, bank credit also becomes available to the Group, to augment its resources for lending to its members. It needs to be emphasised that NABARD sees the promotion and bank linking of SHGs not as a credit programme but as part of an overall arrangement for providing financial services to the poor in a sustainable manner and also an empowerment process for the members of these SHGs. NABARD, however, also took a conscious decision to experiment with other successful strategies such as replicating Grameen. Starting with a NABARD led limited scale Pilot Project (with the support of the Central Bank of the country, i.e., Reserve Bank of India) in 1992 that aimed at promoting and financing 500 SHGs across the entire country, the SHG- bank linkage strategy has come a long way. The strategy includes financing of SHGs promoted by external facilitators like NGOs and government agencies, as also promotion of SHGs by banks themselves and financing SHGs indirectly where NGOs and similar organisations act as financial intermediaries as well.

Research Studies and Action research projects by NABARD resulted in evolution of the 'Self Help Groups (SHGs)- bank linkage model' as an appropriate mechanism. Other delivery modes include replication of Grameen, networking of NGOs, federations of SHGs, cooperatives, etc. Against the back cloth of different structures, diverse legal framework and varied approaches, the need for a national policy framework arose.

Task Force on Micro Finance

A High level Task Force on microFinance was constituted under the Chairmanship of Mr. Y. C. Nanda, Managing Director, NABARD. MicroFinance was defined by the Task Force as "provision of thrift, credit and other financial services and products of very small amounts to the poor in rural, semi-urban or urban areas for enabling them to raise their income levels and improve living standards".

SHIFT TO THE NEW PARADIGM

The Poor

Perceived thrift as their strength as also as the bonding factor among themselves. Realised that timely and adequate credit was preferable and productive than subsidies and doles.

They needed hassle-free delivery mechanisms.

NGOs

Acted as catalysts of change. Combined social and economic agenda with synergistic effect. Recognised sustainability as the core factor in development.

Banking System

Accepted SHG-bank linkage as a cost effective means of reaching the poor. Accepted peer pressure as collateral substitute for excellent recovery of loans.

Government

Formulated supportive policy framework. Encouraged routing of social programmes through SHGs.

Reserve Bank of India

RBI policy inputs on micro Finance led to increased involvement of banks. Liberalised interest rates and deregulated interest rate structure for micro credit, leading to flexibility in lending rates.

NABARD

Provided inputs in capacity building for banks and partner agencies. Promoted the idea of organising thrift and credit groups among the NGOs as an add-on activity and encouraged linking them with banks. Provided loanable funds to banks and financial support to eligible mFIs, to ease the fund flow position to the sector.

Micro Finance - NABARD's Vision and Mission

Vision

Empowerment of rural poor by improving their access to the formal credit system through various mF innovations in a cost effective and sustainable manner.

Mission

To extend financial services to one third of India's unreached and underserved rural poor numbering nearly 100 million through one million SHGs with focus on women during a ten year period through various microFinance interventions

Micro Finance- NABARD's Strategy

Overall Strategy

Forming and nurturing small, homogeneous and participatory self help groups (SHGs) of the poor has today emerged as a potent tool for human development. This process enables the poor, especially the women from the poor households, to collectively identify and analyse the problems they face in the perspective of their social and economic environment. It helps them to pool their meagre resources, human and financial, and prioritise their use for solving their own problems.

The emphasis on regular thrift collection and its use to solve immediate problems of consumption and production not only helps to meet their most urgent needs, but trains them to handle larger financial resources more skillfully, prudently and with a more lasting impact.

The SHGs have also become a forum for many social sector interventions.

SHG-Bank Linkage Programme

The availability of bank loan to the group helps fulfill their needs further. SHG-Bank Linkage Programme has proved to be the major supplementary credit delivery system with wide acceptance by banks, NGOs and various government departments.

Region-specific Initiatives

NABARD has intensified its efforts in identifying potential districts in the Southern Region and for enlarging its partner spread.

The coverage of districts/ partners in Western and Northern Regions are being widened.

Priority has been assigned to awareness- building and for identification of NGOs and other partners in Eastern and North Eastern Regions.

Capacity Building Initiatives

Sensitisation of senior executives of commercial banks and Chairmen of RRBs have been taken up by NABARD.

Under the direct training programme for staff of banks/ NGOs, over 25,000 field level functionaries have already been trained by NABARD. NABARD provides training inputs on SHG financing to training establishments of participating banks, to help them to internalise the training requirements at their level.

NABARD gives technical support to banks to evolve suitable intermediate structures like Farmers' Clubs (Vikas Volunteer Vahini Programme of the National Bank) to increase the outreach of their branches in promotion and linking SHGs

NABARD supports and helps banking institutions (especially RRBs) to take on the role of Self Help Promoting Institutions (SHPIs)

Support to Governments

Necessary assistance is provided to the governments by NABARD for dovetailing mF practices with the poverty alleviation programmes

NABARD also encourages the association of Panchayati Raj Institutions (PRIs) in adopting group processes for maximisation of empowerment.

Support to NGO Partners

Several steps have been taken by NABARD for capacity building of NGOs which partner in promotion and nurturing of SHGs. The emphasis is on involving a large number of NGOs. Special focus is on those NGOs participating in watershed development, health, literacy and women development, to encourage them to take up promotion, nurturing and linkage of SHGs as an 'add-on' activity.

NABARD has a scheme of part-financing the cost of promotion of groups by NGOs.

Alternate Micro Finance Practices

The NGOs and other local bodies at village, block and district levels in the North Eastern States are encouraged to take up alternative micro-credit delivery mechanisms through direct funding.

Formation and operation of SHG Federations is supported and encouraged by NABARD. Similarly, networking of NGOs is also encouraged.

Policy and Regulatory Initiatives

The recommendations of the Task Force on microFinance are being followed up and implemented, to spawn a supportive and conducive policy mechanism for sustained growth of mF initiatives in India. These steps include facilitating emergence of standards for Micro Finance in India, Supporting graduation of Micro Finance - NGOs to pure Micro Finance Institutions, etc..

Coordinating Micro Finance Efforts in India

NABARD coordinates the mF activities in India at international/ national/state/district levels. These include organising international/national Workshops, Seminars, etc for experience sharing, Organising National and State level Meets of Bankers and NGOs, etc..

Monitoring and Review

Block/district/state level review meetings are organised and/ or organised by NABARD. The relative documentation and data base is also carried out by NABARD. In addition, periodical Monitoring studies are conducted through NABARD/Bank Officers.

10

INDIAN BANKING REFORM

Since financial reforms were launched in 1991, there have been several favorable changes in India's highly regulated and repressed banking sector. This paper assesses the results by examining (1) whether India's gradual approach to the privatization of dominant public sector banks has been successful, (2) what factors have contributed to improving the performance of the banking sector, and (3) whether foreign and private domestic banks perform differently from public sector banks.

This paper shows that public sector banks have become more profitable and cost-efficient in the reform period; while diversification into nontraditional activities has improved the performance of the banking sector as a whole, investment in government securities has had the opposite effect; and foreign and private domestic banks performed better than public sector banks initially, but their differences have diminished over time.

INTRODUCTION

Strengthening financial systems has been one of the central issues facing emerging markets and developing economies. This is because sound financial systems serve as an important channel for achieving economic growth through the mobilization of financial savings, putting them to productive use, and transforming various risks (Beck, Levin and Loayza [1999], King and Levin [1993]), Rajan and Zingales [1998], Demirigüç-Kunt and Maksimovic [1998]), Jayaratne and Strahan [1996]). In this context, many countries adopted a series of financial sector liberalization measures in the late 1980s and early 1990s, which included interest rate liberalization, entry deregulations, reduction of reserve requirements, and removal of credit allocation.

In many cases, the timing of financial sector liberalization coincided with that of capital account liberalization; domestic banks were given access to cheap loans from abroad and allocated those resources to domestic production sectors.

Since the Asian financial crisis of 1997-1999, the importance of balancing financial liberalization with adequate regulation and supervision prior to full capital account liberalization has been increasingly recognized. The crisis was preceded by massive, unhedged, short-term capital inflows, which then aggravated double mismatches (a currency mismatch coupled with a maturity mismatch) and undermined the soundness of the domestic financial sector. A maturity mismatch is generally inherent in the banking sector, since commercial banks accept short-term deposits and convert them into relatively longer-term, often illiquid, assets.

Nevertheless, massive, predominantly short-term capital inflows— largely in the form of inter-bank loans—shortened banks' liabilities, thus expanding the maturity mismatch. Further, a currency mismatch was aggravated, since massive capital inflows denominated in foreign currency were converted into domestic currency in order to finance the cyclical upturn of domestic investment in manufacturing equipment, real estate, and stocks (Asian Policy Forum and [2000] and Yoshitomi and Shirai [2000]).

In other words, many share the view that the proper sequencing of financial sector and capital account liberalization is one of the most important policies in preventing another Asian-type "capital account" crisis. It is now widely accepted that capital account liberalization should follow current account and domestic financial sector liberalization (Mckinnon [1973]). This sequence issue is even more important for countries such as the People's Republic of China and India, which have not yet launched full capital account convertibility and where public sector banks still remain dominant. In such countries, financial sector liberalization comes against more politically difficult issues than those that have already opened up their capital account to a substantial degree, since they have to first restructure predominant public sector banks.

This chapter focuses on India's banking sector, which has been attracting increasing attention since 1991, when a financial reform program was launched. It assesses whether the reform program has been successful so far in restructuring public sector banks and if so, what elements of the program have contributed. This paper tackles the following fundamental questions. In what way has the reform program affected the behavior of public sector banks? To what extent have foreign and new domestic banks contributed to the performance of the whole banking sector? Has India's gradual approach to the privatization of banks been successful? What policy implications can we derive from India's experience?

Table 1: Performance of the Banking Sector: 1993–2000

ROAA	1993	1994	1995	1996	1997	1998	1999	2000
All Banks	-0.1	0.1	1.1	0.8	1.1	1.0	0.5	0.4
Foreign	2.0	2.0	2.0	1.6	1.6	1.1	0.4	-0.2
Private	-0.2	0.5	1.2	1.2	1.3	1.1	0.7	1.0
Public Sector	-1.3	-2.3	0.1	-0.4	0.4	0.8	0.4	0.6
COST								
All Banks	81.5	78.4	82.6	162.7	84.8	76.8	83.8	78.3
Foreign	67.7	60.9	80.7	308.1	87.2	68.6	81.2	72.4
Private	86.4	83.9	80.3	80.1	80.5	80.1	85.0	80.0
Public Sector	93.8	92.2	87.3	88.1	86.7	84.9	86.6	85.3
$INCOME_1$								
All Banks	12.4	11.5	10.4	11.6	12.0	12.1	11.4	11.2
Foreign	14.5	12.9	12.1	13.2	13.3	13.8	12.3	12.5
Private	11.2	10.1	8.7	11.0	11.4	11.4	11.0	10.4
Public Sector	10.9	11.1	10.7	10.6	10.9	10.7	10.4	10.2
$INCOME_2$								
All Banks	7.6	7.3	5.0	5.5	6.3	5.8	5.3	4.0
Foreign	12.9	9.1	7.1	5.1	6.3	6.8	6.9	4.3

Private	5.2	7.6	3.9	5.1	6.5	5.6	4.2	3.7
Public Sector	3.5	5.1	4.1	6.4	6.3	4.7	4.2	3.6
DIVERSE								
All Banks	1.3	1.2	1.2	1.2	1.4	2.1	1.4	1.6
Foreign	1.8	1.6	1.4	1.5	1.9	3.2	2.0	2.1
Private	1.0	0.9	1.0	1.1	1.1	1.5	1.0	1.3
Public Sector	1.1	1.1	1.1	1.1	1.1	1.1	1.0	1.1
GBOND								
All Banks	20.4	23.8	20.7	19.1	21.3	22.0	23.3	24.3
Foreign	19.5	24.4	20.5	16.3	18.0	19.4	21.6	22.4
Private	21.0	20.5	17.5	17.5	20.6	21.2	22.0	23.5
Public Sector	21.1	25.8	24.6	24.6	26.9	26.6	27.4	28.0
PROV								
All Banks	2.4	2.3	1.5	1.1	0.8	1.2	1.5	1.7
Foreign	3.8	3.0	2.3	0.9	0.8	1.9	2.7	3.0
Private	1.1	1.0	1.2	1.0	0.7	0.8	0.5	0.7
Public Sector	1.8	2.6	1.2	1.6	0.9	0.8	0.8	0.7
EQUITY								
All Banks	4.1	4.6	8.7	13.6	14.4	13.3	13.6	11.4
Foreign	6.8	7.9	17.4	25.0	28.4	25.2	25.4	20.3
Private	1.7	2.2	3.6	3.3	4.0	4.8	4.4	4.2
Public Sector	3.2	3.4	5.3	10.0	6.5	6.0	5.8	5.7

Source: PROWESS Database, Center for Monitoring Indian Economy Pvt. Ltd.

Note: All indicators are estimated from PROWESS Database with the available data.Main Issues and Hypothesis

India's Pre-Reform Period and Financial Reform

Since 1991, India has been engaging in banking sector reforms, which aimed to increase the profitability and efficiency of the then 27 public sector banks that controlled about 90% of all deposits, assets, and credit. The reforms were initiated in the middle of a "current account" crisis that occurred in early 1991. The crisis was caused by poor macroeconomic performance, characterized by a public deficit of 10% of gross domestic product (GDP), a current account deficit of 3% of GDP, inflation rate of 10%, and growing domestic and foreign debt, and was triggered by a temporary oil price boom following the Iraqi invasion of Kuwait in 1990.

Prior to the reforms, India's financial sector had long been characterized as highly regulated and financially repressed. The prevalence of reserve requirements, interest rate controls, and allocation of financial resources to priority sectors increased the degree of financial repression and adversely affected the country's financial resource mobilization and allocation.

After Independence in 1947, the Government took the view that loans extended by colonial banks were biased toward working capital for trade and large firms (Joshi and Little [1996]). Moreover, it was perceived that banks should be utilized to assist India's planned development strategy by mobilizing financial resources to strategically important sectors.

Reflecting these views, all large private banks were nationalized in two stages: the first in 1969 and the second in 1980. Subsequently, quantitative loan targets were imposed on these banks to expand their networks in rural areas and they were directed to extend credit to priority sectors. These nationalized banks were then increasingly used to finance fiscal deficits. Although non-nationalized private banks and foreign banks were allowed to coexist with public sector banks at that time, their activities were highly restricted through entry regulations and strict branch licensing policies. Thus, their activities remained negligible. In the period 1969-1991, the number of banks increased slightly, but savings were successfully mobilized in part because relatively low inflation kept negative real interest rates at a mild level and in part because the number of branches was encouraged to expand rapidly. Nevertheless, many banks remained unprofitable, inefficient, and unsound owing to their poor lending strategy and lack of internal risk management under government ownership. Joshi and Little (1996) have reported that the average return on assets in the second half of the 1980s was only about 0.15%, while capital and reserves averaged about 1.5% of assets. Given that global accounting standards were not applied, even these indicators are likely to have exaggerated banks' true performance.

Table 2: Testing the Differential Behavior between Public Sector and Foreign and Private Banks

	Foreign Banks vs. Public Sector Banks	Private Banks vs. Public Sector Banks		Foreign Banks vs. Public Sector Banks	Private Banks vs. Public Sector Banks
1993			**1997**		
ROA	4.213***	0.951	ROA	3.875***	3.537***
COST	-6.435***	-1.865*	COST	0.037	-2.745***
INCOME[1]	3.704***	0.301	INCOME[1]	1.414*	0.245
INCOME[2]	5.128***	1.274	INCOME[2]	-0.066	0.455
PROV	2.487**	-1.945**	PROV	-0.288	-1.812*
EQUITY	9.688***	1.469*	EQUITY	-0.008	0.263
1994			**1998**		
ROA	4.390***	2.637***	ROA	0.295	1.270
COST	-9.475***	-2.169*	COST	-5.456***	-2.266**
INCOME[1]	1.565*	-0.821	INCOME[1]	4.854***	1.089
INCOME[2]	3.957*	0.976	INCOME[2]	2.116*	2.861***
PROV	0.674	-3.785***	PROV	1.559	-0.184
EQUITY	4.435***	2.599***	EQUITY	0.541	1.436*
1995			**1999**		
ROA	6.684***	2.852***	ROA	0.057	1.355
COST	-0.530	-2.008**	COST	-0.835	-0.853
INCOME[1]	1.255	-1.694**	INCOME[1]	3.087***	0.967
INCOME[2]	4.392***	-0.395	INCOME[2]	2.615**	0.047
PROV	3.899***	0.037	PROV	1.608*	-2.008**
EQUITY	0.639	-0.231	EQUITY	0.687	0.025
1996			**2000**		
ROA	3.704***	2.870***	ROA	-1.299	2.361**
COST	0.971	-2.950***	COST	-4.127***	-2.797***
INCOME[1]	1.297	0.188	INCOME[1]	3.020***	0.351
INCOME[2]	-1.161	-1.637*	INCOME[2]	0.630	0.557
PROV	-2.024**	-2.026**	PROV	3.159***	0.065
EQUITY	-0.225	-0.461	EQUITY	0.273	0.234

Source: PROWESS Database, Center for Monitoring Indian Economy Pvt. Ltd.

Note: The values reported are t-test values and *, **, *** indicate significance at 10%, 5 % and 1% significance level respectively.

Further, in 1992/93, non-performing assets (NPAs) of 27 public sector banks amounted to 24% of total credit, only 15 public sector banks achieved a net profit, and half of the public sector banks faced negative net worth. Major factors that contributed to deteriorating bank performance included: (1) too stringent regulatory requirements (i.e., a cash reserve requirement [CRR] and statutory liquidity requirement [SLR] that required banks to hold a certain amount of government and eligible securities); (2) low interest rates charged on government bonds (as compared with those on commercial advances); (3) directed and concessional lending; (4) administered interest rates; and (5) lack of competition.

These factors not only reduced banks' incentives to operate properly, but also undermined regulators' incentives to prevent banks from taking risks via incentive-compatible prudential regulations and protect depositors with a well- designed deposit insurance system.

While government involvement in the financial sector can be justified at the initial stage of economic development, the prolonged presence of excessively large public sector banks often results in inefficient resource allocation and concentration of power in a few banks.

Further, once entry deregulation takes place, it will put newly established private banks as well as foreign banks in an extremely disadvantageous position. Against this background, the first wave of financial liberalization took place in the second half of the 1980s, mainly taking the form of interest rate deregulation. Prior to this period, almost all interest rates were administered and influenced by budgetary concerns and the degree of concessionality of directed loans.

To preserve some profitability, interest rate margins were kept sufficiently large by keeping deposit rates low and non-concessional lending rates high. Based on the 1985 report of the Chakravarty Committee, coupon rates on government bonds were gradually increased to reflect demand and supply conditions. Following the 1991 report of the Narasimham Committee, more comprehensive reforms took place that same year. The reforms consisted of (1) a shift of banking sector supervision from intrusive micro-level intervention over credit decisions toward prudential regulations and supervision, (2) a reduction of the CRR and SLR, (3) interest rate and entry deregulation, and (4) adoption of prudential norms.

Table 3: Concentration Indicators: 1993 – 2000

M-Bank Concentration Ratio	1993	1994	1995	1996	1997	1998	1999	2000
1 bank concentration Ratio	24.7	24.3	22.0	22.2	21.9	21.7	23.7	24.2
5 banks concentration Ratio	50.2	48.5	47.3	47.4	46.9	46.7	47.7	48.1
10 banks concentration ratio	65.4	63.3	63.6	65.5	64.4	63.4	64.2	65.0
Herfindahl Index								
All Banks	11.2	9.9	7.9	7.2	6.6	6.5	7.1	7.0
Foreign Banks	14.1	12.6	11.5	11.9	10.8	10.9	11.7	12.2
Private Banks	11.3	10.8	7.8	5.8	4.8	4.6	4.8	5.2
Public Sector Banks	15.1	13.4	10.7	9.8	9.4	9.4	10.1	10.1

Source: PROWESS Database, Center for Monitoring Indian Economy Pvt. Ltd.

Note: All indicators are estimated from PROWESS Database with the available data.

Further, in 1992, the Reserve Bank of India (RBI) issued guidelines for income recognition, asset classification and provisioning, and also adopted Basle Accord capital adequacy standards. The Government also established the Board of Financial Supervision in the RBI and recapitalized public sector banks in order to give banks sufficient financial strength and enable them to gain access to the capital markets. In 1993, the RBI permitted private entry into the banking sector, provided that new banks are well capitalized and technologically advanced, and at the same time prohibited cross-holding practices with industrial groups.

The RBI also imposed some restrictions on new banks with respect to opening branches, with a view to maintaining the franchise value of existing banks. As a result of the reforms, the number of banks increased rapidly. In 1991, there were 27 public sector banks and 26 domestic private banks with 60,000 branches, 24 foreign banks with 140 branches, and 20 foreign banks with a representative office.

Table 4: Regression Results of Public Sector Banks

EXPLANATORY VARIABLES	DEPENDENT VARIABLES		
	ROAA	COST	$INCOME_1$
Constant	-4.67 (-1.47)	119.91*** (10.15)	9.15** (2.43)
Time93	-1.87*** (-2.75)	9.65*** (4.16)	0.62 (0.84)
Time94	-2.67*** (-4.87)	5.55*** (2.68)	0.82 (1.24)
Time95	-0.38 (-0.72)	1.83 (0.91)	0.33 (0.51)
Time96	-0.85 (-1.63)	2.69 (1.37)	0.19 (0.31)
Time97	0.13 (0.27)	-0.05 (-0.02)	0.7 (1.16)
Time98	0.24 (0.51)	-0.14 (-0.07)	0.36 (0.61)
Time99	-0.04 (-0.09)	0.23 (0.13)	0.38 (0.66)
DIVERSE	1.24*** (3.12)	-10.92*** (-7.33)	2.27*** (4.77)
GBOND	-0.08*** (-3.18)	0.66*** (6.59)	0.004 (0.12)
PRIORITY	0.07** (2.48)	-0.49*** (-4.34)	-0.008 (-0.24)
PUBLIC	0.03 (1.08)	-0.15 (-1.45)	-0.03 (-0.91)
SIZE	0.32 (1.55)	-2.18*** (-2.84)	-0.09 (-0.38)
R^2	0.36	0.53	0.14

Note: *** indicates significant at 1% significance level
** indicates significant at 5% significance level
* indicates significant at 10% significance level

Between January 1993 and March 1998, 24 new private banks (nine domestic and 15 foreign) entered the market; the total number of scheduled commercial banks, excluding specialized banks such as the Regional Rural Banks rose from 75 in 1991-1992 to 99 in 1997-1998. Entry deregulation was accompanied by progressive deregulation of interest rates on deposits and advances.

From October 1994, interest rates were deregulated in a phased manner and by October 1997, banks were allowed to set interest rates on all term deposits of maturity of more than 30 days and on all advances exceeding Rs200,000. While the

CRR and SLR, interest rate policy, and prudential norms have always been applied uniformly to all commercial banks, the RBI treated foreign banks differently with respect to the regulation that requires a portion of credit allocated to priority sectors. In 1993, foreign banks—which used to be exempted from this requirement while all other commercial banks were required to earmark 40% of credit—were required to allocate 32% of credit to priority sectors.

Table 5: Regression Results of the Whole Banking Sector

EXPLANATORY VARIABLES	DEPENDENT VARIABLES		
	ROAA	COST	$INCOME_1$
Constant	0.49 (0.46)	273.52** (2.28)	6.49*** (3.49)
Foreign	0.79** (2.05)	-60.36 (-1.36)	2.65*** (3.87)
Domestic	0.96*** (3.02)	-60.48 (-1.63)	0.58 (1.01)
Time93	-0.62 (-1.24)	3.22 (0.07)	1.69** (2.29)
Time94	-0.14 (-0.36)	-17.46 (-0.39)	0.64 (0.92)
Time95	0.72** (2.01)	4.18 (0.098)	0.14 (0.22)
Time96	0.25 (0,74)	100.99** (2.47)	1.27** (2.01)
Time97	0.67** (2.07)	13.87 (0.36)	1.44** (2.39)
Time98	0.30 (0.97)	15.70 (0.41)	0.82 (1.37)
Time99	0.12 (0.37)	8.32 (0.22)	0.62 (1.05)
DIVERSE	0.36*** (4.98)	-17.38** (-2.09)	0.79*** (6.20)
GBOND	-0.08*** (-5.46)	7.71*** (4.89)	0.08*** (3.29)
PRIORITY	-0.003 (-0.31)	-1.61* (-1.83)	-0.003 (-0.21)
PUBLIC	0.014 (0.99)	0.199 (0.12)	-0.04* (-1.74)
AGE	-0.23 (-0.93)	16.91 (0.59)	-0.77* (-1.73)
SIZE	0.08 (0.92)	-34.83*** (-3.56)	0.11 (0.71)
R^2	0.15	0.07	0.17

Note: *** indicates significant at 1% significance level

** indicates significant at 5% significance level

* indicates significant at 10% significance level

DRASTIC VERSUS GRADUAL PRIVATIZATION APPROACH

While India's financial reforms have been comprehensive and in line with global trends, one unique feature is that, unlike with other former planned economies such as Hungary, Poland, and Russia, the Indian Government did not engage in a drastic privatization of public sector banks. Rather, it chose a gradual approach toward restructuring these banks by enhancing competition through entry deregulation of foreign and domestic banks. This reflects the view of the Narasimham Committee that ensuring integrity and autonomy of public sector banks is the more relevant issue and thatthey could improve profitability and efficiency without changing their ownership if competition is enhanced.

Since this approach was introduced, some criticisms have been expressed (Joshi and Little [1996]).

First, public sector banks continue to be dominant thanks to their better branch coverage, customer base, and knowledge of the market compared with newcomers.

Second, public sector banks would find it more difficult to reduce personnel expenditure because of the strong trade unions.

Third, the Government would find it difficult to accept genuine competition within public sector banks. In response to these concerns, the Government decided to gradually expand private sector equity holdings in public sector banks, but still avoided the transformation of their ownership.

The 1994 amendment of the Banking Act allowed banks to raise private equity up to 49% of paid-up capital. Consequently, public sector banks, which used to be fully owned by the Government prior to the reform, were now allowed to increase non-government ownership. So far, only eight public sector banks out of 27 have diversified ownership.

Meanwhile, a consensus is emerging that state ownership of banks is bad for financial sector development and growth (World Bank [2001]). Based on data of the 10 largest commercial and development banks in 92 countries for 1970-1995, La Porta et al. (2000) have found that greater state ownership of banks in 1970 was associated with less financial sector development, lower growth, lower productivity, and that these effects were greater at lower levels of income. Barth et al. (2001a, 2001b) have shown that greater state ownership of banks tends to be associated with higher interest rate spreads, less private credit, less activity on the stock exchange, and less nonbank credit, even after taking into account other factors that could influence financial development.

This suggests that greater state ownership tends to be anticompetitive, reducing competition both from banks and nonbanks. Barth et al. have also noted that applications for bank licenses are more often rejected and there are fewer foreign banks when state ownership is greater. Moreover, Caprio and Martinez-Peria (2000) have shown that greater state ownership at the start of 1980-1997 was associated with a greater probability of a banking crisis and higher fiscal costs.

With respect to privatizing banks, moreover, the World Bank (2001) takes the view that privatization can yield real benefits to economies provided that an appropriate accounting, legal, regulatory infrastructure is in place. It should be noted that premature privatization may give rise to banking crises.

Clarke and Cull (1998) have demonstrated that Argentina promoted privatization of public sector banks in a reasonably developed regulatory and infrastructure environment, and thus, privatized banks improved productivity remarkably. Considering the implications derived from the above studies, this paper examines whether India's gradual approach has been successful so far by examining whether public sector (commercial) banks have improved their performance (profitability, efficiency, and soundness) in the reform period.

This paper adopts two hypotheses in this regard. The first hypothesis (H1) is that the degree of concentration in the banking sector has been declining in the reform period. The second hypothesis (H2) is that the performance of public sector banks may have deteriorated initially during the adjustment period, but performance improved later on. This paper adopts three types of performance indicators: (1) profitability, (2) cost efficiency, and (3) earnings efficiency.

It tests this hypothesis by analyzing trend patterns and empirically testing the performance of public sector banks.

DIVERSIFICATION OF BANKING ACTIVITIES

The second unique feature of India's banking sector is that the RBI has permitted commercial banks to engage in diverse activities such as securities-related transactions (e.g., underwriting, dealing, and brokerage), foreign exchange transactions, leasing activities, etc. The 1991 reforms lowered the CRR and SLR, enabling banks to diversify their activities. Diversification of banks' activities can be justified for at least five reasons.

First, entry deregulation and resultant intensified competition may leave banks with no choice but to engage in risk-taking activities in the fight for their market shares or profit margins. As a result, risk-taking would reduce the value of banks' future earnings and associated incentives to avoid bankruptcy (Allen and Gale [2000]).

Second, banks need to obtain implicit rents in order to provide discretionary, repetitive, and flexible loans.

Also, banks attempt to reduce the extent of information asymmetry by processing inside information on their clients and monitoring their performance. Such roles are unique to the banking system and important particularly for small and medium enterprises (SMEs), since information on them tends to be highly idiosyncratic. Without sufficient rents, however, banks are likely to cease providing these services and the implication for SMEs and economic development can be enormous. Thus, it is important for bank regulators to ensure adequate implicit rents to banks in order to encourage them to provide such unique services. Moreover, banks may lose an opportunity to collect implicit rents if their clients switch to capital markets once they become larger and profitable.

Diversification of banking activities helps banks to mitigate the two problems raised above by providing them with an opportunity to gain non-interest income and thereby sustain profitability. This enables banks to maintain long-term relationships with clients throughout their life cycles and gives them an incentive to process inside information and monitor their clients.

Third, banks can stabilize their income by engaging in activities whose returns are imperfectly correlated, thereby reducing costs of funds and thus lending and underwriting costs.

Fourth, diversification promotes efficiency by allowing banks to utilize inside information arising out of long-term lending relationships.

Thanks to this advantage, banks are able to underwrite securities at lower costs than nonbank underwriters. Also, firms may obtain higher prices on their securities underwritten by banks because of their perceived monitoring advantages. Further, banks can exploit economies of scope from the production of various financial services, since they can spread fixed physical (i.e., branches and distribution channels) and human capital costs (Steinherr and Huveneers [1990].

Fifth, diversification may improve banks' performance through diluting the impact of direct lending (through requiring banks to allocate credit to priority sectors). Direct lending reduces banks' incentives to conduct information processing and monitoring functions. As a result, this not only lowers banks' profitability by limiting financial resources available to more productive usages, but also results in a deterioration of efficiency and soundness by discouraging banks from functioning properly.

These five advantages, however, can be offset by the following disadvantages.

First, public sector banks' engagement in securities business may promote a concentration of power in the banking sector, since the asset size of banks expands. This is partly because banks have a natural tendency to promote lending over securities, thereby indirectly deterring the development of capital markets. Further, the reputation and informational advantages enjoyed by public sector banks put them in an even more favorable position, preventing other banks and investment firms from competing on a level playing field.

Second, banks' engagement in underwriting services may lead to conflicts of interest between banks and investors. Banks may decide to underwrite securities for troubled borrowers so that the proceeds of the issue of securities can be used to pay off these banks' own claims to the companies. Banks may dump into the trust accounts they manage the unsold part of the securities they underwrite. Further, banks may impose tie-in deals on customers by using their lending relationships with firms to pressure them to purchase their underwriting services (e.g., using the threat of increased credit costs or non-renewal of credit lines). Banks may also use the confidential inside information that they possess when they underwrite firms' securities in a way that the firms do not contemplate, such as disclosing the information directly or indirectly to the firms' competitors.

Third, diversification may expose banks to various new risks. For example, banks may end up buying the securities they underwrite. They may also face greater market risks as they increase their share of securities holdings and market making activities. Further, derivatives involve higher speed and greater complexity, which may reduce the solvency and transparency of banking operations.

The presence of these three potential disadvantages suggests that measures are needed to balance the advantages and disadvantages. The RBI tries to cope with the disadvantages by encouraging banks to engage in securities business through subsidiaries, thereby putting in place firewalls between traditional banking and securities services.

Also, the RBI prohibits cross-holdings with industrial groups to minimize "connected lending"—one of the causes of the East Asian crisis.

To assess the overall impact of banks' activities, this paper examines whether diversification improves bank performance. In particular, the impact of disadvantages can be assessed indirectly by examining how soundness is associated with diversification. It is also important to examine whether diversification has led to even greater dominance of public sector banks by examining whether banks' asset portfolios differ between public sector and private banks. This paper examines the following three hypotheses with respect to diversification. The first hypothesis (H3) is that banks' engagement in foreign exchange and securities business improves their performance. The second hypothesis (H4) is that investment in government securities has worsened banks' performance, since it limits the realization of the diversification effect. The last hypothesis (H5) is that lending to priority sectors and the public sector has lowered banks' performance.

IMPACT OF FOREIGN AND PRIVATE DOMESTIC BANKS

One interesting feature of India's banking sector is that some large public sector banks appear to have been performing reasonably well in the post-reform period. This could be attributed to:

(1) the importation of better risk management skills from foreign and private domestic banks,

(2) intensified competition,

(3) the diversification effect described above,

(4) reorganization (e.g., mergers and acquisitions [M&As]), and

(5) goodwill.

In India, however, given the virtual absence of an exit policy, large-scale M&As among problematic banks have not occurred so far.

It is generally viewed that the entry of well-capitalized new banks is likely to improve the quality and variety of services, efficiency of bank management, and prudential supervisory capacity (Levine [1996), Walter and Gray [1983], Gelb and Sagari [1990]). The entry of foreign banks tends to lower interest margins, profitability, and the overall expenses of domestic banks (Clarke, Cull, D'Amato, and Molinari [2000]; Claessens, Demirguc-Kunt, and Huizinga [2000]).

Further, Claessens, Demirguc-Kunt, and Huizinga (2000) have reported that the number of entrants matters compared to their market share, indicating that foreign banks affect local bank competition upon entry rather than after they have gained a substantial market share. Moreover, these banks may be able to provide a source of new capital for enterprises and thus reduce government restructuring costs, especially when the domestic banking sector is devastated in the aftermath of a crisis.

Some studies also find that foreign banks tend to go for higher interest margins and profitability than domestic banks in developing countries, while the opposite is true in developed countries (Claessens, Demiriguc-Kunt, and Huizinga [2000]). On the other hand, premature deregulation and foreign entry may cause some downside effects.

First, they may increase the risk of a banking crisis in the presence of macroeconomic or regulatory weakness, as was experienced in Argentina, Brazil, and Chile in the 1970s (Demirguc-Kunt and Detragiache [1998]).

Second, foreign banks may exhibit a home country bias, leading them to retreat promptly and massively at the first sign of difficulty. In the East Asian crisis, for example, it is widely believed that foreign banks, such as Citibank, played a major role in supporting the capital outflow without consideration as to the national damage caused.

This paper assesses whether their performance shows statistically different results from that of public sector banks through three steps:

(1) analyzing trend patterns,
(2) testing the null hypotheses that the average level of each indicator is the same between public sector and foreign and private domestic banks, and
(3) using OLS regression.

The first hypothesis (H6) is that foreign and private domestic banks have performed better than public sector banks, and thus have contributed to an improvement in overall banking sector performance. The second hypothesis (H7) is that new banks perform better.

APPRAISAL OF BANKING SECTOR PERFORMANCE

India's financial market has been gradually developing, but still remains bank-dominated in the reform period. The extent of financial deepening measured by total deposits in GDP has risen only modestly from 30% in 1991 to 38% in 1999. Capital market development has also been quite sluggish. Outstanding government and corporate bonds as a share of GDP rose from 14% in 1991 to 18% in 1999 and from only 0.7% in 1996 to 2% in 1998, respectively, while equity market capitalization dropped from 37% in 1995 to 28% in 1999.

Nevertheless, the Government's commitment on restructuring the highly regulated banking sector appears strong. Since financial reforms were launched in 1991 and particularly when the entry of new banks was permitted in 1993, public sector banks appear to have become more conscious of the need for greater profitability and efficiency, suggesting that the reform has had a non-negligible favorable impact on India's financial market.

According to an analysis of the overall performance of state-owned, domestic, and foreign banks based on trend patterns in 1993-2000, the overall performance of public sector banks appears comparable to foreign and private domestic banks.

In general, foreign banks performed better than domestic banks (public sector and private domestic banks) in terms of cost, earnings efficiency, and soundness. However, domestic banks overtook foreign banks in terms of profitability in 1999-2000. Moreover, all banks are comparable in terms of the scale of medium- to long-term credit and liquidity. These results are summarized as follows:

Profitability

Foreign banks' profitability (defined as the ratio of profits after tax to average assets [ROAA]) exceeded that of private domestic and public sector banks in 1993-1997, despite a declining trend.

However, private domestic banks have become more profitable than foreign banks in 1999-2000. The International

Monetary Fund (IMF) (2001) has also reported that foreign and new private domestic banks maintained higher profitability (about 1-2%) than public sector and old private domestic banks (0.6-0.8%) during 1995/96- 1999/2000. Also, profits from securities and foreign transactions, and brokerage/commission services have increasingly contributed to profitability for all banks, suggesting that the diversification effect is positive.

Cost and Earnings Efficiency

Foreign and private domestic banks are generally more cost-efficient than public sector banks.

The ratio of operating expenditure to operating income (COST) in 2000 was 72% for foreign banks, 80-85% for domestic banks, and 84% for public sector banks. While foreign banks are more cost-efficient, their efficiency level has somewhat deteriorated.

Instead, the latter two types of banks improved efficiency over the sample period. As for earning capacity, foreign banks are generally better performers. The earning indicator proxied by the ratio of income to assets (INCOME1) shows that foreign banks have consistently performed better than private domestic and public sector banks. However, foreign banks' income generating capacity deteriorated somewhat from 14.5% in 1993 to 12.5% in 2000, while the two other types of banks maintained their performance at a level of about 11%. The inferior performance of domestic banks relative to foreign banks can be attributed to:

(1) the larger share of credit extended to the public sector,

(2) more stringent requirement imposed on direct lending,

(3) a lesser degree of diversification, and

(4) lower interest rate margins.

Implicit interest rate spread (defined as the difference between implicit lending and deposit rates [INCOME2]) has been shrinking for all banks over the sample period. While foreign banks have received higher interest rate spreads than private domestic banks and public sector banks, their margins have become comparable in 2000.

An alternative indicator (the difference between interest income and expenditure) shows that while all types of banks reduced interest rate margins over the sample period, those of public sector and private domestic banks have generally remained negative and recently even worsened. This suggests that domestic banks must obtain income from other activities to maintain profitability and thus extend credit to the private sector.

CAPITAL, ASSET QUALITY, MANAGEMENT, AND LIQUIDITY

The balance sheets of foreign banks appear to be more structurally sound than those of domestic and public sector banks based on the following criteria: capital adequacy, asset quality, management, and liquidity.

First, on the capital adequacy ratio proxied by equity plus reserves over liabilities, the ratio of foreign banks increased from 7% in 1993 to 20% in 2000. While the ratios increased moderately for domestic banks, it still remains small. This suggests that foreign banks have greater incentives to lend prudently and remain well capitalized than the two other kinds of banks.

This reflects that foreign banks steadily reduced their deposit dependence ratio from 67% of liability in 1993 to 47% in 2000, while the two other types maintained their dependence ratio at about 85% throughout the sample period. Nevertheless, IMF's report (2001) indicates that the risk-weighted capital ratio has been comparable among all banks and has improved from 1996/97 to 1999/2000: from 10.4% to 11.9% for foreign banks, from 11.7% to 12.4% for old private domestic banks, and from 10% to 10.7% for public sector banks, while that of new private domestic banks declined from 15.3% to 13.4%.

Second, by contrast, the assessment on asset quality based on:

(1) the ratio of contingent liabilities to assets,

(2) asset growth,

(3) the ratio of investment in securities to assets,

(4) the ratio of provisions for NPA to assets (PROV), and

(5) the ratio of medium- and long-term credit to assets reveal mixed results.

The first indicator reports that the ratio of foreign banks (at around 25-30%) has been greater than that of domestic banks and public sector banks. While this indicates that foreign banks are more exposed to high potential losses in cases of default, this outcome may simply reflect that foreign banks provide more complex and sophisticated services than the two other types of banks, given that their activities are concentrated on urban areas, wholesale markets, and large clients.

The second indicator reports that foreign and private domestic banks faced rapid credit growth in1993-1997, signaling some kind of risk-taking behavior. However, this may be explained simply by their early stage of establishment. The third indicator shows that all three banks invested about 30-40% of assets in securities in response to the SLR, indicating that all of them have a large cushion against NPAs. In particular, public sector and private domestic banks increased their share of investment in government bonds in assets during 1993-2000 from 21% to 23% and from 21% to 27%, respectively.

This may be due to their preference for more liquid, safe assets as the Basle accord was applied. The fourth indicator reports that foreign banks generally allocated greater provisions for NPAs. Given that more stringent accounting and auditing standards of their mother countries are applied to foreign banks, the foreign banks are more resilient to adverse shocks. IMF (2001) has reported that foreign and new private domestic banks maintained small NPA ratios (about 2-4%) during 1995-2000—below the level of public sector and old domestic banks, with the former declining from 9.2% in 1996/95 to 7.4% in 1999/2000 and the latter remaining at around 7%. The final indicator reports that foreign and private domestic banks increased medium- to long-term credit in 1993-2000 from 7.5% to 17% and from 10% to 13%, respectively, suggesting their increased confidence in India's financial market. Public sector banks maintained the same level of exposure throughout the sample period.

Third, management performance is assessed based on two indicators:

(1) the ratio of credit to deposits, and

(2) the ratio of equity and reserves to debt (inverse of leverage).

The first indicator reports that foreign banks attempt to improve their income by expanding their lending operations as compared with other domestic banks. The ratio of foreign banks surged from 56% in 1993 to 94% in 2000, while the two other types of banks maintained the ratio at about 40% over the same period. Given that foreign banks' ratio of credit to assets is similar to other domestic banks (about 35% of assets), however, this simply suggests that foreign banks lowered the deposit dependence ratio. Based on the second indicator, foreign banks are generally less leveraged than domestic and public sector banks. Fourth, all three types of banks maintain a similar liquidity position, accounting for about 15% in terms of cash and balances with banks; and about 50% in terms of the sum of cash, balances with banks, and investment. This reflects the CRR and SLR.

Testing the Differential Behavior between Public Sector, Foreign, and Private Domestic Banks As a second step, a statistical test was conducted to see whether the average levels of the following indicators are the same for public sector, foreign, and private domestic banks: ROAA, COST, INCOME1, INCOME2, and PROV. The results report that foreign banks have generally performed better than public sector banks in terms of all indicators (Table 2). A similar pattern is observed for private domestic banks against public sector banks. However, such differences were more pronounced in the earlier period compared to later periods. This may suggest that public sector banks have made greater efforts to improve their performance as reforms have progressed.

TESTING HYPOTHESES

This section assesses the extent of concentration in the banking sector and conducts empirical estimation to test seven hypotheses.

Concentration Index: Testing the First Hypothesis

This paper tests this hypothesis by adopting two approaches:

(1) the m-bank concentration ratio adopted by Sarkar and Bhaumik (1998) and

(2) Herfindahl Index adopted by Juan-Ramon, Randall, and Williams (2001).

The m-bank concentration measures (a) one bank concentration ratio (market share of the largest bank or the State Bank of India [SBI]), (b) five-bank ratio, and (c) 10-bank ratio. This paper uses deposits to estimate the m-bank concentration indicator. The Herfindahl Index is defined as 100×i=1i=Nki2 where ki=Ki/i=1i=NKi and N=number of banks during the period under consideration. This indicator can be calculated for the whole banking sector as well as public sector, foreign, and private domestic banks, respectively. The higher the indicator, the greater the concentration of the banking sector. The lower limit of this indicator is obtained as 100 divided by N and the upper limit is 100.

The m-bank concentration indicator reports that the degree of concentration in the banking sector has barely changed during 1993-1999. Since most of these large banks are public sector banks, this indicates that public sector banks continue to be dominant and enjoy scale advantages over new banks. On the other hand, the Herfindahl Index reports that the degree of concentration has declined consistently in the whole banking sector, more or less in line with H1. In addition, the concentration has declined even within foreign banks, private domestic banks, and public sector banks. Since the lower limit (100/N) has also declined, this suggests that a number of new banks have entered the market and exerted some competition at the lower end.

Empirical Estimation

There are two studies that assess the impact of India's reform program. Based on data of 1993/94 and 1994/95, Sarkar, Sarkar, and Bhaumik (1998) have shown that foreign banks are more profitable than public sector banks, based on two indicators (profits divided by average assets and operating profits divided by average assets). Profitability of private domestic banks is similar to that of foreign banks, but private domestic banks spend more resources on provisions for NPAs. Second, foreign banks are more efficient than private domestic and public sector banks, based on two measures (net interest rate margins and operating cost divided by average assets).

Based on data of 1980-1997/98, Sarkar and Bhaumik (1998) have concluded that foreign banks, despite the superior quality of services they offer, have not been a competitive threat in Delhi, West Bengal, and Maharashtra, where their presence is greatest. This reflects that competition has emerged only at the fringe, since the entry of new banks has been at the lower end. Domestic private banks have gained some market share in these regions, but the impact on public sector banks was small and instead, gained at the expense of foreign banks.

In Uttar Pradesh, Madhya Pradesh, Bihar, Orissa, Gujarat, and Punjab, public sector banks have been predominant before and since the reforms, thus no apparent impact of new entries was observed. In Tamilnadu, Kerala, Andhra Pradesh, Karnataka, Jammu and Kashmir, and Rajasthan, private domestic banks have been more concentrated than in other regions and have experienced an increase in market share at the expense of public sector banks. But the presence of foreign banks was small. This paper investigates the progress of India's financial reforms via two steps. In the first step, it assesses the overall impact of the financial reforms on public sector banks by using pooled data. The performance measures adopted in this paper are ROAA, COST, and INCOME1. Some of these indicators were employed from Claessens, Dmirguc-Kunt, and Huizinga [2000]; Dmirguc-Kunt and Huizinga [1997]; Sarkar, Sarkar, and Bhaumik [1998]; and Sarkar and Bhaumik [1998].

The time dummy (TIME) has been introduced to capture time differences in the sample. This paper includes five control variables that account for banks' specific features and behavior:

(1) diversification (proxied by the sum of profits from securities and foreign exchange transactions and brokerage and commissions/assets [DIVERSE]),

(2) investment in government securities/assets (GBOND),

(3) lending to priority sectors (proxied by lending to priority sectors/assets [PRIORITY]),

(4) lending to the public sector (proxied by lending to the public sector/assets [PUBLIC]), and

(5) size of the bank (proxied by the log of each bank's asset size [SIZE]).

This paper uses data from the Prowess database for 1993-2000 compiled by Center for Monitoring Indian Economy Pvt. Ltd. (CMIE), which includes most of the major banks in India.

The results from this estimation are reported in Table 4. A significant coefficient of the time dummy variable would indicate that the particular year was different, which could be due to numerous factors, including regulatory changes, if any, that happened during that year. First, the time effect on ROAA (and COST) given in columns 1 and 2 was negative (positive) and statistically significant initially. Since many of the regulatory changes took place during the earlier period of reforms, the significance of the time effect could reflect the initial negative impact of the reform, which has disappeared in the later period.

Based on these outcomes, the financial reforms appear to have had a non-negligible impact on the overall performance of public sector banks. While the reforms lowered their profitability and cost efficiency at the initial stage, this negative effect has disappeared later on as they have adjusted to a new environment, supporting H2.

Second, DIVERSE has exerted a statistically positive (negative) contribution to ROAA and INCOME1 (COST), indicating that the diversification effect on the performance of public sector banks is favorable and thus H3 is supported. The statistically significant and negative (positive) impact of GBOND on ROAA (COST) is present.

This suggests that investment in government bonds limits banks in the diversification of their asset portfolios and thus H4 is supported. On the other hand, PRIORITY has made a statistically significant and positive (negative) impact on ROAA (COST), contrary to H5. This implies that while lending to priority sectors is generally regarded as the cause of NPAs, some lending activities may generate high income and allow banks to improve cost efficiency.

As a next step, this paper examines the overall impact of the whole banking sector by using pooled data of all commercial banks for 1993-2000. In addition to the approach adopted above, this paper uses ownership dummy variables ([FOREIGN] and [PRIVATE]) to capture differences in ownership.

FOREIGN (PRIVATE) equals 1 if the bank is foreign (domestic)-owned and equals 0 otherwise. Moreover, the age dummy (AGE) has been used to capture the differences between new and old banks. AGE is equal to 0 if the bank existed before 1991 and equals 1 otherwise.

The estimation results reported in Table 5 are summarized as follows. First, if the entry of foreign and private domestic banks brings in more skilled banks, the profitability and efficiency of the banking sector is expected to be higher. The results reported in columns 1-3 indicate that the coefficients of FOREIGN and PRIVATE in ROAA equation were statistically significant and positive, although their coefficients were not significant in the COST equation. Further, coefficients of FOREIGN are positive and statistically significant in INCOME1 equation.

These results suggest particularly that foreign banks perform better than domestic banks, and that ownership matters, thus supporting H6. Second, the coefficient of TIME is negative (but statistically insignificant) initially in the ROAA equation of the whole banking sector, but is positive and statistically significant in 1995 and 1997. TIME coefficient was also positive and statistically significant in INCOME1 equation.

Third, DIVERSE has improved profitability and the cost and earnings efficiency of the whole banking sector, in line with H3. The coefficient of DIVERSE shows that the diversification impact on ROAA and INCOME1 (and COST) was positive (negative) and statistically significant.

Fourth, GBOND helps banks to increase holdings of safe, liquid assets, and thus improve their liquidity position. At the same time, however, it reduces the opportunity to allocate limited financial resources toward more needed sectors and hence profitability and cost and earnings efficiency. The results indicate that the coefficients of GBOND on ROAA (and COST) were negative (positive) and statistically significant, supporting H4. Contrary to our expectations, however, the impact of GBOND on INCOME1 was positive and statistically significant.

Fifth, lending to priority sectors and the public sector would be expected to lower the profitability and earnings efficiency of the whole banking sector, reflecting that this type of lending is characterized by direct lending. Despite the share of credit extended to priority sectors accounting for more than 20% of their total credit, the coefficients of PRIORITY and PUBLIC with respect to ROAA turn out to be insignificant, contrary to H5. Moreover, the coefficient of PRIORITY on COST was negative and statistically significant, implying that some types of those credits enhance cost efficiency.

However, the coefficient of PUBLIC on INCOME1 was negative and statistically significant, suggesting that such lending lowers banks' income earnings capacity.

Sixth, the coefficient of AGE with respect to ROAA and INCOME1 was negative but statistically insignificant.

CONCLUSIONS

Since the financial reforms of 1991, there have been significant favorable changes in India's highly regulated banking sector. This paper has assessed the impact of the reforms by examining seven hypotheses. It concludes that the financial reforms have had a moderately positive impact on reducing the concentration of the banking sector (at the lower end) and improving performance.

The empirical estimation showed that regulation (captured by the time variable) lowered the profitability and cost efficiency of public sector banks at the initial stage of the reforms, but such a negative impact disappeared once they adjusted to the new environment. In line with these results, Tables 1 and 2 shows that profitability turned positive in 1997-2000, cost efficiency steadily improved over the reform period, and the gap in performance compared to foreign banks has diminished.

Moreover, allowing banks to engage in non-traditional activities has contributed to improved profitability and cost and earnings efficiency of the whole banking sector, including public sector banks. By contrast, investment in government securities has lowered the profitability and cost efficiency of the whole banking sector, including public sector banks. Lending to priority sectors and the public sector has not had a negative effect on profitability and cost efficiency, contrary to our expectations. Further, foreign banks (and private domestic banks in some cases) have generally performed better than other banks in terms of profitability and income efficiency. This suggests that ownership matters and foreign entry has a positive impact on banking sector restructuring.

The above results suggest that the current policy of restructuring the banking sector through encouraging the entry of new banks has so far produced some positive results. However, the fact that competition has occurred only at the lower end suggests that bank regulators should conduct a more thorough restructuring of public sector banks. Given that public sector banks have scale advantages, the current approach of improving their performance without rationalizing them may not produce further benefits for India's banking sector. As 10 years have passed since the reforms were initiated and public sector banks have been exposed to the new regulatory environment, it may be time for the Government to take a further step by promoting M&As and closing unviable banks. A further reduction of SLRs and more encouragement for non-traditional activities (under the bank subsidiary form) may also make the banking sector more resilient to various adverse shocks.

11

BANKING FOR GROWTH OF ECONOMY

ROLE OF BANKING

The role of banking in growth of the economy is sizeable and significant. Economic history indicates that banks have played a stellar role in supporting economic growth across a broad spectrum of countries.

Countries such as the United States and Japan have enormously benefited from strong banking systems which not only helped the domestic economic systems to grow and prosper but also pursue international ambitions and business expansion. Among the mature economies such Germany and France, even today, banks are majorly responsible for financing growth. The recent evidence of dramatic growth of south East Asia that now enjoys the distinction of rapidly growing economic region is also on the back of massive role played by the respective banking system.

There are several indicators that show the importance of banking system in the world of finance.

Bank assets account anywhere upto to 50 percent of the total size of the world capital markets. Banks and Bonds account anywhere upto 85 percent of the total activity in the capital markets worldwide today The size of activity of banks is more than the size of the economy in several countries experiencing rapid economic growth. For instance, for the world as whole, bank assets to the gross domestic product is as high as 132 percent. In some regions such as the EU, it is as high as 212 percent. Several mature countries have very high bank assets/ GDP ratio and these include; United Kingdom (262 percent), France (255 percent), Japan (168 percent), and Canada (152 percent)

For the emerging markets, the bank/GDP ratio is subdued at about 95 perent, though, Asia has a very high ratio of 144 percent, followed by Middle East and Africa.

The imperative is that banks do play a very important role in financing growth.

The issue is how India could take advantage of its banking systems to pursue the desired growth of the economy.

INDIA AND DOUBLE DIGIT GROWTH

All economies that have experienced rapid economic development in the recent period experienced double digit or very high single digit growth for a very long and sustained period. For instance, China has been experiencing an average growth of 9 to 10 percent for almost a decade and following the liberalization of the economy, it had experience double digit growth as well for several years.

East Asian economies too experienced prolonged growth of respective domestic economies for a very long period.

Double digit growth thus becomes imperative for India too to enable it to join the league of growth countries.

An important aspect of the double digit growth is that, notwithstanding the aspirations, which every country has, but also the presence of enabling conditions or possibilities for harnessing the potential and reaching that target.

The possibilities that make India to enter the realm of double digit growth include;

- Opening up of the economy and growing investment from within and outside.
- Increasing international interest on Indian economy
- Growth in infrastructure development

- Promotion of private enterprise and streamlining of the public sector
- Leadership in service sector growth and expansion
- Resurgence of the industry and in particular the manufacturing sector.

Above all, India is viewed a major opportunity and value which the world financial community is keen to unlock for the benefit of the mutual advantage.

BANKS AND DOUBLE DIGIT GROWTH

The recent years have been remarkable for the growth of Indian banking and its role in the domestic economy. First and foremost has been the significant recovery of banks with very less fiscal costs that makes the turnaround of the Indian banking one of the most efficient in the world.

Profitability and productivity of the banks have been rising at rapid pace and so as the stock prices of banks. I think about ten years ago, Indian banking depicted a very disappointing and dismal picture. Today more investors invest in bank scrips than others and I am sure that members of the FICCI must have made sizeable gains from their investments in banks. Which means banks show more confidence than others, which is a matter of great satisfaction for the banking industry in India that was ridiculed as the most inefficient just a decade ago. While on profitability and productivity the progress has been quite smart and spectacular, on the growth front, Indian banking still could do more. For instance, between 1990 and 2003, domestic credit provided by the banking sector for the world as a whole (average) rose from 139 percent to 162 percent. This ratio for several emerging countries was much more. In Korea, during this period, bank assets/GDP ratio from 63 percent to 106 percent, in Malaysia from 75 percent to 152 percent, in South Africa from 98 percent to 158 percent, in China from 90 perent to 178 percent. In several other countries the growth of bank assets has been very rapid and fast

The experience of India however is very subdued. The domestic credit provided by banking sector in India as a percent of gross domestic product between the last 13 years rose just by 10 percentage points from 52 percent in 1990 to 62 percent in 2004.

The growth of bank assets in India is growing but still not that rapid. For instance in 2004, bank assets in India grew at an average of 16 percent, but that is due to very high growth of 24 percent showed by the private sector banks, since assets in the public sector in 2004 grew at about 14 percent. Compared to this, world wide, bank assets in 2004 grew at an average rate of about 20 percent and regions such as EU showing a growth rate as high as 27 percent. Several transition economies in the Africa and Europe too showed growth in the region of over 25 percent. It is imperative that Indian banks step up growth in the assets that is would be critical from the point of view of supporting the double digit growth of the economy.

As there are several enabling features that could make double digit growth of the economy possible, equally relevant is the enabling features that could enable banking to support such a growth rate in the economy. These include;

- Smart turnaround in Indian banking. They are now more profitable and productive than anytime in the past.
- Efficiency levels are continuously improving.
- Able to function in an intensely competitive environment
- Product range is fast expanding
- Professional competencies and capabilities are growing
- Greater thrust on regulatory compliance and best practices
- Better management of assets and credit monitoring
- Growing international relations and business opportunities

In the background of these, I would now attempt to touch upon a few aspects that would be of significance to Indian banking, that would equip and enable them to meet the challenges of the financing double digit growth of the economy.

Size has a Meaning in Global Context

There was a time when it was considered small is Beautiful. It is true even today, but not so necessarily in banks. Banks worldwide are once again acquiring to growth both in stature and size. Globalisation and deregulation offer banks a host of opportunities for business and growth but smaller banks would not be able in take full advantage of these due to limitations of capital and regulatory restraints. A lot of churning out is happening at the banking systems in a number of regions primarily focused on getting into proper size which could withstand competition and command greater market share.

Indian banks should be able to grow at more than 20 percent a year for the next 10 years that would be relevant to pursue not only their respective growth but also relevant for financing the economy that is aiming at double digit growth. In this context, it would not be out of context to say that banks should seriously examine the issues of right size that makes them competent and capable to meet the emerging challenges.

Need for Innovative Instruments

Capital is the most important constraint for the growth of bank assets. For public sector banks, it is much more important since there is a limit to which the government stake could be reduced. Even today, public sector banks account for about 80 percent of the bank assets in India and these are also the banks which provide a major chunk of bank credit.

To enable to them expand the assets, it becomes important that their capital positions too are boosted and accessing stock markets, though helps, but cannot provide complete solution to the challenge at this juncture. In this background, it is important that some innovative instruments of financing the public sector banks towards capital be evolved to make the growth process much easier and efficient.

Financing Agriculture

Despite predominance of service sector in the Indian economy, and its rapidly growing share in the overall economy,.

Agriculture is the sector which will make the success of the reforms more meaningful and relevant. It is because a large proportion of people are still employed in the agriculture sector. In this background, it becomes imperative that this sector attracts large investments. When I say large investments, it does not necessarily mean financing crops and other allied activities.

There is enormous scope for financing agri business and also play a useful role in the development of commodities markets. Commodities futures markets in India are already experiencing rapid pace of growth and banks could play a very important role in stepping financing towards this sector. Financing innovative crops and cultivation techniques also becomes very pertinent in this context. The overall focus should be in improving the both production and productivity of the agriculture sector that would be of great help for the rest of the economy to march ahead.

Reinforce Retail Lending

Indian economy now shows growing signs of being led by consumption which is largely bank financed. Personal loans as a percent of bank credit in India shot up significantly from about 10 percent in 1997 to about 15 percent now.

What is more interesting is household balance sheets in India are still robust and household debt as a percent of gross domestic is still at a very low level of about 5 percent, which gives a lot of leg room for the retail lending to boom. Banks should step up this segment, of course with all the precautions and due credit monitoring systems in place, which will be useful for speeding up the momentum of the economic growth.

Resurgence in Manufacturing

For any economy to remain robust for long, it is important that it has a strong manufacturing base. India scores very high on the growth of service sector, but equally important is bringing back high growth in the manufacturing sector. For instance, credit to manufacturing which formed 45 percent of the bank credit in 1996-97 slipped to 33 percent by 2003. The fall has been particularly more in the engineering sector where the share of bank credit fell from 8 perent to 4.5 percent during this period.

Banks should look at this challenge with greater intensity and care. Enhancing manufacturing competence and capabilities would strengthen the growth process and also its competitiveness.

Support SMUs

SMU development is critical for any growth process to be robust and sustained. In India several attempts in the past were made to develop SMU development but the need is still large. Banks can play an important role in supporting SMU development.

However, to make it a long lasting process, it is important that capital markets too complement the efforts of the banks in this regard. World over, many leading stock exchanges have set up exclusive platforms/exchanges for the SMUs and India also made a beginning with the Indonext Platform, under the aegis of the Bombay Stock Exchange and 18 other regional stock exchanges.

It is hoped that a vibrant stock markets exists for the small and medium companies which would fasten the involvement and participation of banks in the process of their growth and development

Product and Service Range

Banks should focus on a continuous development on the product side, particularly for the corporates and other major segments of the customers. Product range enables to banks to offer a wide range of on and off balance sheet services that could increase the overall reach and access, that will be of great relevance for the real economy. Banks could consider interesting collaborations and joint initiatives with institutions in India and abroad for this purpose, subject to the regulatory guidelines and compliance standards.

People to Take Risks

Banks need more professionals who could read, assess and manage risks that are not only domestic in nature but global in reach and perspective. This requirement is more pertinent in the public sector banks.

At the same time, it must be added that PSBs are a big repository of skilled people, and what is more relevant is reorientation in approaches, attitudes and skills. Banks should invest in this process to a great length.

Look Ashore

It might not sound too ambitious, if it is said that banks in India could also look with greater intensity opportunities available abroad both for business and growth.

Transition economies offer excellent opportunities for making acquisitions, creating new assets and also extending the reach and influence.

Banks in India could keep this at the back of mind, though there might be touch challenges for pursuing them at present. Another aspect of this could be helping Indian companies to acquire and expand business in international markets that would bring enormous benefits to the domestic economy.

INITIATIVES AT DENA BANK

Let me now take this opportunity to outline a few of the initiatives that our bank is taking to play a meaningful and purposeful role in the growth process of the Indian economy and its pursuit of double digit growth. At Dena Bank, we are geared to take advantage of several opportunities that a growing economy offers.

Among the various strategies that have been drawn up, Retail, Agriculture and SME have been extended a focused attention. To push the Retail Credit further, the Bank opened 40 FinMarts, a unique concept in Indian Banking, at various centers to provide all retail services to its customers under one roof.

These "FinMarts" provide one-stop state-of-the-art customer experience in delivery of the array of Retail Banking products spanning a customer's life cycle. These "FinMarts" which operate in "Branch within Branch" concept have been exclusively designed to present a highly enriched customer ambience for state-of-the-art customer experience. All retail- banking products are available in this one-stop shop where dedicated and smart staff are deployed to deliver.

Dena Bank has over 1123 branches and has a dominant presence in the industrially and economically vibrant Western Region with presence of about 70 percent of the branch network.. About 61% of the branches are situated in rural and semi-urban areas and hence agricultural and related activities remain part of the key business strategies.

Dena Bank has carried out wide ranging initiatives in pushing agricultural credit. Dena Bank was the first to launch credit card to farmers in the name of "Dena Krishi Shakh Patra". To empower the farming community to avail hassle-free credit facilities, the Bank launched "Dena Kisan Gold Credit Card Scheme".

A unique feature of this card is that it covers both production and investment credit. As a part of its rural development activities, Dena Bank opened Rural Development & Self Employment Training Centre at Bhuj and Mehsana and the centre imparts vocational trainings to budding entrepreneurs to take up gainful activities in rural areas.

In addition to simplification of procedures, easing of credit terms and incentives for prompt payment, the Bank has established several forward and backward linkages to enable the farmers to reap the benefits thereof.

The knowledge services has been given a thrust by setting up Rural Kiosks and this again is a unique and pioneering initiative by Dena Bank. The Scheme envisages loans to the rural youth in collaboration with the service provider for setting up Rural Internet Kiosks and this would provide gainful employment to the educated rural youth.

Recognising the importance of SME in the economic growth and the opportunities that it would provide to the Banks, Dena Bank is in the process of entering into a tie up arrangement with SIDBI for financing of SMEs. A strategic business unit has been set up with a pre-defined role to push the SME credit.

Apart from these, the Bank has also taken several technological initiatives to keep pace with the growing expectations of the industry and customers. In addition to the growing number of ATMs, Dena Bank has launched several technology enabled services like Dena Bill-Pay, Dena M-banking, Dena Internet Banking, Multi-City Cheque facility and value added services through ATM.

THE ROAD AHEAD

The importance of banking systems in many emerging economies stems from a host of factors that include;

Prevalence of a high degree of financial intermediation Lack of suitable financial instruments that support and spur growth Regulatory and policy restrictions on range of financial instruments and market participants.

Absence of a vibrant and fully functioning and efficient capital markets Restrictions in access to the international financial markets and global capital flows.

In India however, the situation is rapidly changing with capital markets growing both in stature and size. Today stock markets in India have some of the best practices anywhere relevant in the world, both in terms of practices and procedures. The risk management has been robust and there are no major default in the system.

A debate that has gained enormous influence in the recent period is on the relative efficiencies of the banking and capital markets. Evidence throws up that market based financial systems are found to be emerging more efficient but the underlining message is that a combination of efficient banking systems that provides fast and cheaper payment settlement systems and a capital market that acts as an efficient resource mobilization and allocative mechanism would prove beneficial for the long term growth of the economy.

My message today is that Indian banking should grow more faster but not just alone. Simultaneous with its growth. equally rapid and robust should be the growth, role and responsibility of other segments of the financial sector. Which is when the real economy benefits enormously and it could reach double digit growth and stay there for quite some time.

BIBLIOGRAPHY

Ariel Buira: *Challenges to the World Bank and IMF: Developing Country Perspectives*, London, Anthem Press, 2003.

Besley, T.: *How do Merket Failures Justify Interventions in Rural Credit Markets?*, Washington, D. C., World Bank, 1994

Davidson, P.: *Money and the Real World*, London: Macmillan, 1978.

Desai, Vasant: *A Study of Rural Economics: A Systems Approach*, Bombay, Himalaya, 1983.

Guhan, S.: *The World Bank's Lending in South Asia*, Washington, Brookings Institution, 1995.

Jack Kemp: *A Monetary Agenda for the World Economy*, Boston, Quantum, 1984.

Le Prestre, Philippe: *The World Bank and the Environmental Challenge*, London, Associated University Presses, 1989.

Magliveras, Konstantinos D.: *Banks, Fraud and Crime*, Lloyd's of London Press, London, 2000.

Peet, Richard, Born, Beate: *Unholy Trinity: The IMF, World Bank, and WTO*, New York, Zed Books, 2003.

Ranade, Sudhanshu: *Rural Banking Adrift*, Bombay, Jaico Publishing House, 1984.

Swoboda, A. : *Monetary Problems of the International Economy*, Chicago, University of Chicago Press, 1969.

Wolfe, J.N.: *Value, Capital and Growth*, Chicago, Edinburgh University Press. 1968.

INDEX

□□□